HINDU TALES

AN ENGLISH TRANSLATION OF JACOBI'S AUSGEWAHLTE ERZAHLUNGEN IN MAHARASHTRI

HINDU TALES

AN ENGLISH TRANSLATION OF JACOBI'S AUSGEWAHLTE ERZAHLUNGEN IN MAHARASHTRI

JOHN JACOB MEYER

GYAN

Published by

Gyan Publishing House
5, Ansari Road
Daryaganj, New Delhi-110002
Phone: 011-47034999, 9811692060
E-mail: books@gyanbooks.com

Distribution Network
gyanbooks.com
India, USA, Canada, UK, Australia

ISBN: 978-93-6780-371-4 (PB)

First Published, 1909

2nd Impression 2024

Printed at: Gyan Press, Delhi.

Hindu Tales: An English Translation of Jacobi's
Ausgewahlte Erzahlungen in Maharashtri
Author: JOHN JACOB MEYER

HINDU TALES.

HINDU TALES.

AN ENGLISH TRANSLATION OF

JACOBI'S AUSGEWÄHLTE ERZÄHLUNGEN IN

MĀHĀRĀSHṬRĪ.

BY

JOHN JACOB MEYER.

LONDON
LUZAC & CO., 46, GREAT RUSSELL STREET,
1909.

INSCRIBED TO

Geheimrat Prof. Dr. H. JACOBI.

PREFACE.

This modest work has been suggested by Prof. C. R. Lanman. I am glad that I took it in hand. The tales here presented are of no small interest to the student of Indian antiquity and of folklore, and Jacobi's collection is such an excellent primer for the beginner in Prākrit that an English translation seems really a desirable thing, especially as the stories present many a difficulty and Jacobi's vocabulary is hardly sufficient to clear up all doubtful points. A number of words are missing in his glossary; sometimes he is wrong. Doubtless he himself has quietly rectified many a mistake since the publication of the Erzählungen 20 years ago. "Wir sehen auf niemand so sehr herab als auf die, auf deren Schultern wir stehen", says Jean Paul Friedrich Richter. I hope the reader will not impute such a spirit to me, although I take Jacobi to task quite often. In my Prākrit studies, which, alas, have been all too limited as yet, this eminent scholar was my earliest guide, for his Ausgewählte Erzählungen were my first Prākrit reading, and from his many invaluable contributions to our knowledge of Jinism I have derived the greatest profit. If I dedicate my little volume to that reverend scholar it is but an inadequate acknowledgement of all I owe him.

I regret that I could not peruse the linguistic articles

bearing on Prākrit which have been published by him and by other scholars in various journals; but for almost twenty years, since the days of my boyhood, my health has been such that I had to refrain from many things. Doubtless a great number of the etymologies that I propose in my notes have been laid before the public by others already. Not a few of the identfications at which I arrived some years ago, I saw confirmed by Pischel's Prākrit grammar (Grammatik der Prākrit-Sprachen von R. Pischel. Strassburg, 1900) when this book came out. Whereever I found that somebody else gives the same derivation I have called attention to the fact. A conscientious study of Pischel's grammar, that most magnificent monument of German scholarship, is presupposed. For brevity's sake I refer to Pischel's work simply by quoting the paragraphs, omitting the title of the book itself. Whenever anything may be found by consulting the index to the Prākrit grammar no remark was, as a rule, considered needful. Constant appeal to the index is therefore indispensable. But the index to a work of such a nature cannot contain all the references desirable for some purposes. So I have tried to supply the necessary indications. To some scholars I may seem to have overdone the thing; but perhaps I should have offered even more of such help.

Some words not given in Jacobi's glossary may have escaped me. There are quite a number of them. But I hope that those which I fail to explain in the notes may become clear from my translation. This book is intended to smooth the way a little for the beginner. But the free play of our own powers delights us most.

So room should be left for it. And students of Prākrit are usually Sanskrit scholars. They will hardly require more assistance. The Appendix is to be noted.

These are tales of the Jainas. Some knowledge of the theology of this old Hindu sect is necessary to understand the stories. Quite a deal of information may be gathered from books the greater number of which are easily procured. I mention Colebrooke's Miscellaneous Essays, Vol. I, 404—413, with Cowell's appendix 444—452; Vol. II, 194—195; 198—201; H. W. Wilson, Selected Works, Vol. I, pp. 297—302; 305—317; Jacobi's extremely important introductions to his "Jaina Sutras" Vols. XXII and XLV of the Sacred Books of the East; Bühler's Vortrag über die Indische Sekte der Jainas; Tawney's introduction to his Kathākoça; A Lecture on Jainism etc. by Lala Benarsi Dass (Jain Itihas Series. N°. 1. Agra 1902; a very noteworthy treatise). I hope, that such of my notes as are intended for the more advanced student of Prākrit literature will contain at least a few serviceable hints. Exhaustiveness could nowhere be my object. I know too little for that. But in the present state of our knowledge of these matters we can ill afford to miss any information that may be had. So I venture some remarks that perhaps have been made by others already.

Both the translation and the notes were prepared four years ago. But poor health prevented me from getting the manuscript quite ready for the printer. After years of involuntary idleness I could now return to my long-abandoned Hindu studies if external circumstances permitted. Present conditions and prospects for the future being as they are, it seems to be to no purpose to keep the work longer in my desk. I have carefully gone over the whole once more and now offer it to the public.

As regards the style of the translation, I have to remark that elegance of diction was a very subordinate consideration. Faithfulness, above all, I considered the thing to be striven after. Very frequently the "outlandishness" is in the matter and not in the words. If you try to adapt yourself to our modes of expression you destroy too much of the thought conveyed by the original. Perhaps even a little more "wooden literalness" would have done more good than harm, at least to the beginner in Prākrit. Still it is a pity that the many charms of style that beautify the stories in the Prākrit have been lost.

The first story in the following collection is decidedly the poorest — a most insipid and tiresome performance. The tales increase in interest as we go along. The *novella* of Mūladeva, which comes toward the end of the book, will fascinate many a reader. From the literary and from some other points of view the best of all these selections is the last — the poem of Agaḍatta. So I hope the general reader will not despair when he is confronted at the very outset by that wooden statue of a sensualist called Bambhadatta. The student will find much valuable matter in all the stories.

A few inconsistencies in the treatment of proper nouns and in other things will be noticed in this book. I consider them of no account at all.

I have to thank Prof. C. R. Lanman for assistance most kindly and disinterestedly rendered.

J. J. Meyer.

BAMBHADATTA.

BAMBHADATTA [1]).

In the town of Soma there lived the son of king Caṇḍavaḍiṃsa, Muṇicanda by name. And becoming disgusted with the enjoyment of pleasures he at the feet of Sāgaracanda, renounced the world. Once upon a time, while leading the austere life of a religious mendicant and wandering about with his teachers [2]), he set out for another country and entered a village to beg alms. He was left behind by the company and later on lost his way in the wilderness. Four herdsmen boys saw him fainting from thirst and hunger. While ministering to him, they suffered a spiritual awakening [3]) from his religious discourse and embraced the life of religious

1) The story of Bambhadatta has been exhaustively dealt with by Leumann in the Wiener Zeitschrift für die Kunde des Morgenlandes (WZKM) in Vols. V and VI. Prof. Pavolini gave an Italian translation with notes in the Journal of the Italian Asiatic Society. (La novella di Brahmadatta). A Sanskrit form of our tale is found in Uttarajjh. (i. e. Uttarajjhayaṇasutta. Calcutta, Samvat 1936 [1880 A.D.], with the dīpikā of Lakshmīvallabha) pp. 378 sqq. Cf. pp. 127—147.

2) Or perhaps rather, "teacher" (Plur. majest.)

3) For paḍibuddha Jacobi gives "converted", and for boheï and paḍiboheï "to convert". This is perfectly correct. I need only quote Uttarajjh. p. 1099, l. 6: bodhi = Jainadharmaruci (faith in the Jaina religion) and p. 1100, l. 3: bodhi = Jainadharmaprāpti. Nevertheless I usually try to come as near the original meaning of budh as possible. "To convert" is so colorless.

mendicants. Two of them, loathing this world[1]), went to the world of the gods [when they died]. Thereupon both of them were born as the twin sons of Jasamaī, the slave girl of the Brahman Saṇḍilla in Dasapura town, begot by this same Brahman. They passed the age of childhood and entered that of adolescence.

Once upon a time they went to the woods in order to guard the fields. While they were asleep under a fig tree a snake crept out of a hollow in the fig tree and bit one of the boys. The other too was bitten by the same serpent as he ran about in order to catch the reptile. Then, no remedy being applied, they both died and were born again as the twin fawns of a deer on Mount Kāliṇjara. On account of the attachment growing out of their former love they always grazed in each other's neighborhood, and thus both of them were killed by a hunter with one and the same arrow. And so dying, both of them were conceived in the womb of a swan on the bank of the Ganges, were born, and in the course of time passed beyond childhood. One day when in the same manner they were roaming about there together a fisherman caught them suddenly in one snare, wrung their necks, and killed them. Then, in the city of Benares, they again entered existence as the sons of a very rich Caṇḍāla chief, Bhūyadinna by name. There also they

1) Dugañchā for "disgust for the world" is not the common expression. Maybe the dīpikā is correct. It gives malaklinnavastrādijugupsā kṛitā p, 378, l. 8. "They loathed the soiled garments and other disagreeable things [connected with their monastic life]". But their antipathy against dirt that was rendered sacred by religion was a sin and resulted in the many low births that followed. Cf. l. 9. So better translate: "Having conceived a loathing".

were bound in close friendship to each other, and Citta and Sambhūya were the names of the two brothers.

Now there was a king in Benares, Sankha by name, and his minister of state was called Namui. One day as it chanced a crime committed by the minister being such [as to merit death] [1]), Bhūyadinna, the head of the Caṇḍālas, was commanded by the king to put him to death in secret. He concealed him and said to him: "I will save you if you stay in an underground dwelling and instruct my boys". For the sake of his life he consented. While he was engaged in this, some time passed.

One day Bhūyadinna found out that his wife lay with him. He resolved [2]) to kill him. Citta and Sambhūya, thinking: "He is our benefactor", let him escape. Later on he became the counsellor of the universal sovereign Saṇāṃkumāra in the city of Hastināpura.

Now these two Caṇḍāla boys, Citta and Sambhūya. excelling [3]), in beauty, youthful bloom, grace, dancing,

1) The sequel clearly shows that the minister, a kind of Don Juan, had tasted the sweets of love in the king's harem. That was by no means a rare offence of royal counsellors in Ancient India, and their lords were not always as severe as our king Saṅkha. Of course, the *secret* execution was intended to preclude scandal ("sensational revelations"). — Caṇḍāla is about the same as Pariah.

2) Āḍhatta past passive participle of ā + dhā "to undertake, resolve, begin". So Pischel. Whether āḍhatta is really formed from the present stem dadh, as he supposes, or simply in analogy with datta (in which, for that matter, we have the present stem dad + ta too), āḍhatta would be a kind of fossil form. For the present stem in Prākrit is nowhere dadh, and instead of datta, although this form is taught by Hemacandra, we find only dinna (diṇṇa). So after all, it would be preferable to derive āḍhatta from the causative passive āḍhappaï (a possibility also pointed out by Pischel). [Jacobi refers me to Zeitschr. f. vgl. Sprachforsch. N. F. VIII, 253].

3) Lit., "having attained pre-eminence".

singing, and the other arts, gladdened the hearts of all the people of Benares by singing songs that were accompanied by the tisaraya, the flute, and the lute. One day when the great festival of love had come and various parties of singing people had started and companies of youths and maidens were dancing, a chorus consisting of Citta, Sambhūya, and other Caṇḍālas also set out. Then, hearing their excellent songs and plays, which ravished the hearts even of beasts, the whole population of the town, especially the young women, gathered about them. Thereupon those among the people of the town whose was the lore of the four Vedas, inspired by jealousy, said to the king in humble manner, "Your majesty, all the people have been tainted by contact with these boys"[1]). They were forbidden to enter the town. Some time went by.

One day on the great festival of the full moon, being carried away by curiosity on account of their covetous senses, they forgot the king's order, took no account of their own station, and entered the town. Thereupon, while they looked at the spectacle[2]), they, on account of their exquisite taste, heard [only] the cries of

1) Cf. Uttarajjh. p. 379, ll. 2 and 3 from bottom: Tataç caturvedavidbhir brāhmaṇair nagarasvāmina evaṃ vijñaptam: "Rājann, etābhyām Citra-Sambhūtābhyāṃ caṇḍālābhyām sarvo 'pi nagarīloka ekākāraṃ prāpitaḥ".

2) Pecchaṇaya (prekshaṇaka) seems to be a kind of dramatic performance accompanied by music and singing. But Uttarajjh. p. 688, l. 2 we read: Bhagavatpuro veṇuvīṇāgītaninādaiḥ pravaraṃ prekshaṇakaṃ kartum ārabdhavān. So perhaps "concert" would be the correct rendering. That would accord well both with the present passage and with Erz. p. 25, l. 32; cf. with p. 20, ll. 29, 30. (Erz. stands for Jacobi's Ausgewählte Erzählungen in Māhārāshṭrī). [Jacobi, "Any *show* with or without music". So also in Skt.].

jackals[1]), and they broke out into words, and a song burst forth[2]). Then, covering their faces with their garments [in order not to be recognized], they began to sing. Thereupon, hearing in a certain place their song, which was a delight to the ear, all the people surrounded them on all sides and said: "Who is it that has, as by a stream of nectar, created this pleasure for our ears by his sweet song, which is like [the song of] the Kinnaras?" [3]) Now when they pulled away their upper garments[4]) and looked at their faces, lo, there were these

1) That is, the music and singing seemed so to them. The reading of B points to the correct interpretation although it is not clear and a part of it, at least, is apparently a gloss. Kolhuyāṇaṃ may either be gen. pl. "of jackals", or it may mean "the music (voice, vāṇaṃ) of jackals". Aṇhakolhagasarisaṃ I translate: "like hungry jackals" — aṇha = açna; kolhaga = kroshṭṛi + ka (cf. § 600).

2) Bhanjeūṇa vayaṇaṃ neither Jacobi nor Pavolini understand. It corresponds to Pāli vācaṃ bhindati "to speak". See for instance, Majjh.-Nik. I, 301, 207; Saṃyutt.-Nik. IV, 293; Kathāvatthu 195 ff.; Vinaya Vol. III, p. 266; V, p, 175; IV, p. 286. The accusative though is hardly the acc. of direction so common in Skt., Pāli, and Prākrit, as it would seem judging from my translation, but the underlying idea is probably this: Speach is thought. As unuttered thought it is a compact whole in our minds. Speaking (articulating) breaks up thought (which is the same as speech) into pieces. Cp. Appendix.

3) The song of the Kinnaras (a kind of mythical beings) is celebrated for its beauty, and so sweetly sing these wood and mountain dwellers that even the deer in ecstasy close their eyes and stop chewing the cud; and only after a long time does the hair on their bodies, which bristles with joy, return to its natural position. Setubandha IX, 87. But, on the other hand, human speech is denied the Kiṃpurushas (or Kiṃnaras). Why? Every one who speaks the language of men lies. Angutt.-Nik. II, IV, 9.

4) Uttarijjāiṃ. The neuter plural ending in -āiṃ I take to be one of the many interesting double formations in Prākrit. It is -ā (as in the Veda, = Skt. -āni) + the i of the consonantal stems (e. g. nāmāni) + the anusvāra, which is so often added in the Prākrits. Thus this form corresponds to the plurals puttāo and mālāo (i. e. mālās + as). — Kaḍḍhai is a denominative from kaḍḍha (common also in Pāli). See Goldschmidt's Rāvaṇavaha sub voce. Such denominatives are numerous in Prākrit. Kṛishṭa > kaṭṭha > kaḍḍha.

very same Caṇḍāla boys. Crying: "Strike them! strike them!" they belabored [1]) them with kicks, with blows, with slaps with the open hand, etc. And so they ran out of the town and came to the park outside. Then, sad and gloomy, they began to reflect: "Out upon our beauty, youth, skill in the arts, and the multitude of our others excellences! For merely by this one stain of our birth as Caṇḍālas all of them have been made naught of and we have been shamed by the people". They were seized with a deep disgust for life. Without telling their relatives they resolved to die and set out in a southern direction. When they had gone a great distance they saw a magnificent mountain. Ascending it, they saw on a slab of rock a great ascetic whose body was withered by protracted penances, who was absorbed in meritorious meditation [2]), whose hands were hanging down, and who practised austerities in the kāyotsarga posture [3]). Seeing him they were filled with

1) Literally, "struck".

2) Çubhadhyāna often leads to the state of a kevalin, or a pefect, all-knowing sage, who has already in this life attained final emancipation.

3) Pralambitabhujadvandvam
ūrdhvasthasyāsitasya vā
sthānaṃ kāyānapeksham yat
kāyotsargaḥ prakīrtitaḥ.

"The posture of one who stands upright or sits with his two arms hanging down and without any regard for his body is called abandonment of the body" (kāyotsargh). Hemacandra's Yogaçāstra IV, 132.

Sayaṇāsaṇaṭhāṇe vā
je u bhikkhū na vācare
kāyassa viussaggo
chaṭṭho so parikittio.

"If a monk remains" (= vyācaret) motionless when lying down, sitting or standing upright this is called abandoning of the body, which is the sixth kind (of internal austerities)". Jacobi's translation. Uttarajjh. XXX, 36. Concerning the special fruit of this penance we read Uttarajjh.

joy and went up to him. Thereupon they saluted the venerable one with devotion and respect. At the completion of his meditation he gave them the Blessing of the Faith [1]) and addressed them: "Whence have you come". They related their previous story to him and then told him their intention, saying: "We want to cast ourselves from this magnificent mountain". Then the great sage said: "It is not meet for people like you whose intellects have become clear by the knowledge of many sciences to act as common people do [2]) Con-

XXIX, 12: Kāussaggeṇa ṇam, bhante, jīve kiṃ jaṇayai? Kāussageṇaṃ tīyapaḍuppannaṃ pāyacchittaṃ visohei. Visuddhapāyacchitte ya jīve nivvuyahiyae ohariyabhāru vva pasatthajjhānovagae suhaṃ suheṇaṃ viharai. "Sir, what does the soul (or, a living being, a man) realize by Kāyotsarga? By Kāyotsarga he cleanses away past and present sins that require expiation. And a soul that is cleansed of sins requiring expiation lives most happily, engaged in praiseworthy contemplation, having his heart filled with peaceful bliss, like unto the carrier of a burden whose burden has been taken off".

1) What this blessing was like appears from passages like the following, "Dharmalābhaḥ syat", says one to the king and departs. Hemacandra's Pariçishṭaparvan VIII, 77. "Dharmalābhas tavānaghe", are the words of another to a woman. Pariçishṭap. VIII, 165. "Dharmalābhāçishaṃ dattva" we read in the same work XII, 371; XIII, 67. Cf. Prabandhacintāmaṇi transl. by Tawney pp. 10—11.

2) The giripaḍaṇa (bhṛigupāta), so very popular in India, is given as one of the twelve deaths of the fool in Webers Fragment der Bhagavatī p. 266; and in the Kathākoça (transl. by Tawney) p. 8 we are told that people who commit suicide become demons when they have expired. But there is no uniformity of view on this point, and voluntary death because one cannot resist temptation is glorified as the "death of the wise". Bühler, Ueber die indische Sekte der Jaina, p. 12 and note 10. Cf. Hopkins, Religions of India p. 291. It is well known that death by starvation is the correct way of leaving the world for a Jaina saint. The real object of life is nirjarā, the wearing away or destruction of karman. There are two kinds of nirjarā: voluntary and involuntary. The ascetic engages in the former, other people undergo the latter. Involuntary nirjarā never produces Nirvāṇa, but may, at best, only bring about a new life in the heaven of the Vyantara gods. Criminals who have been put to death for their misdeeds become Vyantara gods,

form to the Law of monks preached by the prince of the Jinas [1]), which is able to burn up the forest of karman, the karman that is the seed of the many pains both of body and mind". Thereupon they accepted his words without any doubt, just as sick people tormented by a serious disease accept the words of the physician, and they said: "Reverend, sir, grant us your own vow" [2]). And he thinking, "They are fit, "consecrated them. And

and as such will enjoy celestial glory for twelve thousand years. Aupapātika-Sūtra §§ 69, 70. Cf. Pariçishṭaparvan II, 618. Also in Bhavabhūti's Mahāvīracarita (ed. T. R. Ratnam Ayar, S. Rangachariar, and K. Parab, Bombay 1892) IV, 26—27 (p. 151) we read: "The teachers of the Law think that a redemption from sin takes place in suffering capital punishment just as in penance". "Penance" is here prāyaçcitta, which ordinarily means a particular act to atone for a particular sin. But Rāghava's commentary takes it here as equivalent to tapas. It may be that in the passage from Bhavabhūti we have a parallel to Schopenhauer's famous doctrine. But the Jaina idea certainly differs toto coelo from the German philosopher's magnificent conception and from the beautiful thought of Bṛihadaraṇyakopanishad 5, 11, that the pain of this life and dying and being burned are the highest kind of ascetism (paramaṃ tapas). With the Jainas the matter simply amounts to an arithmetical operation, a thing worked out in accordance with the numeration table. I give only one illustration: A jackal is beaten most unmercifully and dies from these blows; on account of this nirjarā he is born as a god. Uttarajjh. p. 108, l. 6. Cf. my translation of the Daçakumāracaritam p. 31 note; Yogaçāstra IV, 85 ff.; Ziegenbalg's Malabarische Götter (ed. Germann) pp. 164, 176, 188; Jolly, Recht und Sitte (in Bühler's Grundriss) p. 121.

1) Or, "the princes of the Jinas", or perhaps rather, "the princely Jinas"; for the Jainas say that there have been twenty four Jinas. Jinism is the religion preached by all of these.

2) Or, "confer your vow upon us", i. e. ordain us as monks. I see in niyavaya the equivalent of nijavrata. According to Jacobi the translation would seem to be: "Grant us your own station" (pada), i. e. permit us to become monks. Pavolini understands him differently. He offers the rendering: "Assign us our posts". That is clearly wrong. Lanman approves of my taking vaya as vrata, but would like to translate: "Induct us into the way of life which you yourself practise" (vrata = course of action).

in the course of time they became fully instructed monks. Thereupon perfecting themselves by fasting for two days and a half, for three days and a half, four days and a half, five days and a half, a half-month, a whole month, and by other austerities of various sorts[1]), and wandering from village to village, they came in the course of time to Hastināpura. They stayed in the park outside.

One day the monk Sambhūya entered the town in order to break his fast after a self-mortification of one month. Making the round from house to house, careful in his walk[2]), and coming upon the king's highway, he

1) The Jainas eat two times a day. One who performs the chaṭṭhatava, "the penance of the sixth meal" therefore does not eat for five meals, or for two days and a half; and so with the other terms.

2) Īryāsamita. This refers to the first of the five samitis a Jaina monk has to observe. They are: "Īryāsamiti, going by paths trodden by men, beasts, carts, etc., and looking carefully, so as not to occasion the death of any living creature; 2) bhāshāsamiti, gentle, salutary, sweet, righteous speech; 3) eshaṇāsamiti, receiving alms in a manner to avoid the forty-two faults that are laid down; 4) ādānanikshepaṇasamiti, receiving and keeping of things necessary for religious exercises" (i. e. of the monk's begging bowl etc.) "after having carefully examined them" (and the place where anything is to be put down lest living beings be harmed); "5) pari- (prati-)sthāpanasamiti, performing the operations of nature in an unfrequented place" (after having carefully examined the same lest any living being be killed by the discharges of the body). Bhandarkar, Report on the Search for Sanskrit Manuscripts in the Bombay Presidency during the year 1883—1884, p. 98, note †. [The words in brackets are mine]. Cf. Sarvadarçanasaṃgraha transl. by Cowell and Gough p. 57. Weber already has pointed out that samita is Skt. çamita. Bhagavatī p. 279. But it seems to me that it might equally well represent çramita "subdued". That would connect it with çramaṇa, the ordinary word for a Jaina monk. The two last samitis are better described by the words so common in the Jaina books: āyāṇabhaṇḍamattanikkhevaṇāsamie and uccārapāsavaṇakhelasiṃghāṇajallapariṭṭhāvaṇiyāsamie. The former is variously explained by the commentators, but the word itself seems to mean simply: "circumspect in the putting down of one's receiving-vessel-outfit" (i. e. the begging bowl). Cf. Āyāranga-suttaṃ II, 15, II, 4: āyāṇabhaṇḍanikkhevaṇasamie "careful in the setting

was seen by Namui, the minister. The minister recognized him and thinking: "This Caṇḍāla boy will make disclosures to the king and the others", from fear for himself he sent his men and had him tormented with blows of stick, fist, and cudgel and had him chased out [of the city]. Then while the guiltless man was being beaten he assumed a terrible mien on account of his anger, and a flame of fire issued from his mouth to burn these men with. Then the city was darkened all around by the volumes of smoke as by masses of black clouds. Thereupon the townsmen came in fear and curiosity to worship, and together with their attendants they began to propitiate him. The universal sovereign Saṇaṃkumāra, too, came in order to propitiate him. Bowing, with his hands folded on his forehead, he said: "Reverend sir, forgive it that we poor ignorant[1]) people have sinned

down of his utensils of begging". So Jacobi. But we could also translate: "of his receiving-bowl". The latter compound means: "Circumspect in the depositing (disposing) of his excrements, urine, saliva, mucus, and dirt (of the body)". A detailed treatment of the samitis we have in Uttarajjh. XXIV. See especially Jacobi's note to stanza 12 (Sacred Books of the East, Vol. 45, p. 131 ff.). But I have to make the following remarks on his words. Prāmitya (Prākrit pāmicca) and uddhāraka both mean "debt". N°. 9 on p. 132 should therefore read: "Prāmitya, when one has to contract a debt (or make a loan) in order to give to the mendicant". N°. 3 on the sáme page ought rather to run somewhat in this manner: Nimitta, when one gets food by fortune telling". Lakshmīvallabha says: Yadā lābhālābhajīvitamṛityusukhaduḥkhādinimittaṃ trikālasthaṃ gṛihasthāgre uktvā āhāraṃ gṛihṇāti tadā nimittadoshaḥ. Uttarajjh. p. 731, l. 4. N°. 13 on p, 133 (mantradosha) is better explained by the dīpikā: Yadā kārmaṇam, yantramantraṃ sādhayitvā, kṛitvā, dattvā āhāradikaṃ grihṇāti tadā mantradoshaḥ (p. 731, l. paenult.).

Īryāsamiti requires also that a monk look only a yuga ahead — the well-known yugamattaṃ pekkhati of the Buddhists.

1) Possibly aṇejja is = a + jňeya, lit. "being without that which is to be known". The development of jňeya to ṇejja is good Prākrit. See §§ 276, 252. [Jacobi suggests aṇajja (anārya), which is the reading of C].

against you. Withdraw your fire; bestow your gracious favor in granting us life. We shall not do so again".

As he would not be appeased, the monk Citta, who heard the talk of the people and saw the heavens covered with dense smoke, approached him. He said: "O Sambhūya, exstinguish, exstinguish this fire of wrath. Peace of soul is the chief characteristic of great saints [1]). Even if they have been wronged they do not give way to anger; for anger ends in misery, is the cause of all misfortunes and a forest fire for the wood of good conduct.

"And it has been said:

> "As the forest fire kindled by the forest fire burns the essence of the forest in a moment, so the soul changed by passions consumes asceticism and self-control [2]).

1) Uvasamasāraṃ khu sāmaṇṇaṃ, "peace of soul is the essence of monachism". Kalpasūtra III, 59.

2) I do not think that the stanza needs emendation. In the first two pādas the second vaṇadava may be = vanadrava, taking drava as "juice, essence". A forest fire often leaves only the black trunks of the larger trees, which tower in the vast, ash-covered, smouldering cemetery like gigantic mourners draped in sable habiliments, dead themselves; their sap (drava) is gone, the branches and the leaves and the manifold beauty of the forest are gone. Such a spectre of a wood is the fit symbol of a soul ravaged and ruined by the unchecked sway of passions (kasāyapariṇao jīvo). One passion, if indulged in, engenders other passions, the corrupted soul begets, so to speak, a soul still more corrupted, just as the fire is propagated by the fire (davassa jalio lit. kindled of the fire). So vaṇadava would be a punning word and not a bad one if we bear in mind that the soul itself destroys the soul, just as vaṇadavo vaṇadavaṃ. Cf. Dhammapadam 240:

Ayasā va malaṃ samuṭṭhitam
taduṭṭhāya taṃ eva khādati,
evam atidhonacāriṇam
sāni kammāni nayanti duggatiṃ.

"As the rust which has sprung from the iron eats the iron itself, though sprung from it, so his own deeds lead to misery him who transgresses purity" (lit. that which is pure. Dhona "pure" is either *dhā-

"And another saying:

"Anger destroys love, anger increases misery, anger causes pain to one's self and to others.

"Even if one practises manifold fasts lasting a month, gives himself up to dwelling in the woods, studies, perfects himself continually by knowledge and meditation, keeps the hard vow of chastity, and eats alms-food, this will all prove of no avail to him if he is overcome by anger".

By such floods of the water which consisted of the words of the prince of the Jinas, and which had peace of soul for their chief content, the fire of wrath was extinguished. Sambhūya was seized with a great displeasure for the world. Then he returned from that place. And he went to the park. And they thought: "We have undertaken mortification, therefore it is now meet to abstain entirely from eating." They engaged in continued fasting.

vana = pāvana, or *dhauna = dhauta, and it reccurs, for instance, in Majjh.-Nik. I, p. 386; Theragāthā 1271). Or we may translate: "Just as the forest fire burns up the forest fire", i. e. consumes itself, "so the depraved soul destroys the true self of the soul: asceticism and self-control". Cf. Uttarajjh. p. 108, l. 1, where attagavesae (Lecture II, Stanza 32) is beautifully explained: ātmagaveshakaḥ ātmānaṃ saṃyamajīvaṃ gaveshayati. Leumann, as Pavolini informs us, proposes to read: jaha vaṇadavo vaṇaṃ davadavassa jalio, "as the rapidly kindled forest fire burns up the forest" etc. Davadavassa (from dru) occurs, e. g., in Daçavaikālikasūtra V, 1, 14: davadavvassa na gachejjā, "he shall not walk rapidly"; and in Uttarajjh. XVII, 8: davadavassa carai, "he strides on rapidly". Cf. sarasarassa, Uvāsagadasāo § 108 (= Pāli sarasara and sassara, i. e. sarasara > sarsara > sassara Majjh.-Nik. I, 128; Journal of the Pāli Text Society 1889, p. 209. Sarasara "a rustling, rattling noise" occurs also in Skt. Samayamātṛikā VI, 34).

Kasāya is fourfold: anger, conceit, deceit, desire. "Impurity, taint" would suit the etymology and the sense better than the usual translation. Deceit is hardly a passion. Cf. Pāli kasāya.

Thereupon Saṇaṃkumāra, finding out these doings of his minister and becoming angry, had him bound with strong ropes and conducted into their presence. But out of compassion Namuḷ was set at liberty by them. Saṇaṃkumāra too, together with his harem, came to this park to pay them reverence. Accompanied by his harem he did homage to them with devotion and respect. Thereupon Sambhūya began to conceive a wordly thought [1]) because he enjoyed exceedingly the touch of the locks of Suṇandā, [Saṇaṃkumāra's] "Pearl Among Women", who fell at his feet. Then the saint Citta thought: "Alas, how hard it is to conquer delusion! Alas, how hard it is to control the senses! Alas, how the objects of the senses agitate us, since this man, although he has so well done penance, although he has

1) He resolved or desired: "Let the fruit of my asceticism be this that I become a universal sovereign in the next birth, so that I may enjoy such women". A wish of this kind is sinful as being at war with the very nature of asceticism. Its technical name is niyāṇa, nidāṇa. Lakshmīvallabha says: Nidānaṃ tapasaḥ vikrayaḥ. Mamāsya tapasaḥ phalaṃ syāt tarhi rājyendrādibhāg ahaṃ syām itirūpaṃ nidānaṃ (Uttarajjh. p. 828, l. 3). "Nidāna is the selling of penance" etc. But it seems such a wish of bartering away asceticism for sensual pleasures in a future existence must and will be realized; and I consider Citta guilty of a pia fraus when he says to Sambhūya: "Eteshu mā nidānaṃ kuru! Nidānam ghorānusthānaṃ; naiva tādrikphaladaṃ bhavishyati. Uttarajjh. p. 381, ll. 3 and 4 from below. From the hoary days of the Veda down to the present time Hindu sages have declared: "Man is God and the only creator and fashioner of his own being". A remarkable case of āveça, an idea or desire that takes entire possession of a man and that is destined to attain its end, we will meet with in the story of Mūladeva. It is also but natural that the thought which engages a dying man's soul should be deemed of mystic power, especially in the shaping of his future condition. The doctrine of the Bhagavadgītā is well known, and Lakshmīvallalha quotes a rhymed adage that reads: Maraṇasamaye yādṛiçī matiḥ syāt, tādṛiçī gatiḥ syāt. Uttarajjh. p. 1099. l. 6.

so well understood [1]) the words of the prince of the Jinas, has resolved on such a thing, induced by the touch of the tips of a young woman's hair!" Then desiring to awaken his soul he said to him: "Hear! desist from this impure resolution; for the enjoyments of pleasure are unsubstantial, terrible in their consequences, the causes of wandering about in the saṃsāra. Even while they are being enjoyed they cause very great disturbance; and sorrow in reality is their nature. The idea that there is pleasure in them is a manifestation of delusion. And it has been said:

> "As the scabby man scratching his scab deems pain a pleasure, so men fevered with delusion call the pain of sensual enjoyment a pleasure.

"Furthermore: Dependent on eating and drinking [2]) is the body of man and only of impure nature wholly and entirely, and hence there is no reason for being attached to it.

For it has been said:

> "Sprung from semen and blood, caused to grow by impure fluids, consisting of skin, blood, flesh, fat, bones, marrow and semen, dripping impure fluids from nine openings for fluids, a store-house of filthiness — that is the body, charming to the mind only in appearance [3]).

1) Suciiya = *sucitita, from cit, cetati. But maybe we have here one of the many cases where c and v are confused (on account of their great similarity in the Devanāgarī alphabet). Viiya would either be = vidita (known, understood) or = vicita (sifted, investigated, discerned).

2) Lit. "on feeding".

3) Or: on account of the beauty of the skin, (lit. with regard merely to the skin; chavimettaṃ adverb. But the reading of C chavimetta-maṇoharaṃ seems preferable).

"There are an āḍhaya of blood, half an āḍhaya of fat, a kuḍava of bile and phlegm, and half as much of semen, seven hundred veins, nine hundred sinews — in such a body there is no purity.

"Delicious food and drink and the most excellent dainties and sweetmeats, they all grow impure by coming in contact with the body.

"The finest garment, the finest flower, the finest perfume and ointment, the finest bed and seat are destroyed by the body [1]).

Ill-smelling moisture [2]) continually flows on the teeth, and impure fluid in the mouth, and sticking mucus in the nose.

"Only marrow runs in the bones, nasty filth in the ears, ill-smelling sweat from the pores.

"With such a body, the abode of all diseases, do you, O foremost among saints, not become infatuated after you have fully fathomed sacred knowledge:

Although he was instructed with such and other similar words his soul did not awake. And by reason of his excessive delusion Sambhūya formed the wordly thought: "If there is a fruit of this penance [of mine] then may I become [3]) a universal sovereign in another birth." By him was proved what has been said:

1) Cp. the story how Bharata, the first cakravartin, became a monk Uttarajjh. pp. 515, 516.
2) For ulla = unna see Pischel § 111.
3) For hojjā see § 466.

> The most dangerous tree of delusion, whose roots are spread out for the bringing forth of beginningless existence is only with difficulty uprooted by the most zealous.

Then dying they both became gods in the Sodhamma heaven. Thence the soul of Citta fell and was born as a rich merchant's son in Purimātala. Sambhūya's soul having fallen thence — there was a king in Kampillapura, named Bambha, his queen consort was named Culaṇī — was conceived in her womb and born in the course of time, announced by the fourteen great dreams [1]). And the name of Bambhadatta was given him. He increased in growth of body and in [knowledge of] the multitude of the sciences.

And this king Bambha had for his friends four great kings, descended from the most exalted lines. They were:

> Kaḍaya, the lord of the realm of Kāsī; Kaṇeradatta, the ruler of Gayaura; Dīha, the lord of the realms of Kosala; Pupphacūla, the ruler of Campā.

In their exceeding great love, unwilling to be separated from one another, delighting only in one another's company, they lived by turns always one year in the kingdom of one of them [2]), engaged in various kinds of amusements. One year, being so fond of one another's com-

1) The fourteen great dreams that every pregnant woman dreams who is going to give birth to a tīrthakara (Maker of a Ford, Founder of the Faith, Jaina Prophet), or to a universal monarch. See Kalpasūtra ed. Jacobi p. 32 ff.; Nirayāvaliyasuttaṃ ed. Warren, Aanteckningen pp. 22—23.

2) Lit. "in their own kingdoms".

pany, they came to Bambha. And while they stayed there, Bambha — since the end of death is appointed for the world of the living — was attacked by a disease of the head that would yield neither to spell, nor witchcraft, nor medicine, nor anything else. Then he had Kaḍaya and his other friends called; on their lap he put Bambhadatta and said to them: "You must make it possible for him to rule the realm". Having thus provided for his kingdom he died. His friends performed the funeral rites etc. for him. Then Kaḍaya and the others said: "Until this boy becomes able to bear the burden of government we must guard this kingdom"; and thus taking counsel together they, with the consent of all, appointed Dīha [regent]; and the rest went home to their own realms. And when they had gone this Dīha maintained the royal power with all its appurtenances, looked after the treasury, entered the harem and talked with Culaṇī. Then by reason of the uncontrollability of the senses, not heeding his friendship for Bambha, and disregarding reproach, he had a love intrigue [1]) with Culaṇī. While thus their enjoyment of sensual pleasure increased, the days passed by.

Then a minister of king Bambha, called Dhaṇu, who had been his second heart, found out the truth and thought: "How should he who does such an improper thing desire the welfare of prince Bambhadatta!" Having thus reflected he privately said to prince Varadhaṇu [his own son]: "Son, his mother has become a wicked woman; therefore let the prince secretly know of this affair." He did

1) Sampalagga = Skt. sampralagna.

so. Then the prince, not being able to bear his mother's evil conduct, in order to make her understand put a crow and a hen kokila together and taking them with him went straight into the harem and said: "If any one else acts thus I shall punish him." The next day he took a male elephant of mean extraction [1]) together with the female elephant of state, and came to the same place. Then Dīha knew [what he meant] and said to Culaṇī: "I am the crow, you the hen kokila." She prated: "The prince is a child; he babbles out anything." Then he said: "It is not otherwise; therefore the prince, who hinders the enjoyment of our love, must die. As long as I am at your disposal you will have other sons" [2]). Then because she was a slave to her love for sexual enjoyment she consented even to such a thing, although it is not to be thought of even in one's heart. For:

> Woman is the little stream that destroys families, woman in this world is the field where wicked conduct grows, woman is the door to misery, woman is the womb of misfortunes.
>
> A bad woman fevered with passion kills her fond husband, undoes her son, likewise destroys wealth, and sets fire to her own house.

1) Saṃkīrṇa > saṃkiṇṇa (mixed), if used of an elephant, is said to mean "rutting." But saṃkīrṇanāga denotes an "elephant of mixed characteristics"; and here the connection speaks rather for "mongrel, not of pure blood".

Concerning the crow and the kokila the dīpikā informs us: kākakokilamithunaṃ çūlāprotaṃ kṛitvā (in explanation of saṃgrahaṇa). This is almost certainly wrong.

2) According to Jacobi, who is followed by Pavolini, we would have to translate: "As long as I am independent (free) you will have other sons". I think this interpretation is not as good as mine.

And she said: "If only he were killed somehow by such a strategem that the censure of the people would be avoided!" He replied: "This is the way the thing must be done. We will celebrate the marriage of the prince; along with all that is needful for it, we will make ready a house built of resinous material, resting on many pillars, and having a hidden entrance and exit. When after the wedding he sleeps there soundly we will do the deed unnoticed by setting fire [to the house]". Having thus taken counsel together, they asked for a great king's daughter and prepared everything necessary for the nuptials.

Now Dhaṇu, who was attentive to the affairs of Bambhadatta, respectfully told king Dīha: "My son here, prince Varadhaṇu, is able to take care of the burden of government; I, on the other hand, will bring about my welfare in the other world". Then Dīha deceitfully said: "Enough of travelling [1]) to other places! Stay right here and acquire merit by alms-giving and by other good actions".

And consenting to this, Dhaṇu on the bank of the Ganges had a great shed with water reservoir made. And they set about to give food and drink in plenty to travelers, religious mendicants, etc. And he bade trustworthy men whom he won over by gifts, honors, and favors dig an underground passage of two gavyūti in length till they would reach the resin house. And now the bride, surrounded by her retinue, which was attired in various costumes, reached the good town

1) For pauttha = pavuttha cp. Pāli vuttha and § 564.

and was conducted into the city with great splendor.

The wedding took place forthwith. Immediately after, the hosts of attendants were dismissed and the prince together with his bride was conducted to the resin house. Accompanied by his young wife and attended by Varadhaṇu, who sat down on a seat, he dismissed the rest of the servants[1]) and spent two watches of the night.

Then the bedchamber was set on fire all around. Woeful cries arose. Then the prince, whose mind was troubled as to what should be done, questioned Varadhaṇu: "What is the matter?" He said: "That princess was warned by sending her a letter; this woman is somebody else. You should not regard her[2]). Give the resin house here a kick with your heel that we may escape". He did so. Thereupon having broken through the resin house, he escaped by way of the underground passage and came to the place near the door.

Now two trusty men, mounted on steeds, were kept in advance at the door of the underground passage by the minister Dhaṇu. These bade the princes mount on the horses which they had brought with them[3]) by appointment with Varadhaṇu, and then went away. The princes too started to go and they travelled a distance

1) Or, "all the servants", if the reading given by Jacobi in the Verbesserungen und Druckfehler is that of the MSS. [So MS. C].

2) According to Jacobi the passage means: "You should not bestow your love on her". Paḍibandha is perhaps better taken as "hindrance" ("let not yourself be hindered by her"); or, as imāe in all probability is a loc. sg., "do not trouble about her" (mach bei ihr keinem Aufenthalt). The dīpikā has: Tasmād asyām moho manāg api na kāryaḥ (p. 383, l. 2 from bottom).

3) Lit., "which had come together" (had been brought together).

of fully fifty yojanas. Exhausted by the long journey the steeds dropped. They started to go on foot and came to a village called Koṭṭa. Then the prince said to Varadhaṇu: "Hunger torments me: I am sorely wearied". Stationing him there Varadhaṇu entered the village; he returned with a barber. He had the prince's head shaved and attired him in a dark red robe. A band consisting of a strip of cloth four fingers in breadth covered his breast, adorning it with a sirivaccha [1]). Varadhaṇu too changed his attire. They entered the interior of the village.

In the meanwhile a slave servant came out of the fine house of a Brahman and accosted them: "Come, eat!" Going thereupon they were fed there [being treated] with marks of distinction that would have befitted a king. And at the end of the meal a most beautiful woman threw akshata [2]) on the prince's head pointing to [his marriage with] Baṇdhumaī And she said: "That is the bridegroom of this maiden". When Varadhaṇu had heard this he said: "Why do you trouble yourselves on account of this stupid lad?" Then the master of the house said: "Hear, Sir. Formerly an astrologer announced to us: He whose breast is covered with a strip of cloth and who, together with his friend, eats the food of this girl, will be her husband" [3]). Addressed in such wise the

1) The sirivaccha, an auspicious figure (maṅgala) is often mentioned in the Jaina writings. A picture of one may be seen in Schlagintweit's Indien in Wort und Bild Vol. II, p. 105.

2) "Whole grain, entire unhusked and unpounded rice washed with water and used as an article of worship in all religious and sacred ceremonies". Apte. Cp. Shankar Pandit's note to Raghuvaṃça II, 21.

3) Probably the next sentence also belongs to the speech of the master

prince was married to her on that day. On the second day Varadhaṇu said to the prince: "We have to travel far". Thereupon they told Bandhumaī the real state of affairs and went away.

Travelling on they came to another village far away. There Varadhaṇu entered in order to get water. Returning quickly he said: "I have heard here the common talk of the people which declares: "King Dīha has closed the roads against Bambhadatta in every direction." Therefore let us flee, O prince." Then setting forth on a by-path [1]) they got into a great forest. Thereupon leaving the prince, who was overcome with thirst, under a fig tree Varadhaṇu went for water. And in the meanwhile Varadhaṇu in the evening was seen by men in Dīha's employ, as it were by the servants of Yama. Being beaten [by them] he went a long way. He made a sign to the prince. Bambhadatta fled and strayed into a pathless wildwood.

Thereupon, exhausted by thirst, hunger, and fatigue, he traversed the great forest and on the third day saw an ascetic. At the mere sight of him hope of life sprang up in him. And he asked him: "Reverend sir, where is your hermitage?" He told him and conducted him to

of the house. "The prince having been thus announced on that day was married to her". But bhaṇio in this sense would be unusual. B reads bhaṇiyam. "Thus he spoke. On this day I have married the prince to her". This rendering too is open to objections.

1) Ummagga does not only mean "Abweg", but also "Umweg, Seitenweg", a signification of the word that is common in Pāli (e. g. Majjh.-Nik. I. pp. 171, 237; Vinaya, Vol. I, p. 8; Angutt.-Nik. II, pp. 177, 189; Therīgāthā p. 203); but also "wrong way", as in Skt. Cp. Theragāthā 1232; Therīg. 94; and "the way up to, the way of attacking a problem" etc. Angutt.-Nik. II, pp. 177, 189).

the head of the community of ascetics [1]). He made a low obeisance to the head of the community. And he was accosted by him: "Child, where do you come from? This wilderness is full of untoward things". Then he told him everything truthfully just as matters stood. Thereupon the head of the community said to him: "I am your father's uncle [2]); therefore my hermitage is yours. Dwell here at ease". Knowing the sentiment [3]) of his heart he began to live there. And in the meanwhile the rainy season came. By his grandfather [4]) he was instructed in archery and all the other great sciences of arms.

One day in autumn time when the boys of the ascetics rambled about on the borders of the wildwood in order to gather fruits, bulbs, roots, flowers, and fuel, he, from curiosity, went into the wildwood, although the head of the community forbade him [5]). While he was looking there at the woods that abounded in fresh fruits and flowers he saw a great elephant. And the animal uttered

1) Jacobi's "Hausherr" for kulavai is at least misleaping. The word also denotes the head of a community of ascetics (cp. Ṛishabhapañcāçikā 20; Zeitschr. d. deutsch. morgenl. Gesellschaft 33, p. 461, where the commentator correctly transscribes it by "tāpasācārya). Kulapati is frequently used the same way in Skt.

2) Cullapiu and cullatāo (little father) do not mean "father-in-law", as given by Jacobi, but "uncle", just as cullapitā in Pāli. The dīpikā correctly has: Aham bhavajjanakasya kshullabhrātā. Uttarajjh. p. 385, l. 4.

3) Ahippāya in all probability is = abhiprāya, since abhippāya is also used in Pāli. Still there is a possibility of its being equivalent to Pāli adhippāya (e.g. Majj.-Nik. I, pp. 234, 305; Angutt.-Nik. III, p. 156; Vinaya Vol. I, p. 301 (metaph. used of that which is *intended* for one, i.e. one's share). Cp. also adhippeta, Jāt. I, 103; Sumangalavil. I, 104, and Childers.

4) His "grandfather", of course, is his father's uncle.

5) §§ 266, 546.

a roar that came rumbling from the throat. Then the elephant turned towards him and started in pursuit. Thereupon he rolled up his outer garment and threw it down before the beast. And it seized it that very moment with its trunk and flung it up into the air. At the very time when the elephant had become blind with rage the prince caught the garment, baffling the elephant by his dexterity. Then having wearied the elephant with different kinds of play he let it go.

Thereupon he started on the way back, bewildered as to which was the eastern or the western direction. Straying hither and thither he saw a fine ruinous town situated on the bank of a mountain stream and visible only in the broken walls of the old, decayed houses. And filled with curiosity at the sight of this, looking about with eyes cast in every direction, he saw a strange bower of bamboo with shield and sword thrown down beside it [1]). And having seen this he playfully brought that sword to bear on this bamboo bower [2]). At one stroke the bamboo bower tumbled down. And a severed lotus-like head with slightly quivering lips and charming in appearance, which had been in the midst of the bamboo

1) Kuḍanga is extremely common in Prākrit. It designates not only a bower, an arbour, but very frequently a thicket, a coppice. Jaina writers use it also in Skt. So Hemacandra, Pariçishṭap. XI, 152; that very same kuḍanga he calls a vana in stanzas 154 and 166. In the text too we most probably ought to translate: "a bamboo thicket".

For kheḍayakhagga and kheḍagaasi Jacobi offers "Hirschfänger". Maybe he is right. But as I do not know of this use of the word I have preferred to take it as a dvandva compound.

2) Vāhia, I think, is = Skt. vāhita, set in motion, swung, brandished etc., although we have ohariá, brought to bear, wielded, geschwungen in Rāvaṇavaha XIII, 3, 28. The ṭīkā, too, has vāhita, though this counts for little. But we find vāhai, "to wield, to use" in Uttarajjh. XVII, 18.

reeds, dropped down[1]). When he saw this he was confused and blamed his own strength of arm, saying: "Woe is me! Out on my violence!"[2]) Then as he looked about, seized with regret, he saw a headless body fastened with the feet up, desirous of drinking smoke[3]). He began to feel extremely distressed. When he looked again he saw a fine park and in it a palatial mansion of seven stories surrounded on all sides by fine açoka trees. And having seen this he gradually ascended to the seventh story. And there he saw a magnificent woman with eyes like the petals of the full-blown blue lotus flower, who seemed a fairy woman that had lost her magic. And he asked her: "Beautiful lady, who are you?" Then she began to speak, full of fear, in the following manner: "Most excellent sir, my story is very long;

1) Ruṇḍa cannot stand for "trunk" here. It is an adjective, meaning "mained". Maṇoharāyāra is = manoharākāra.

2) Vavasiya most probably corresponds to vyavasita, "determination, energetic effort, violent act".

3) This does not refer to the burning of the dead body on the funeral pile, as Pavolini thinks, but to a well-known mode of doing penance, consisting in the man's hanging from the bough of a tree with his head downward, over a fire lighted below. See, for instance, Raghuvaṃça XV, 49, 50:

> Atha dhūmābhitāmrākshaṃ
> vṛikshaçākhāvalambitam
> dadarça kaṃcid Aikshvākas
> tapasyantam adhomukham.
>
> Pṛishṭanāmānvayo rājñā
> sa kilācashṭa dhūmapaḥ
> ātmānaṃ Çambukaṃ nāma
> çūdraṃ surapadārthinam.

In Uttararāmacarita ed. R. Ayar and K. P. Parab, Bombay 1899, p. 53 we read: Çambūko nāmādhomukho dhūmapaḥ çūdro 'sminn eva sthāne janas tapaç carati. The object of the man's austerities appears later on in our tale.

therefore do you tell me, Who are you? And where do you go?" Thereupon having heard her speech which was as sweet as the melodies of the kokila, his heart was won and he told her the truth: "Beautiful lady, I am the son of king Bambha, the ruler of Pancāla, and Bambhadatta is my name". Then immediately on hearing these words she suddenly rose, and her eyes being filled with tears of joy and opening wide from delight, she fell at his feet and began to weep. Then his heart was seized with pity and lifting up her face and saying: "Do not weep", he quieted her and asked her: "Fair lady, who are you?" Then she wiped [1]) her eyes and commenced to speak: "Prince, I am the daughter of your maternal uncle king Pupphacūla, [and am] bestowed on you. Waiting for the wedding day I was brought hither by a wicked Vidyādhara while I played on the sandy beach of the lake in the park of our house. And while I dwell here burned [2]) with the fire of separation from my relatives, you have suddenly arrived here like an unexpected rain of gold. Because you have been seen by me, therefore hope of life has sprung up in me".

1) Phusai "to wipe" is rather rare; usually we have pusai. Etymologically it can, of course, not be equivalent to proñchati. Puṃsai (phuṃsai) also occurs. See Gauḍavaha, ed. Shankar Pandit, sub voce. The Skt. commentary translates it by puṃsati (utpuṃsati). Puṃs abhimardane will hardly do. I think phuṃs, phus, puṃs, pus connect with spṛç. The developement of meaning is parallel to maḷai "to touch" and "to rub". The difference of import would also account well for pus instead of phus. Rovai is from ru, not from rud § 473. — I see now Pischel offers the same etymology of pus (§ 486). Puṭṭha = phuṭṭha "touched" occurs frequently too.

2) § 244. The same change we have in Pāli, e.g. ālimpati and ālimpeti, "to kindle, set on fire, to heat". Vinaya Vol. I, p. 204; II, p. 138; Anguttara-Nik. III, 100, 13; Milindapañho p. 43 (ālimpanaṃ conflagration).

Thereupon he addressed her: "But where is this enemy of mine, so that I may try his redoubtable strength?" She said: "My lord, he gave me a charm, called Saṃkarī, which works when it is recited. And he said: "As soon as the charm is simply remembered by you it will become surrounded by friends, servants etc. and do your bidding. Coming to your side it will keep off an enemy and it will announce to you what I am doing if it be asked[1]). And I have remembered it, so I am its master[2]). Naṭṭumata is the name of the Vidyādhara by whom I have been brought here. And he cannot bear the splendor of me who excels in virtue; therefore he left me in a palace created by magic and decorated with white and red flags, and sent a charm called Jāṇāvaṇī to his own sisters in order to tell them my story; he himself went to the bamboo bower. Having made himself master of a magic spell[3]) he will come out and marry me[4]). And to-day, you know, the attainment of this spell will come to pass". Thereupon when Bambhadatta had heard this he told Pupphavaī the story of the Vidyādhara's death. Full of joy she said: "You have done well in that you killed this villain". Then he married her according to the Gandharva marriage rite. And he remained with her for some time.

1) That is, the charm or spell will *speak*, a common idea. Cf. Uttarajjh. p.p. 386, 394 and see the note on p. 71 of my Daçakumāracaritam.

2) Sāhei vijjaṃ is very frequent in Prākrit. It answers to Skt. sādhayati vidyām (cp. sādhayati mantram in Monier-Williams sub sādh). Idānīṃ sādhayishyāmi vidyām udyogavān aham. Pariçishṭaparvan II, 664. Cp. VII, 61 ff.; VIII, 262, and many other passages in this work.

3) Vidyāṃ sādhayituṃ vaṃçakuḍange gato 'sti. Uttarajjh. p. 386, l. 10.

4) The careful reader will see that ti (tti) = iti in our tales is often inserted somewhere in the direct speech, instead of being added at the end.

One day he heard the talk of heavenly women[1]). And he asked her: "Whose voice is that?" She answered: "Husband, these are the sisters of your enemy Naṭṭumatta, two fairy maidens, Khāṇḍā and Visāhā by name, who have come bringing all the wedding paraphernalia for him. Do you, therefore, quickly withdraw till I find out[2]) their disposition[3]). If they are attached to you I shall wave a red flag on the roof of the palace — that is the signal; otherwise a white one."

Then, after a short while, seeing a white flag, he softly slipped away from that place and came into the midst of a mountain-thicket. And he saw a great fine lake. He duly bathed in it and stepped out on the north-western bank. And there he saw a most beautiful maiden. And he thought: "Ah, what good luck of mine[4]) that she has come into the range of my sight!" Then she also looked at him with ardent love. Then gazing[5]) she departed from that place, while after a short time a female servant sent by her alone handed over to him a pair of garments, flowers, betel etc. And she said: "She who has been seen by you on the bank of the great lake, she sent this. And she told me:" "Friend Vanalaiā, let this noble man attend to the

1) I see no reason whatever why vilayāṇa should be changed to valayāṇa in accordance with Lakshmīvallabha's divyavalayānām çabdaḥ, as Pavolini has done. [C also reads vilayāṇa].

2) Lit, "approach".

3) — tti because the preceding words express her idea (purpose, their agreement).

4) Lit., "Ah the ripening (reward) of my good works (done in a former existence)!"

5) Paloyantiyā = *prolokayantikā, fem. of pralokayantaka, Skt. pralokayat. [Cf. asohantiyā = açobhamānā, C fol. 242 *b*].

care of his body in the house of my father's minister". Therefore, come you!" Then the prince, dressed and adorned, went to the house of Nāgadeva, the minister. And she said to the minister: "He has been sent by your lord's daughter Sirikantā. Therefore look upon him with regard." The minister did precisely so.

On the second day he was taken into the presence of the king. He too rose to greet him and gave him a seat in front. He questioned him as to his history. And after the meal he said: "People like us can do no other notable thing to bid you welcome". After these words he gave him the maiden Sirikantā in marriage with marked honor. On a preeminent day the wedding took place.

One day the prince asked his beloved: "Why have you been given in marriage to me, a lonely man?" "She replied:" "Dear lord, my father here, driven away by a mighty kinsman [1]), has taken refuge in this inac-

1) Dāiya according to Jacobi here means an adversary, and the ṭīkā has balavattaravairisaṃtāpitaḥ. In our passage it is not perfectly clear how we should translate. But one thing seems certain — dāiya is = Skt. dāyaka in both cases. A kinsman is the natural and most redoubtable enemy of an Eastern ruler. Kshemendra has a number of stanzas on this matter which I cannot forbear to quote. They are so excellent and so much in the Hindu vein.

Marmajñaḥ svajanaḥ puṃsāṃ
kshaye jāgarti nāparaḥ;
çikshāpakshibhir ākrishṭah
kshayaṃ yāntyeva pakshiṇaḥ.

Sadā dārūṇi dahyante
dārujena ca vahninā,
krimiṇā svāngajātena
pātyante prauḍhapādapaḥ.

cessible hamlet. And when he has destroyed towns and villages he enters the fortress. I was born of Sirimaī, my father's wife, in addition to four sons, and my father is exceedingly fond of me. And when I had attained the bloom of youth the king said to me: "Daughter all the kings are my enemies; so the bridegroom who captivates your heart while you live here, must be announced to me". Now while I, leaving the hamlet and going to the great, fine lake, looked at the men, I saw you by virtue of my merit [acquired in a former life]. This is the state of affairs." The days then went by for him while he together with Sirikantā enjoyed the pleasures of the senses.

One day the lord of the hamlet accompanied by his army went to devastate a country [1]). Bambhadatta too went with him. In the meantime he suddenly saw Varadhaṇu on the bank of a lotus lake near the outs-

Mṛijjātalohakuddālaiḥ
khanyate mṛiṇmayī mahī,
svajātair nirjharair nītāḥ
kashadbhir bhūdharāḥ kshayam.

Jnātiprahāro niḥçarma-
marmapātī parādhikaḥ;
lohādhikāṃ vyathām asthnaḥ
karotyasthimukhaḥ çaraḥ.

Sahabhogyām api jñāter
necchanti jñātayaḥ çriyam;
kāṅkshanti bhūtim anyeshāṃ
dūrālokananishphalam.

Daçāvatāracritam VIII, 108 ff.

Cp. also bhrātrivya, "cousin, enemy". — Pellāi (pellei), I think, is = *preryati, in Skt. prerayati. Weber in his Hāla has already suggested either prer or pīḍ. See § 285.

1) Lakshmīvallabha has: svavirodhinṛipadeçabhangāya calitaḥ. Uttarajjh. p. 388, l. 1.

kirts of the village there. And he, recognizing him, whom he had not expected to see, fell to weeping. Bambhadatta quieted him. Varadhaṇu, who sat down comfortably, asked the prince: "What have you experienced in my absence?" And he told him everything. When Varadhaṇu also was questioned by him he answered: "Prince, listen. At that time, having left you below a banyan tree, I went for water. Then I saw a great lake. When I had taken some water in the hollow of my hand[1]) and had set out toward you I was suddenly beaten by the hirelings of Dīha, who were armed and buckled in mail and who said: "Ho there! ho there! Varadhaṇu, where is Bambhadatta?" I answered: "I don't know". Then, being beaten by them still more severely, I said: "He has been devoured by a tiger." "Show us the spot!" Then I wandered hither and thither and by a trick came into the range of your sight. I made you a sign that meant: "Flee!" I myself put a [magic] pill into my mouth that had been given me by a religious mendicant. By the power of that I became senseless. Then they thought: "He has died," and went away. And after a long while I took the pill out of my mouth. Then I set out to search for you, but did not see you. I went into a village. There I saw a religious mendicant, He said: "I am your father's friend, Vasubhāga by name." And he related [the story] to me: „Dhaṇu has fled[2]) and your mother has been banished to a Caṇḍāla village". Thereupon, having

1) Perhaps more probably: "in an (improvised, cornucopia-shaped) vessel made of a lotus leaf" (or of some other leaf).

2) Palāo = *palāta, Skt. palāyita.

heard this, I went in great sorrow to Kampillapura. Putting on the dress of a kāpālika ascetic and deceiving the Caṇḍāla village magistrate [1]) I took my mother away. Then leaving my mother in a village in the house of my father's friend, the Brahman Devasamma, I came hither to search for you".

While thus they tarried there deeming happiness a misery [2]) a man came there. He spoke as follows: "Most excellent sir, you must not stroll about anywhere; men in Dīha's employ have arrived here in search of you". Then they quickly left that forest thicket and wandering about went to Kosambī. There in the park outside of the city they saw a cock-fight gotten up [3]) by two merchant's sons, Sāgaradatta and Buddhila by name, who had made the stake a hundred thousand pieces. Buddhila's cock was struck by Sāgaradatta's cock and then Sāgaradatta's cock was struck by the cock of Buddhila. Thereupon Sāgaradatta's cock was cowed and did'nt want to fight, although he was moved toward the cock of Buddhila; and therefore Sāgaradatta lost his lakh. At this point Varadhaṇu said to Sāgara-

1) Leumann (Literaturblatt für orientalische Philologie Vol. III, p. 81) declares: mayahara aus mahayara = mahattara. The phonetic difficulties are too great. Mark also maikara = mayahara. I think, it is matadhara (matidhara), or less likely, — hara; i. e., either: he who represents (lit. holds, carries) the opinion of the community, or: he who carries (i. e. gets, is honored by) their opinion (approbation). It is true we find mahattara for mayahara in Jaina Skt. But that proves nothing; and mahattara remains unchanged in Prākrit. See Kalpasūtra I, 110 and Pischel § 414. In a way similar are German Stimmführer and Finnish äänenkannattaja (lit., Stimmenträger).

2) They were impatient that they had to remain in the little hamlet, but in reality it was for their best. Cp. Erz. 4, ll. 4 and 5; Erz. 53, l. 1,

3) Sampalagga = Skt. sampralagna.

datta and Buddhila: "Why has this cock, although of good breed, been cowed by the second cock?[1]) So I'll look [into the matter], if you do not take it amiss". Sāgaradatta said: "Most excellent sir, look, look! For I am not at all greedy for the money in this affair, but I care that my honor should prosper". Thereupon Varadhaṇu examined Buddhila's cock. And he saw bright fine needles made of iron fastened to his feet. And Buddhila observed that he noticed them. Then he went up to him and secretly told Varadhaṇu: "If you do not speak of the affair of the needles I shall give you half of the lakh". But although he prated: "Hear, I have investigated, but seen nothing", in such a manner that Buddhila did'nt notice it he made the matter known to Sāgaradatta somehow or other, by employing [certain] movements of the eyes and the fingers. And Sāgaradatta freed his own cock from the needles[2]) by taking them off [the feet of Buddhila's cock] all unnoticed. And thus

1) Bīyakukkuḍa Leumann takes = bījakukkuṭa, "Samenhahn, Zuchthahn" (Literatturbl. f. oriental. Philol.. III, p. 81). I hardly think a cock used for breeding purposes will be a very good fighter. But even if he were, how about the first cock? The two cocks cannot have been so different, for these sportsmen of Ancient India knew something about that matter. Cp. my Daçakumāracaritam pp. 281 ff.; R. F. Burton, Sind Revisited, Vol. II, pp. 78—83. Burton sees nothing wrong in this sport, which George Crabbe condemns so eloquently (The Parish Register, Part I: Here his poor bird th' inhuman cocker brings etc.). Our fellow citizens in *spe* on the Philippine Islands are very fond of this kind of sport. Most interesting notes on this amusement of theirs are to be found in a number of the Revue des deux mondes of 1876, if my memory serves me right. See also Haberlandt's Daçakumāracaritam p. 158, note 46. In Pullés Un progenitore Indiano del Bertoldo (p. 4 of the text) a cock is made to fight with himself (by being placed before a mirror).

2) I. e. from the annoyance caused him by the needles of his adversary. [Cp. Appendix].

the second cock was defeated. So Buddhila lost the lakh. Thereupon the two were astonished[1]). And highly gratified, Sāgaradatta said with eyes opening wide: "Noble sirs, let us go home". With these words he made both mount into his fine carriage and went to his own house. Having performed all the proper duties [of hospitality] he always looked upon them with love.

While they were thus knit to him in affection one day a slave servant came to them. He called Varadhaṇu and took him aside. Saying thereupon: "On account of the half of a lakh that Buddhila promised you in case you would not speak of the affair of the needles he sent you here a necklace of pearls worth forty thousand pieces", the slave servant handed over to him the little bamboo box containing the necklace and went away. Varadhaṇu took it, went to Bambhadatta, told how the matter was, and showed him the necklace, drawing it out of the box[2]). When the prince examined it he saw hanging from one part of it a letter addressed to Bambhadatta[3]) and he asked: "Friend, whose is this letter?" Varadhaṇu said: "Who knows? There are many men called Bambhadatta. What is there to wonder about?"[4])

1) For sarisarī Jacobi conjectures the meaning "astonishment". Unfortunately we do not know who is intended by doṇha. Only Bambhadatta and Buddhila can have been surprised at the issue. Sari is found in the sense of sadṛç (see § 245). So sarisarī could perhaps denote "friendship" (lit. "a like-and like"). Cp. my books Kshemendra's Samayamātrikā p. 52 note 1) and Dāmodaragupta's Kuṭṭanimatam p. 148 (additions). The translation then would run: "A friendship between the two (Sagaradatta and Varadhaṇu) sprang up". The context favors such an interpretation. [Possibly noise, hubbub, Skt. sarasara?]

2) Concerning kaḍḍhittu see § 577; darisei §§ 135, 554.

3) Lit. "marked with the name of Bambhadatta".

4) Cojja is = codya (lit. inciting, exciting etc.). Cp. Çiçupālavadha

Then as the prince was all absorbed in musing he took him aside and opened the letter, and they saw the following stanza contained in it:

"Although Rayaṇavaī is being wooed by the people in the world, who put forth their exertions for a union with her, nevertheless she means to honor only thee, the fortunate" [1]).

And while Varadhaṇu reflected: "How shall I find out the truth about her?" [2]), on the second day a female religious mendicant came to him. She threw akshata and flowers on the head of the prince, and saying: "Son, mayest thou live a thousand years", she took Varadhaṇu aside; and after speaking about something with him, she went back. Then the prince questioned Varadhaṇu: "What does she say?" He answered: "This is what she said: "Hand me over a reply to the letter that came together with the necklace Buddhila sent

IX, 16; Hāla 406. But maybe the Skt. codya is a wrong translation of cud + ya > cujja > cojja. — For avaherī from stem avadhārya cp. § 176. But I am not sure of the etymology.

1) The reading of A. [and C.], which is confirmed by Uttarajjh. p. 389 l. 3 from bottom, is to be preferred, and the passive patthijjai connects with prārthyate. Dhaṇiyaṃ can also here mean "much, exceedingly" (so Jacobi), which may perfectly well correspond to Skt. dhanyam "reichlich" = sehr. My translation is better in sense.

2) Bhāvattha would be literally: "the matter of her being (i. e. of her condition, station in life etc.), the particulars about her". For these, it seems, he would naturally have applied to Buddhila. Very likely the delicate nature of the affair forbade him. Bhāvartha usually means "sense". In that case we would have to translate: "the meaning of this stanza". So Pavolini takes it, and Lakshmīvallabha declares: Sūkshmabuddhyā dhyāyatā Varadhaṇunāsyā gāthāyā artho 'vagataḥ. Uttarajjh. p. 389, ll. 2 and 3 from bottom. The import of the metrical missive however is perfectly clear; and no subtle intellect was necessary to grasp that.

you in a little bamboo box". I said: "This letter is addressed to king Bambhadatta. Therefore tell me: Who is this Bambhadatta? She said: "Listen[1]), but you must not tell this to any one. There is here in the city a merchant's daughter, a maiden named Rayaṇavaī. And from the very time of her childhood being extremely attached in love to me she has reached the bloom of youth. And I saw her the other day pondering over something[2]). Then I went up to her and said: "Daughter Rayaṇavaī, what are you thinking about?" Her attendants said: „It is many days since she has been so melancholy". When she said not a word to me, although I asked her again and again, her friend Piyangalaiā declared: "Reverend lady, she is so ashamed that she cannot tell you anything; therefore I relate the matter. A few days ago she went to the park in order to amuse herself, when her brother, the merchant Buddhila, made [his cock] fight for the stake of a lakh, and she beheld a fine prince never seen before[3]), who somehow or other had come to that place. And since she beheld him she has become thus". And when I had heard this I noticed her love-sickness. And I said to her tenderly: "Daughter, tell me the truth". Then with very great difficulty she became affectionate[4]) and said: "Reverend lady, you

1) In regard to summau see § 536. Perhaps summai is to be looked upon in the same way as hammai etc. (for which see § 540), i. e. * çrūman parallel with * dūman, * nūman, * (hnūman). Hāla 91.

2) Or according to Jacobi's corrections (p. 159): "Being extremely attached to me from the time of her chilhood, she has reached the age of puberty. And I saw her the other day pondering about something."

3) I. e., 1) a stranger to her; 2) extraordinary, wonderful.

4) So if we follow Jacobi. But it seems preferable to translate: "She approached the truth, faced the truth, resolved to tell me the real state

are my mother; so there is nothing that I could not tell you. If that Bambhadatta of whom Piyangulaīa spoke does not become my husband, then I shall surely die". Thereupon having heard this, I said: "Child, take courage. I shall make it possible for your desire to be realized" [1]). Then she grew a little better [2]). And yesterday I said to her in order to comfort her heart: "Child, I have seen that prince Bambhadatta". When she had heard this she said, her heart reviving: "Reverend lady, through your grace everything will be well. But in order to inspire him with confidence do you, in the name of Buddhila, put this jewel of a necklace into a box and send it and this letter addressed to Bambhadatta". And yesterday I performed [3]) this accordingly. So the affair of the letter has herewith been told you, illustrious sir. Now give me the reply". And I handed her the following reply:

> "Bambhadatta too, accompanied by an excellent bow that has a mighty string [or, accompanied by Varadhaṇu who appears in the quality of a teacher] means to honor Rayaṇavaī as the moon united with Çiva the earth [4]).

of affairs." Less likely is the rendering: "She entered (regained) her real (i. e. her natural, usual) state (of confidence in me)". The dīpikā reads: Mayā uktam: "Putri, kathaya sadbhāvam!" Punaḥ punar evaṃ mayoktā sā katham api sadbhāvam uktvā prāha' etc.

1) Lit., "I shall so act that your desire will be realized."

2) Lit., "became well somewhat." Or perhaps better, "became a little herself again."

3) Nirūvia = nirūpita, exactly, "to perform" (give form to); cp. the stage sense of nirūpayati, "to perform, present, enact, play"; and thence "sich etwas gestalten, vergegenwärtigen, to perceive, to consider" etc.

4) This stanza seems to bristle with equivoque. We could also translate: "Accompanied by Varadhaṇu, who possesses great virtues." The third

And having heard what Varadhaṇu announced to him, the prince's heart was captured by Rayaṇavaī, although he had never seen her. And while he sought a means of seeing her and of meeting her a few days went by.

And on another day Varadhaṇu returned from outside. Being perplexed he started to speak as follows: "Prince, some trusty men have been sent here to the ruler of this town by the lord of Kosala in order to search for us, and the ruler of this town has raised the hue and cry against us [1]). This is the rumor that is heard repeatedly". Thereupon, when Sāgaradatta knew of this matter, he hid them both in an underground dwelling. The night came. The prince said to Sāgaradatta: "Bring it about that we may run away". And hearing this Sāgaradatta left the city [with them]. They traveled a short distance. Then having made Sāgaradatta somehow or other return although he did not wish to

pāda may be = "Means to honor the lady skilled (lit., rich, abounding in) literary composition" (racanavatī). The greatest difficulty confronts us in the last pāda. Candaṇī cannot be intended as a feminine, notwithstanding the candamāyoga of Lakshmīvallabha (Uttarajjh. p. 390, l. 2 from bottom). A masculine is required to answer to Varadhaṇu. I take Candanī = Skt. candanin, Çiva. The long vowel is perfectly legitimate and occurs numberless times in poetry. In our own tales we have it on page 39, l. 27; p. 55, l. 29. If I liked to tamper with the text other suggestions might be made. I suspect that rayaṇavaī in the secondary sense is = *rajanavatī = rajanī "night". The earth is a little out of place here. Māṇeuṃ, too, seems to favor this view. The second half of the stanza would thus run as follows: "means to honor (or, to enjoy) Rayaṇavaī as the Moon (masculine in Skt.!) the Night (his beloved)".

1) Or, "a means (plan, strategem) has been undertaken (to find us) by the ruler of this town." The dīpikā has: Nagarasvāminā ca āvāṃ grahaṇopāyaḥ kṛito 'sti. Uttarajjh. p. 391, l. 1 and 2.

do so, the prince and Varadhaṇu set forth. And as they were going along they saw outside of the city a most beautiful woman tarrying among the trees of the park around a Yaksha shrine and sitting near a fine carriage that was provided with a box. Then she rose to greet them with great regard and said: "Why have you come after so *long* a time?" Upon hearing this the prince said: "Who are we, fair lady?" She replied: "Lord, you are Bambhadatta and Varadhaṇu". The prince said: "How did you find that out?" She said: "Listen! Here in the city there is a merchant called Dhaṇapavara. His spouse is named Dhaṇasaṃcayā. She has given birth to me, her daughter, in addition to eight sons. When I had passed childhood no man pleased me. Then I began to propitiate this Yaksha. And the Yaksha, gratified by my devotion, appeared before my eyes and said: "Child, your husband will be prince Bambhadatta, who is destined to be a universal monarch". I said: "How am I to know him?" The Yaksha said: "He whose sight will cause you joy when the cock-fight of Buddhila and Sāgaradatta takes place him you are to know for Bambhadatta". And he told me all that has happened to you and your comrade Varadhaṇu, O lord, since the time of the cock-fight and all the things to be done that I have thus carried out, i. e. the sending of the pearl necklace etc., and how [I should carry them out he told me too]. "Having heard this the prince, filled with loving passion, mounted the fine carriage together with her. And he asked her: Whither shall we go?" [1])

1) Hutta and āhutta I take to be = * bhukta, * ābhukta, Skt. bhugna, bent, turned (hither).

Rayaṇavaī said: "In Magahātown there lives my father's youngest brother, a merchant named Dhaṇasatthavāha; and he, having learnt of this affair, will deem the union of you and me an excellent thing. Therefore let us immediately make the journey thither. As for the time after — as *you* wish [so shall it be]". Then in accordance with Rayaṇavaī's words the prince set forth with his face turned that way. He made Varadhaṇu his charioteer. And travelling on from village to village they left the country of Kosambī and came into a mountain-thicket. And there dwelt two robber-chieftains, named Kaṇṭhaya and Sukaṇṭhaya; and seeing a most excellent carriage and an adorned pearl among women, they armed themselves and set out for the assault because the retinue [of Bambhadatta] was so small. But, attacked by the prince in different ways[1]), they were defeated and fled in every direction. Then the prince again mounted the fine chariot and proceeded, and Varadhaṇu said to him: "Prince, you are sorely wearied; therefore enjoy the comfort of sleep for only an hour right here in the chariot". Thereupon, while the prince lay asleep with Rayaṇavaī, the horses entered a mountain stream and halted. Then somehow or other the prince awoke and rose yawning. He looked about on all sides: he did not see Varadhaṇu. "In all probability he has stepped down[2]) to get some water"; thinking thus he called in perplexity. Not receiving an answer he examined

1) So if we accept Jacobi's view, who understands bhanga in the sense of the Skt. bhaṅgi. Perhaps the literal translation would be: "attacked with various discomfitures (in various discomfiting ways)".

2) Exactly the German: "er wird hinabgestiegen sein". This use of the future is frequent also in Prākrit.

the end of the chariot's shaft [1]) and saw that it was besmeard with much blood. Thinking then: "Varadhaṇu has been killed", he cried: "Woe is me! You are slain" and dropped down on the bottom of the chariot Having gained consciousness again he began to utter laments, saying: "Woe is me, brother Varadhaṇu!" With great difficulty comforted by Rayaṇavaī, he spoke to her as follows: "Fair lady, it is not certainly known whether Varadhaṇu is dead or alive. Therefore I shall go back in order to search for him". She replied: "Dear lord, this is no time to turn back. Why not? Because I am alone and this wildwood is dreadful on account of robbers, wild beasts, etc. And another thing: There must be a settlement near because the kuça grass and the thorns are seen to be crushed" [2]). Then, agreeing to this the prince started with her toward the country of Magadha, and he arrived at a village situated on the border of that realm. And entering there he was seen by the ṭhakkura [3]) of the village, who stood in the middle of the assembly hall of the village. As soon as he had seen Bambhadatta he thought: "This is not a

1) Or perhaps: "the ground before the shaft of the carriage". In the dīpikā we read: Kumārah rathāgrabhāgaṃ rudhirāvaliptaṃ dadarça. Uttarajjh. p. 392, l. 4.

2) Vasama and vasima do not mean "Wohnung", but in all the passages of our tales "Siedelung, Ansiedelung." Parimalia too is wrongly given as "beschmutzt". It is from maḷ = mrad, so common in Prākrit. See §§ 244, 294. The simplex usually means "to rub" or "to crush," sometimes "to touch", whereas "to touch" is the usual signification of parimaḷai. The grass, bushes, etc. are trampled, injured by the feet of men and domestic animals.

3) I. e. the chief man of the community, = gāmapahu (l. 37); gāmāhiva (p. 16, l. 9); grāmādhipati Uttarajjh. p. 392, l. 4 from bottom Cp. my Kshemendras Samayamāṭrikā (Leipzig), p. 38.

common man", and with marks of distinction courteously extended [1]) he honored him and conducted him toward his own house. He gave him lodging. And when the prince was comfortably seated he accosted him: "Most excellent sir, you look as if you were sorely grieved". The prince replied: "It is not known what has become of my brother [2]), who engaged in a fight with robbers. Therefore I must go there in order to search for him". The other said: "Away with distress! If he really is here in the woods we will find him". Having spoken thus he sent out his own men, and when they returned from their expedition they reported: "We saw nobody anywhere; only this arrow, which had dropped on the path, we found". Upon hearing these words the prince was distressed as he thought: "Surely he has been killed"; and while his mind was being distracted with heavy sorrow the night came on and he went to sleep with Rayaṇavaī. When one watch of the night was left suddenly an attack by robbers came upon that village. But sorely weakened by the blows of the prince it was discomfited and beaten off. The prince was congratulated by the chief of the village, who stood at the head of the whole village [3]). And in the morning he took leave of the village ṭhakkura and accompanied by this man's son departed for Rājagaha. In due course he arrived there.

Leaving Rayaṇavaī in a hermitage of female religious mendicants, outside of the city, he started for the interior of the town. And as he was entering it he

1) Or, "shown in polite salutation".

2) Lit., what kind of state he has entered."

3) Or, "praised (hailed with joy by the head of the village, who was accompanied (joined, in his praise) by the whole village."

saw in one place a white palace built with various decorative figures[1]). There he beheld two most beautiful damsels. And when they had seen the prince they began to speak, displaying intense affection: "Is it proper for great men like you to leave people who are devoted and attached to them and to wander about?" He said: "Who are these people, that you speak thus?" They replied: "Do us the favor to take a seat." Then he sat down; the requisites of respectful entertainment, that is, a bath, a repast, etc., were prepared, and when these had been finished the maidens began to speak as follows: "Noble sir, there is here in Bhāraha, in the southern chain of the Veyaḍḍha mountains[2]), a city Sivapura, a king Jalaṇasiha, and his queen, Vijjusihā by name. We are her two daughters. And our eldest brother was Naṭṭumatta. One day when our father was engaged in conversation with his friend, Aggisiha by name, he saw a host of gods and demons (asura) traveling through the air toward Mount Aṭṭhāvaya in order to worship the best of the Jinas. When the king had seen them he too, together with his friend and his daughters, set out and in due course came to the Aṭṭhāvaya. He worshipped the images of the Jinas. He

1) Or, "designs". I take kamma = Arbeit (in erhobne Arbeit, embossed work).

2) See Pischel § 66 and cp. Hemacandra, Pariçishṭaparvan II, 643, 644:

Astīha Bharatakshetre
Vaitāḍhyanāma parvataḥ
saṃpṛikto Bharatārdhābhyāṃ
pakshābhyām iva nīḍajaḥ.

Tatra cāsti puravaram
uttaraçreṇibhūshaṇam
Gaganavallabham iti
dyusadām ativallabham.

did them homage with camphor, aloe wood, frankincense, opened lotus-flowers, and fragrant perfumes. Having performed the triple perambulation from left to right, he went out and saw two perambulating saints under an açoka tree; and making a low obeisance to them they[1]) sat down near them. Then the monks commenced a religious discourse as follows; "Unsubstantial is the saṃsāra, perishable the body, like the clouds of autumn is life, similar to lightning flashes youth, comparable to the fruit of the kiṃpāka tree[2]) are enjoyments, transient as the glow of the evening red is the pleasure of the senses, unstable as the dew drop on the tip of kuça grass good luck, easily obtained sorrow, obtained with difficulty delight, never impeded the progress of death. Therefore, such being the case, let the course of delusion be abandoned, let the mind be fixed on the religion preached by the prince of Jinas".

Having heard this and attained the true faith, etc., the gods and the others returned as they had come. Then friend Aggisiha, getting an opportunity, said: "Reverend sir, who will be the husband of these girls?" They said: "They will become the wives of their brother's slayer". When the king had heard this he became black in the face. At this juncture we said: "Father,

1) The king and his company.

2) I. e., poisonous. The vishavṛiksha of the commentators is *not* "bloss aus dem Zusammenhang erraten" (Leumann, Aupapātika-Sūtra, sub kiṃpāga). Whatever may have been the first meaning of the word it is perfectly clear that it meant, with Buddhists, Brahman writers, and Jainas, a tree bearing poisonous fruit. But probably I do not understand Leumann correctly.

just now the saints have announced the natural character of the saṃsāra. Enough for us of the joy of the senses, that terminates in such a manner!" And our father agreed to this.

While we thus in our fondness for our brother abandoned all things that could give pleasure to our own bodies and continually cared only for his baths, meals, etc., our brother while roaming trough the land the other day saw the maid Pupphavaī, the daughter of your maternal uncle. His heart was distracted by her beauty and other excellences and he returned carrying her off. Not being able to bear the sight of her he went to become master of a magic spell. From this point on the story is known to you. At that time, excellent sir, we were addressed with gentle words by Pupphavaī, who had come from your presence, and she told us what had happened to our brother. Hearing that, we were overwhelmed with sorrow and fell to weeping. We were comforted by Pupphavaī with sweet words. And another thing, having learnt your history from the magical science Saṃkarī, she said:" Remember the words of the saints, accept Bambhadatta as [your] husband" [1]). Hearing that, we were filled with love and agreed. Now, as Pupphavaī, beside herselt with joyous impetuosity, waved the white flag of agreement you departed for some other place; but we wandered through various villages, cities, etc., and when we saw you nowhere we came here, despondent and disconsolate. Thereupon a view of you, which resembles

1) See §§ 92, 143. In mannijjai we have the present stem of the active (middle) in the passive, a common thing in the Prākrits.

an unexpected rain of gold, has here fallen to our lot. Therefore, excellent sir, remembering Pupphavaī's words, let our desire be realized". On hearing that, the prince joyfully agreed to it. Consummating the Gandharva marriage he stayed with them during the night. And in the morning he said to them: "Go you to Pupphavaī; abide with her till my acquisition of the kingdom takes place". "We will do so," declaring thus they went away. When they had gone and he looked about, there was neither that white palace, nor that body of attendants. And he thought: "This is the witchcraft of fairies. Else how could they play such juggler's antics?"

Then the prince, remembering Rayaṇavaī, went toward the hermitage in order to seek her. When he beheld there neither Rayaṇavaī nor anybody else he reflected: "Whom shall I question?" He looked about on all sides and saw no one. Thereupon while he was anxiously pondering about what might have happened to her, after a moment an old man of auspicious appearance came. He was questioned by the prince: "Listen, illustrious sir! Did you not see a girl here yesterday or today who had such and such a particular appearance and dress?" And he said: "Son, are you here the husband of Rayaṇavaī?" The prince replied: "Yes". He said: "Yesterday, in the time of the afternoon, I saw her weeping and I went up to her and asked her: "Daughter, who are you? and whence have you come? and what is the cause of your sorrow? and whither have you determined to go?" Thereupon when she told me something [of her story] I recognized her and said: "You are my own daughter's daughter. And when I had learnt her story I went to her uncle and reported to him. And when he knew the particulars he conducted her respectfully into his own house. You were searched for in every direction, but seen nowhere. Therefore you have now done a beautiful thing in that you came." And talking thus he took the prince to the great merchant's house. And when he had been treated to all courtesies [of entertainment] his marriage to Rayaṇavaī was celebrated. Thereupon he remained with her, enjoying the pleasures of the senses.

One day when the Brahmans etc. ate the food that had been prepared because it was the day [1]) of Varaḍhaṇu, Varadhaṇu himself, dressed in the costume of a Brahman, came on account of the repast [2]) and began to speak as follows: "Listen! Announce to the one who had this food prepared: "If you give food to me then it will come into the mouth of him who dwells in the other world" [3]). And coming to him they reported it to the prince. The prince came out. And with delight the prince looked upon him and recognized him. After embracing him he entered the mansion. At the appropriate time, when Varadhaṇu had finished his bath and meal, he was questioned as to his adventures. He began to relate as follows: "That night when you had yielded to the power of sleep a robber who

1) The ṭīkā reads varshadivasa, "Jahrestag". Bambhadatta, who thought that Varadhaṇu was dead, had his çrāddha, or ceremony of offering oblations to the manes, celebrated.

2) Perhaps better, "in order to get something to eat," although the sense is just the same.

3) The idea that a gift to pious persons accrues to the benefit of one's relatives in the other world is current in India and forms the central thought of the Petavatthu. [Possibly, "into the mouth and stomach"].

had run up from behind and had posted himself in the midst of a dense coppice hit me with an arrow. As I was utterly overcome by the pain of that shot I fell prostrate on the ground. On account of my fearing some misfortune[1]) I did not tell you. In the meantime your excellent chariot passed by. I also softly, softly slipped away through the midst of the space between the dense trees and with the greatest difficulty came to the village where you had stayed over night. And the lord of this village told me your adventures. Delight springing up in my heart and my wound being healed up, I came here under the pretence of begging food and saw you straightway." And while thus they were full of ardent affection the days passed joyfully for them.

One day Bambhadatta and Varadhaṇu were taking counsel together: "How long a time do we have to remain destitute of manly effort?" And while thus they pondered about a means of setting out and were full of longing, spring arrived. And the great festival of Love being celebrated in that season and townspeople and country folk going out into the park, the two, the prince and Varadhaṇu, from curiosity also went. When thereupon the pleasure of sports was at its height and the companies of young men and women were amusing themselves with various pastimes, unexpectedly a royal elephant that was beside himself with rut and had thrown off his driver and [so] was

1) I. e., that might befall you, O Bambhadatta. Pavolini is hardly correct in his "un mal peggiore". Varadhaṇu, the model of a servant, thinks only of his lord. According to the dīpikā the robber shot Varadhaṇu in the foot (pāde).

not curbed by the hook, strayed thither. A confused noise arose; the bands engaged in sportive amusement were broken up[1]). And when thus the hubbub was going on a young girl with high breasts, very large rounded buttocks, and thighs like a rutting elephant's trunk, whose limbs were trembling[2]) with fear and who was seeking a refuge came into the elephant's range of vision. Thereupon woful cries arose; her female attendants screamed. At this point, when she was seized with dread, the prince stepped before the elephant, warded him off, and made him let her go. But the elephant after letting her go suddenly rushed against him, his eyes distended with rage, his frightful trunk stretched out, his ears spread. But the prince formed a ball of his upper robe, and flung it toward the elephant. And he, overpowered by angry impatience, took hold of it and tossed it up into the air. It fell on the ground. While the elephant bent down there in order to strike with his tusks[3]) the prince by virtue of his dexterity mounted his neck, fastened the seat, beat him with the sharp hook, struck him in the region of the frontal globes, and by sweet words made him give up his anger.

Then cries of approbation arose. "Glory to the prince!" a bard recited. The king, who was led to the temporary

1) Or, "the sports and amusements were broken up".

2) § 596.

3) Most likely in order to strike the garment on the ground. The dīpikā tells us: Tadvastraṃ çuṇḍayā gṛihītvā gagane prakshiptaṃ; gaganāc ca punar bhūmau nipatito tadgrahaṇāya yāvat karī punar bhūmyabhimukhaṃ pariṇamati etc. (p. 395, l. ultima and p. 396, l. prima).

pavilion [1]), came to that place. When he saw this deed, which was not like another man's [2]), amazement came upon him and he began to exclaim: "But who is he?" Thereupon the story was told by his minister of state, who knew the affairs of the prince. Then the king being delighted, took the prince to his own palace and had the proper rites [of hospitality] performed, such as giving him a bath, food, etc. Then at the end of the repast he gave his eight daughters in marriage to the prince. On an auspicious day and at an auspicious hour the wedding took place. They remained there at their ease for some days.

One day a woman came into the presence of the prince and began to speak as follows: "Prince, I have something to say to you". He said: "Speak." She said: "There is right here in the city a great merchant, Vesamaṇa by name; his daughter is called Sirimaī. Ever since her childhood she has been taken care of by me. When she whom you saved from the elephant's rage [3])

1) Or, "the temporary pavilions" (erected for the festival). I take khambhuṭṭhāṇaṃ as "post-rising", a collection of raised posts (pillars). The dīpikā reads: Kumāreṇa sa karī ālānastambhasamīpaṃ nīto baddhaç ca. Even if we emendated our text in accordance with Lakshmīvallabha to khambhaṭṭhāṇaṃ it might be understood to speak of the "place of pillars", the place where the temporary pavilions were erected. There is no absolute necessity of recurring to the elephant, which would make the construction of the sentence a rather awkward one. Most probably the Sanskrit commentator, if the form of the tale is really his, could do nothing with khambhuṭṭhāṇaṃ. The compound, though, is intelligible. Cp. Rāvaṇavaha XIII, 37: rauṭṭhāṇa "dust-rising", i. e. raised dust (rajas + utthāna). [C also reads khambhoṭṭhāṇa].

2) Or, "which was unlike another [deed]". I see no reason for changing the reading of the MSS.

3) More literally, "the elephant's agitation". It is not perfectly clear whether that means the flurry and violence (mad onset) of the rut-blinded beast, or the disturbance and fear caused by it.

had escaped from the elephant's rage and had abandoned fear, she cast a longing look on you, thinking: "He gave me back my life". Thereupon, in consideration of your preeminence in exceedingly beautiful form, bloom of youth, grace, and skill in the arts, an ardent love for you arose in her. Then from that instant she, gazing only on you, remained a moment as if paralyzed, as if painted in a picture, as if nailed to the spot, as if carved with a chisel, with eyes fixed motionless. When the rage of the elephant had passed, she was led to her dwelling with great difficulty by her female attendants. There too she pays no attention to the care of the body: to bathing, eating, etc.; but abides entirely in silence. Then I said to her: "Daughter why have you all of a sudden become different from your real nature [1]), so that you heed not even my words?" Thereupon she laughed in an embarrassed way and said: "What is there, mother, that I could not tell *you?* But shame is committing [2]) the offence. Therefore listen. If I am not married by him who saved me from the elephant's rage, then inevitably death will be my refuge". And then having heard this I told the story to her father. By him I have been sent to you. Therefore accept this young damsel". And he agreed to it. On a favorable day the wedding took place. On Varadhaṇu too the minister called Subuddhi bestowed his daughter, Nandā by name, and celebrated

1) Or possibly, "Daughter, why have you who are surely not of a hot temper (or, a fierce, cruel nature [acaṇḍi]) become destitute of affection". But the ṭīkā too has: kathaṃ tvam akāṇḍe īdṛçī jātā?

2) I do not know if avarajjhai *can* mean "hindern" (Jacobi). The usual meaning fits much better, too.

the nuptial festival. And while they both thus enjoyed the pleasures of the senses a few days passed by. Their adventures were noised abroad [1]).

Thereupon they went to Benares. Leaving Bambhadatta outside [the town] Varadhaṇu went to Kaḍaya. Rejoiced, this king went out to meet the prince with a host and vehicles. Thereupon when he had met him he made him mount on an elephant's back and conducted him into his own house. And in due course he bestowed his own daughter upon him, Kaḍayāvaī by name, together with many elephants, horses, carriages, and treasures. On a favorable day the wedding took place. While he enjoyed the delights of the senses with her the time went by.

Messengers being despatched then, there came king Pupphacūla with a host and vehicles, Dhaṇu the minister, Kaṇeradatta and many other kings, beginning with Candasīha and Bhavadatta. They installed Varadhaṇu in the position of general and sent him against king Dīha, and he began to march uninterruptedly. In the meantime Dīha sent a messenger to Kaḍaya and the others. And he was reviled by them [2]). They themselves too moved on in uninterrupted marches and came to Kampillapura. Then they blocked up both exit and entrance all around. Thereupon king Dīha said: "How

1) Or, "the news about them spread all around." Ucchalia from ut + çal, to fly upwards, to rise, fly away, move onward. Cp. § 327a.

2) It was customary to treat disrespectfully an ambassador whose message did not meet with approval, if one wanted war. See e. g. Nirayāvaliyāsuttaṃ ed. Warren §§ 22, 23, where we also find an interesting description as to how an ultimatum (a declaration of war) is delivered.

long a time shall we remain withdrawn in a hole?" And relying on daring courage he issued forth to meet them. A great battle of the two armies took place. Then Dīha, seeing his own army discomfited, and reflecting: "In one's performing a manly deed [there is escape] otherwise there is no escape", drew nigh to meet the enemy. When Bambhadatta saw him the fire of wrath blazed up [1]) in him and he moved against him. A fight ensued. Thereupon, when Bambhadatta had attacked [his adversary] with bow, sword, spear, mace, lance, and other weapons, he hurled the disc. By that the body of king Dīha was made a headless trunk. Then confused cries of: "Hail to the universal sovereign!" arose. The Siddhas and the Gandharvas let a shower of flowers fall. And they declared thus: "The twelfth universal monarch has appeared now". Thereupon he entered his own palace, being hailed with joy by the country folk living about the city and by the townspeople. And all the vassals installed him in the sovereignty of a great universal monarch. In the manner of the former universal monarchs he conquered Bharaha-land, which consists of six parts [2]). His whole seraglio with Pupphavaī at the head joined him. While he thus exercised the rule of a universal monarch the days went by.

One day an actor respectfully addressed him as follows: "Great king, today I shall enact a dramatic

1) Saṃdhukkai corresponds to the Skt. saṃdhukshati. We would expect saṃdhukkhai. But the unaspiratel consonant for the aspirated is not rare. The word could also be a denominative from saṃdhukka (= *saṃdhukna p.p.p.). [C reads saṃdhukhiya with B].

2) For the names of these six see Tawney's Kathākoça pp. 192, 241.

composition called Mahuyarĭgīya". He said: "So be it". "Then in the afternoon he began to act. At this point a slave girl brought an immense wreath of flowers [1]) that abounded in all varieties of flowers to Bambhadatta. When he saw this and listened to [the drama] Mahuyarĭgīya the surmise occurred to him: "Such a dramatic composition I have seen before [2])". While he reflected thus, he remembered his former existence. In the Sohamma heaven, in the celestial region Paummagumma [3]), I have seen it before [4]). And he fell into a swoon and fell to the ground. Then the company of vassals who were at his side brought about his recovery by anointing him with moist sandal. Then the king,

1) In translating gaṇḍa by "immense" I thought of compounds like gaṇḍagrāma, gaṇḍaçilā, gaṇḍamūrkha. Jacobi suggests: gaṇḍa = vana. That would either be a wreath so big that it alone is, so to speak, a forest; or, a forest, as it were, formed by garlands (German "ein Wald von Kränzen"). Maybe gaṇḍa first means "something bulging out" (hence the common meanings of the word) and perhaps also "a bundle, bunch, mass," which would be just the thing in our passage. Cp. Skt. gaṇḍaka, a lump.

2) For suṇanta see § 503.

3) Cp. Hoernle's Uvāsagadasāo Vol. II, p. 40, note 109; Uttarajh. XXXVI, 210 ff. (208 ff. in Jacobi's translation, Sacred Books of the East Vol. 45, p. 226); Weber, Bhagavatī p. 304. A list of the vimāṇas in the Sohammakappa is found in Uvāsagadasāo § 277.

4) Similar scenes are often painted in the Jaina writings. The belief in metempsychosis is most probably *partly* due to that mysterious state experienced sometimes by some of us in which we have the vague, shadowy feeling as if we had once before gone through a certain thing that happens to us at that particular moment, as if we had been in the same surroundings, had been visited by the same sensations before, apparently in a most remote, misty past. Such an abnormal state is not rarely called forth by a peculiar odor or fragrance. The most undeveloped of our senses thus gives rise to that undeveloped sensation. So our passage is very curious, although also here (as elsewhere in Hindu stories) it is rather the sight of the bright flowers that calls forth the trance-like state.

who had remembered the story of his brother [Citta] in his former existence, with the object of seeking him, spoke to his prime minister Varadhaṇu — who was to him entirely as his own heart — hiding his secret, as follows: "Do you spread this half-çloka and have publicly proclaimed [1]) in the city at the places where three roads meet and where four roads meet and on the squares: "Whosoever supplies [2]) the second half of this çloka to him the king will give half of his realm". Thus day after day the proclaiming went on and the verse spread in many places [3]).

At this time the soul of Citra, his brother in a former birth, had become a rich merchant's son and remembered its previous existences, he had taken the vows and had then come from Purimātala to that very place and had repaired to the wood called Manorama. There he put down his outfit: the bowl etc. in a spot free from living beings [4]) and lived sunk in religious meditation in the kāyotsarga posture. At this point the saint heard a man who was working a Persian wheel [5]) recite this half-çloka:

1) Lambiūṇa from the causat. lambei, to cause to settle down, — to take hold, — to rest, — to cling. Or should we translate: "Do you have this half-stanza hung up" (in public places, inscribed on some material, for leisurely inspection)?

2) Lit., "fills up, completes".

3) The rest of the tale is in Skt. For the reason see Leumann, Wiener Zeitschrift für die Kunde des Morgenlandes, VI p. 45 note. — The names Citra and Brahmadatta are the Skt. equivalents for Citta and Bambhadatta.

4) Prāsuka is a wrong translation of Prākrit Phāsuya (Pāli phāsuka), which I derive from *sparçuka, "what may be touched", and Pischel (§ 208) gives the same etymology. The Buddhists have correctly connected it with sparça (see Childers sub phāsu).

5) Araghaṭṭika, a secondary derivative from araghaṭṭa, the Persian wheel (which occurs frequently in the Pāli and Prākrit literatures).

"We two have been two slaves, two deer, two swans, two Caṇḍālas, two gods thereupon ...."

And having heard this the sage said:

"This is the sixth birth of us who are [now] separated from each other".

Then this man working the Persian wheel wrote this half-çloka on a leaf and went to the king's palace, having the lotus of his face opened wide. He recited the supplementary çloka before the ruler. Then the king from excess of love fell into a swoon. Thereupon the assembly was agitated. The body of attendants began to strike the man with their open hands, declaring: "On account of his words the king has fallen into such a state". Being struck by them he wailed: "Not by me has this [çloka] been filled up", and he was released from his tormentors and questioned: "Who is it that filled it up?" He said: "A saint, who lives near the Persian wheel". When thereupon the king had regained consciousness by being sprinkled with sandal liquid, and had learned the tidings of the most excellent sage's arrival, his soul was drawn by devotion and love to him and he departed with his retinue. And he saw the saint in the park. Delighted in his heart he respectfully saluted him. The sage began a religious discourse, showed the worthlessness of existence, described the causes of bondage by karma, extolled the road to final emancipation, proclaimed the excellence of blissful beatitude. The audience was moved. Brahmadatta was not purified [1]) and he said: "Reverend

1) Or, "improved, raised to a holy frame of mind" (Hoernle's Uvāsagadasāo II, p. 41, note 112).

sir, as I have been gladdened by meeting you, so do you, O reverend sir, gladden me by accepting kingship. Later we both will practise asceticism. Just that[1]), indeed, is the fruit of asceticism". The saint said: "That is proper for those who desire to do you a service. Only, this state of being a man is hard to obtain; life is continually ebbing away; fortune is unstable; unsteady is this knowledge of religious truth; bitter in their fruits are sensua enjoyments, those who cling to them surely go to hell; but hard to obtain is the seed of final emancipation, especially the jewel of indifference to wordly objects. To give that up and so to lay hold of kingship, which is the cause of going to hell (from whence it is hard to get out[2]) and which will last a few days, does not gladden the hearts of the wise. Therefore relinguish your evil inclination, remember the sorrow experienced in former lives, drink the nectar-liquid of the Jinas' words, walk in the path declared by them, make your birth as a man bear fruit". He said: "Reverend sir, it is the sign of ignorance to desire unseen pleasures by abandoning the pleasure already attained. Therefore do not direct me thus; fulfill my desire". When Brahmadatta experienced no spiritual awakening, although exhorted repeatedly, the sage reflected: "Ah, I know! In that former existence he, being Sambhūta, by reason of an excessive longing sprung from the feeling of being touched by the locks of the matchless wife of the universal monarch Sanatkumāra, conceived a wordly thought

1) I. e. kingship and similar good fortune.

2) Or, "which is a cause of going to hell hard to shun", which almost inevitably causes men to go to hell.

with the object of obtaining that [1]), although he was exhorted to forbear. That now manifests itself here [in its results]. Hence like one bitten by a black snake he is not amenable to the spells and charms of the Jinas' words" [2]). The saint went away and in the course of time reached final emancipation. But the king passed some time enjoying the pleasures of a universal monarch.

One day a Brahman said to him: "O king, such a desire has sprung up in me that I should like to eat [3]) the food of a universal monarch". The king said: "Listen, Brahman! You are not able to eat my food, for this food is not properly digested by anyone except me" [4]).

1) I. e. the inexpressible delight springing from contact with woman, a delight which a universal monarch (cakravartin) can quaff to his heart's content and in its most delicious form, for he has the pick of the most enchanting women. And not only this, but according to the Jaina belief he is like Kṛishṇa, the happy Don Juan of the later Hindu pantheon — owing to his magic power (ṛiddhi) he can enjoy the transports of love with all the thousands upon thousands of peerless beauties of his harem (64,000 wives is the orthodox number) at the same time. Among this galaxy of stars of womanhood there is one far brighter and lovelier than the rest, and she is the Queen Consort, the cakravartin's "Pearl of Women". Therefore Sambhūta wanted to become a universal sovereign. "That" refers in a somewhat loose way to Sanatkumāracakristrīratnālakasaṃsparça-(vedanā). Pavolini's "oltremodo desideroso di godere la bellissima donna del re Sanatkumāra" is altogether wrong. Naturally, the roused tiger of amorous concupiscence will pant to spring upon such a matchless prey which is so near. But we have to understand the passage by the help of the light thrown on it by the story itself. And our ascetic was a *Hindu.*

2) A person bitten by a black snake cannot be cured. Vetālapañcaviṃçatikā ed. Uhle p. 12, l. 27: kāladashṭā na jīvati kanyeyam, "bitten by a black snake this girl will not live".

3) Lit., "if I [could only] eat"; "[how would it be] if I ate".

4) One thinks immediately of Buddha's words in the Mahāparinibbānasutta concerning that last dish of which the Master partook. Note, too, the kinship between Universal Sovereigns and Founders of the Faith that is to be observed in the Jaina books.

The Brahman said: "Shame upon the grandeur of your royal glory, that you reflectively hesitate [1]) in giving mere food!" Then the king, on account of his indignation, consented and by giving him viands fed the Brahman together with wife, sons, daughters-in-law, daughters, grandchildren, and the whole host of his relatives. The retinue of the Brahman went home. And when the night had come and the food was being digested an extraordinary torrent of madness rushed upon them; not shrinking [2]) from sexual union with mother, daughter-in-law, and sister, deprived of sense by the feeling of mighty amorous passion, the Brahman's people began to commit sinful acts one with the other. In the morning the Brahman and his people, being ashamed, did not dare to look each other in the face, and went out of the city; and the Brahman reflected: "Why have I thus been mocked by the king, who is my enemy without cause?" Thereupon, unwilling to bear this, he wandered about in the wood and saw a goatherd who was making holes in the leaves of a fig tree with peastones [by throwing them at the leaves], and he thought: "He is qualified for doing the thing that I desire" [3]). Thinking thus he waited upon him with gifts, honors, etc. He told him his purpose. And he consented.

One day when Brahmadatta had gone out he hid himself behind a wall and being an unerring shot he tore out both his eyes at the same time with a little ball.

1) Âlocayati, German "sich bedenken".

2) Lit., "not regarding".

3) Or perhaps in accordance with the more original sense of vivakshita, "about which I wish to speak to him". With the passage compare Jâtaka N°. 107. [C has çarkarikâbhir, with pebbles].

Then the king finding out the matter and being filled with wrath, had that priest killed together with his sons and relatives, and after killing other Brahmans said to his minister: "Put their eyes into a dish and set it down before me that I may experience pleasure by crushing them with my own hands". The minister, who understood that the king was in the power of the workings of an evil karma, put fruits of the çakhoṭaka tree into the dish and brought them to him. He, being filled with savage determination, spent his days in crushing them because the thought they were eyes. While he was engaged in this a few days went by. Thereupon, having lived seven hundred years plus sixteen, his life being spent, but his savage determination growing, he died and was born as a hell-being in the seventh hell land destined to live there for thirty-three sāgaras [1]).

1) There are seven narakabhūmi or narakapṛithivī according to the Jainas. The names of these seven "hell earths" and the duration of life allotted to those who dwell therein may be found in Uttarajjh. XXXVI, 157 ff. Cp. Weber, Bhagavatī p. 170. The tortures endured by the unhappy denizens of these worlds of agony are painted in Dantesque colors. The Jaina's soul also here indulges in even more riotous orgies of fancy than that of his brethren, the Brahman and the Buddhist. See Uttarajjh. XIX, 45 ff. (Sacred Books of the East Vol. 45, pp. 93 ff); Sacred Books of the East (abbrev. SBE), Vol. 45, pp. 279 ff.

Sāgara = sāgaropama "ocean-(like)" is the name of one of the immense periods of time in which the imagination of the Jaina revels. Thirty-three sāgaras is the longest period of time which a being may have to live in the 7th hell. Uttarajjh. XXXVI, 167.

SAṆAṂKUMĀRA.

SAṆAṂKUMĀRA[1].

There is here in Bhāratavarsha, in the country of Kurujāngala, a city Hastināpura. There was a king Āsasena of the Kuru line, his wife Sahadevī, and the fourth universal sovereign, Saṇaṃkumāra by name, who had been announced by the fourteen great dreams[2]. Playing together in the dust[3]) with Mahindasīha, the son of Sura and Kalindī, he acquired the multitude of the arts and arrived at the bloom of youth.

One day in the month of spring he went to the park in order to amuse himself, accompanied by princes and citizens. When the princes had amused themselves with various sports they mounted steeds in order to ride about on horseback. But Saṇaṃkumāra mounted a steed called Jalahikallola[4]. They let their horses go at the same time. Thereupon the steed of prince Saṇaṃkumāra, being a horse of inverse training[5], dropped into the

1) The story of Saṇaṃkumāra is also told in the Uttarajjh. pp. 522 (last line) sqq.; Kathākoça pp. 31 sqq.

2) The fourteen great dreams that are seen by the mother of every tīrthaṃkara and of every cakravartin while she is with such a child. Kalpasūtra ed. Jacobi pp. 34 ff.; Nirayāvaliyāsuttaṃ ed. Warren, Aanteckningen p. 22.

3) Or, "with the dust (the mud)". In the Jātaka book we have this phrase frequently.

4) "Wave of the Ocean."

5) A horse that gallops when the reins are pulled and that stops when they are let go (perhaps such an animal also turns to the right, when desired to turn to the left etc.) About an elephant trained in a similar manner for a particular purpose see Jātaka N°. 231.

fifth pace[1]) and in a moment had got out of sight. When the king knew of the affair he followed on the road along with his train. In the meanwhile a fierce wind sprang up. By that the path of the steed's tracks was effaced. Mahindasīha requested the king: "Let the great king return. I shall return when I have obtained full intelligence of the prince". The king returned.

Mahindasīha went on in pursuit of the prince. He entered a dreadful and great forest. While he roamed about, one year passed. And one day he had gone a little distance, when he heard the cries of Indian cranes and smelled[2]) the fragrance of lotus flowers. He set out toward it, saw a great lake, and heard the sweet tones of singing and of a flute. As he went along with eyes wide open from joy he beheld Saṇaṃkumāra in the midst of a company of young women. Astonished in his mind he reflected: "Is this a delusion of the thought, or is that really Saṇaṃkumāra?" As he stood there doubting a bard recited:

> "Hail to thee, moon of Āsasena's heavens, pillar upholding[3]) the house of Kuru! Hail to thee, Saṇaṃkumāra, ruler of the three worlds! Hail to thee, crowned with majesty!"

Thereupon Mahindasīha came to the positive conclu-

1) The "fifth pace" is "Carriere" (Jacobi), hard gallop, full speed.

2) A present formation according the 4th class of the Sanskrit grammarians, āghrāyati; from that p.p.p. āghrāyita > agghāiya is derived.

3) Lit., "pillar for (in) the upholding". If laggaṇa really means "das Stützen" it derives from the causat. laggei (laggeti also in Pāli). Cp. Pāli lakana "anchor" (of a ship), Milindap. p. 377 (from laketi = lageti. Majjh.-Nik. I, p. 127; Angutt.-Nik. III, pp. 230, 233). The double consonant is, of course, due to the present laggati, laggai (§ 488). Cp. the scholiast's explanation of uggīvaṃ Jāt. VI, p. 562, stanza 2255.

sion, "It is Saṇaṃkumāra". And having his soul filled with joy and experiencing a kind of pleasure never felt before, he stepped into Saṇaṃkumāra's range of sight. Even from afar Saṇaṃkumāra recognized him and rose in salutation. And when Mahindasīha had risen from falling at his feet he embraced him closely. They both sat down on seats offered, their souls filled with joy. And the company of fairies stopped their songs and other noise and settled down around them. Thereafter Saṇaṃkumāra wiped both his eyes, that were filled with tears of joy, and said: "Friend, how did you arrive here all alone in this dreadful wildwood? And how did you know that I was staying here? And what are the great king and my mother doing in their separation from me?" Mahindasīha told what had happened. Thereupon Mahindasīha was bathed by most beautiful women. The proper rites [of hospitality] were discharged. At the end of the repast he questioned Saṇaṃkumāra as follows: "Prince, being carried away by the steed, where did you go that time, where did you live, and whence such grandeur?" Saṇaṃkumāra reflected: "It is not meet that good men tell their own deeds by their own mouths. Therefore I shall have them told by the mouth of another". Thereupon he said to his love Vaulamaī, the fairy king's daughter, who was in the midst of hundreds of girls and had been espoused by him: "Darling, do you who have found out my whole history by means of your magic knowledge relate it to Mahindasīha. But as for me, my eyes are unsteady [1]) with sleepiness".

1) Skt. ghūrṇa most probably is a p.p.p. formed with the suffix na and ghūrṇati a denominative. Prākrit ghummāi goes with dūmai,

Speaking thus he repaired to the house of love's pleasure. But Vaulamaī related the adventures of the prince:

"When at that place, at that time, the prince was carried away by the horse before your very eyes [1]) he was taken by it into a gruesome forest. On the second day, when the horse was still pushing ahead in the same manner, noontime came. And distressed with hunger and thirst the horse lolled out its tongue; still just standing upright and having its throat filled with heaving breath, it halted. The prince dismounted. He loosed the straps [2]) and took off the saddle, when the horse reeled, dropped, and was abandoned by the five vital airs, as if they thought: "It is the perpetrator of a sin". And leaving the animal whose service had been cut short [3]), the prince went away and intent solely on looking for water, began to roam about. And

ṇūmai, khammai etc.; it is a denom. from ghūrman. Prākrit gholai therefore represents the original root ghur, ghul.

1) Lit., even while you looked on". Niei, niai I take to be nicayati > niceti > nici (and, going over to the first class, niai) = Skt. niciketi. In Kirātārjunīya XII, 18 we find nicāyati = niciketi. The other root ci also very frequently follows the a-class. § 502.

2) Lit., "the strap-appliance". I think the word consists of paṭṭa + āḍhā (ādhā to put on, to apply etc.). Cp. Skt. saṃdhā, vidhā, upadhā, pradhā, pratidhā etc. and Pāli ādhāna (= mukhādhāna), the bridle or the bit of a horse (Majjh.-Nik. I, p. 446). Of course the appurtenances of the *saddle* are meant.

3) The reading of A is the better one (vukka = vṛikṇa). Cp. Hāla 465, where we have the variant reading vukka for cukka (= cyuta, bhraṣṭa; cp. 183; Zeitschr. d. deutsch. morgenl. Gesellschaft 42, p. 504, l. 31; Rāvaṇavaha I, 9). In all probubility we ought to read cukka. B, v, and c are easily confused in the Devanāgarī, and the Jaina works especially teem with blunders of this kind. The translation then would be: "whose services had ceased" (had been lost). Regarding pesaṇa cp. asamāṇiapesaṇa, Rāvaṇavaha III, 24; kaapesaṇa IV, 13; hīṇapesaṇa, Daçavaikālikasūtra IX, 2, 22. [C fol. 71*b* we read jai kahavi lakkhassa cukkasi "if you in some way miss the mark"].

nowhere he found water. Then because it was such a long way [he had come] and he so very delicate and the noontime come and the wildwood burned by a forest fire, he became extremely faint [1]). Seeing a sattachaya tree in a place far off he ran toward it, arrived there, sat down in its shade, and rolling his eyes [2]), fell on the ground.

And at this juncture, by the power of his merit [accumulated in a former existence] the Yaksha who dwelt in that tree brought fresh, cold water, sprinkled him on all his limbs and made him revive. And when he had regained conciousness he drank water. And he asked the Yaksha: "Who are you and whence have you brought this water?" He said: "I am the Yaksha who dwells here; and the water I brought for you from Mānasa, the most excellent of lakes". Thereupon the prince said:

1) Hallohala properly means "confusion" Cp. Pischel, Materialien zur Kenntnis des Apabhramça p. 24, Nr. 396, 2).

2) More literally, "distorting his eyes" (die Augen verdrehend). Cp. Jātaka II, p. 264 oṭṭhaṃ bhañjati; Kshemendra's Daçāvatāracaritam VII, 210:

> Mṛidor avajñāmukhabhaṅgakārī
> lokaḥ kilāyaṃ bhayabhojya eva.

"The world, which distorts its face in contempt for the gentle, is to be made use of through fear". Compare also mukhamoṭana "making a wry face (PW² queerly "Schnalzen") Pariçishṭaparvan VI, 119; XII, 248; aṅgopāṅgādimoṭana "woman's graceful, playful bending and moving of the body and the limbs" Uttarajjh. p. 919, l. 6, and the dictionaries sub mukhabhaṅga. At Angutt.-Nik. IV, p. 197 we find vanabhaṅga, which seems to mean bendings (movements) of the body that are full of voluptuousness, — full of loveliness" (the scholion is hardly correct).

In conclusion, I mention bhagnamukha and bhagnānana, "having a wry face, — a despondent face, cast down". Kalāvilasa II, 47; Daçāvatāracar. VI, 22. Finnish has the same idiom, e.g. murti suuta, "he made a wry mouth" (lit., broke [his] mouth). Kalevala III, 272 and elsewhere.

"This heat of mine will at best[1]) leave me only by a bath in Lake Mānasa". Hearing that the Yaksha said: "I will accomplish your wish". Speaking thus and putting his hands together so as to form a bowl-like cavity, he conveyed him to Lake Mānasa, and the prince bathed according to rule. And there the Yaksha Asiyakkha who lived on Mount Veyaḍḍha, considering him one who had approached there from viciousness[2]), became angry, and a fight took place with him. He first emitted a wind that was filled with a mighty torrent of pebbles and broke the biggest trees. Thereupon the heavens were darkened with a dense dust. Then he emitted Piçācas, who uttered loud laughter, had hair red as blazing fire[3]), and were terrible on account of whirling flames. As the prince was not afraid of them he bound him with fetters consisting of snakes which flashed flames and sparks from their eyes. Then the prince tore them like worn-out ropes. He made at him with mighty blows with his hands. Thereupon the prince beat him all to pieces with fisticuffs. And again the Rākshasa in a violent rage hit the prince on the chest

1) Paraṃ jai, virtually = yadi param. The literal translation would run as follows: "This heat of mine — it will be a great thing if it leave me, etc."

2) Jacobi has misunderstood this phrase.

3) It is a little strange that both saints and devilish ogres in India have red hair. For also the ṛishis (and Çiva, the ideal holy man) glory in fiery tresses. Kumārasambhava VI, 48; Darpadalana III, 114; Daçāvatarac. VII, 167; Mahāvīracarita II, stanza 26 and between stanzas 32 and 23 (ed. T. R. Ratnam Ayar, S. Raṅgachariar, and K. P. Parab, Bombay 1892); Kirātārjun. III, 1; X, 12; XII, 14; XV, 47; Çicupālav. I, 5; Vikramorvaç. (ed. Sh. P. Pandit) V, stanza 19, etc. etc. I think the ṛishis resemble the Urpriester Agni, who naturally has red hair.

Skt. mathnant > mathunanta (epenthetic u) > mahuṇenta (e-formation) > mahuṇinta, if Jacobi's derivation is correct. I think it is Cp. § 513.

with a hammer that was studded with thick iron. But the prince uprooted a big-trunked sandal-tree and struck him across[1]) the thighs, when he was above; like a tree cut down he dropped on the ground. Then the Rākshasa hurled a mighty mountain high up and let it fall on the prince[2]). By that the limbs of the prince were sorely hurt and he became senseless. When he had regained consciousness he engaged in boxing with him. Hit by the prince with his hand, that was like a hammer, he was turned, as it were, into a hundred shards. But as he was an immortal he did not die. Howling disagreeably, he vanished. The gods and fairies who had come to see the wonderful spectacle let fall a shower of flowers, crying: "Ah, the Yaksha has been vanquished by the prince!"

"Thereupon, when my noble husband had vanquished the Yaksha, the sun having gone to the western region, he departed from the most excellent lake and traveled a little distance. There he saw in the middle of the wood Nandana the eight charming daughters of the Vidyādhara Bhāṇuvega, as it were the eight youthful

1) Ācchoḍia, suggested by Jacobi as an emendation for atthoḍia, does not fit into the context. I propose to retain the reading of the text and to derive from ā + sthuḍ. Sthuḍ, according to the lexicons, means "to cover". The development of meaning therefore answers to English "to lay at, to lay on', i.e. to strike; cp. "to lay about one". Sthuḍ is = skhuḍ (as stabh = skabh etc; § 309), "to strike, to stroke" (if joined with ā or pra). See Daçavaikālikasūtra IV, VIII (Zeitschr. d. deutsch. morgenländ. Gesellsch. Vol. 46, p. 616), and cp. this passage with Ayāraṃgasuttaṃ II, 3, 2, § 7. Khoḍā we have in Uttarajjh. XXVI, 25, and I think it means'. "stroking, gentle beating (Klopfen)". I also call attention to styai = skyai. Skyai we have in saṃkhāya (see Gauḍavaha and Rāvaṇavaha sub styai).

2) Or, "flourished far aloft a mighty mountain and hurled it on the prince".

goddesses of the points [1]). He was regarded by them with tender looks. And he reflected: "But who are these? This I shall ask them after gently approaching them". He went into their presence. He enquired in sweet voice, addressing himself to one of the girls: "Who are you? For what reason do you adorn this desolate wildwood [by your lovely presence]?" They said: "Not far from here is our city, called Piyasaṃgamā. Therefore do you first take a rest there". Having spoken thus they made my noble spouse proceed, the servants showing the way. And the sun set, and he came to the city and they had him taken by the chamberlain to the king's presence, and the king saw him and rose to greet him. The proper rites [of hospitality] were discharged. And he was accosted by king Bhāṇuvega as follows: "Illustrious sir, mine are these eight girls, and you have been pointed out before this by the sage Accimāli as their bridegroom in these words: "He who will vanquish [2]) the Yaksha Asiyakkhạ will be their husband". Therefore marry them". And my noble consort agreed, saying: "Yes", and carried out everything. Thereupon the nuptials were celebrated, the marriage-string [around the wrist] was fastened, and he slept together with them on the couch in the chamber of love's pleasure [3]).

"Straightway at the end of his sleep he saw himself [lying] on the ground, and he mused: "What is this?"

1) Or, "of the regions of heaven"; the four cardinal points and the four intermediate points ('SE., etc.) are meant. These goddesses occur often in Jaina stories.

2) Jiṇai (and Pāli jināti) do not come from ji, but from jyā, jināti "to overpower", etc. The similar meaning led to a confusion with jayati, jeti.

3) Or according to the usual translation, "in the pleasure-house."

And he saw the marriage string on his hand. Thereupon he set out to go on, not dejected in mind. And he saw in the middle of the wildwood, on the summit of a mighty mountain, a heavenly palace resting on jewel pillars. He reflected: "This too in all probability is [1]) full of juggling trickery". And having gone near it he heard the sound of a woman weeping in a pitiful tone. And fearless he entered the palace, and on the seventh story he saw a heavenly damsel weeping in a pitiful tone and saying: "Saṇaṃkumāra, moon of the sky of the Kuru race, mayest thou be my spouse at least in another birth". Speaking thus again and again she fell to weeping. Then my noble consort, who had been given a seat and was amazed at [hearing] his own name, asked her: "What are you to this Saṇaṃkumāra that you have gone to him for protection?" She said: "He is my husband by virtue of my wishes only. That is the reason. For Suraha, the king of the city of Sāketa, has formerly given me in marriage to him by the pouring out of water, considering that I am the beloved daughter of his mother Caṇḍajasā, because I had become infatuated with the beauty of a picture of Saṇaṃkumāra, brought by a messenger. But the nuptials did not take place. And in the meantime I have been taken from the inlaid floor [on the roof of my palace] to this spot by a Vidyādhara prince. And leaving me in this white palace, which he conjured forth by his magic, he has gone away somewhere or other.

"Even while this maiden was speaking thus, that

1) Exactly the German idiom, "Das wird Gaukelei sein."

vilest of Vidyādharas, Vajjavega, the son of Asaṇivega, arrived and flung my noble husband up against the celestial sphere. Then she uttered cries of wail and woe and dropped on the ground, overpowered by a swoon. And in the meanwhile my noble consort had killed this wicked Vidyādhara by a blow with his fist and came to her side with unscathed body. He brought her back to life, told her his tale, and married her. And she will be his "Pearl of Women", named Sunandā.

"After a short time there came Vajjavega's sister, Saṃjhāvalī by name, and having seen her brother slain she flew into a passion. But she remembered again the words of an astrologer that she would be the wife of her brother's slayer, and approached my noble spouse in order to marry him. And with Sunandā's consent he married her in like manner.

"At this juncture two Vidyādharas came to my noble consort. After making a low obeisance they said: "Your majesty, Asaṇivega, who has learnt the tidings of his son's death, comes marching upon you with an army of Vidyādharas. Hence Candavega and Bhāṇuvega have sent us, their own sons, Haricanda and Candaseṇa by name; and they have sent you a chariot[1]) and equipment for the fight. Our fathers too have come here in order to serve your feet". And immediately after, Candavega and Bhāṇuvega arrived for the aid of my noble spouse. Saṃjhāvalī gave him the magic science Pannattī. Thereupon my noble consort and Candavega and Bhā-

1) Raho might also be = rahas, "secretly". So the ṭīkā understands it. For on page 526 of the Uttarajjh. (last line) we find rahasi. Raho = rahasi occurs in Uttarajjh. XI, 8.

ṇuvega, accompanied by their martial hosts of Vidyādharas, started to fight with Asaṇivega's army. Thereupon the two armies being discomfited, and a great personal encounter of my noble husband with Asaṇivega taking place, Asaṇivega hurled the Great Snake Missile; but this the prince beat back by means of the Garuḍa Missile. And again he hurled on him the Missile of Fire; that too the prince repulsed with the Missile of Varuṇa [1]). And again he hurled the Missile of the Wind; this too was driven back by the Missile of the Mountain [2]). Thereupon he rushed forward, bow in hand and discharging arrows. The prince deprived his bow of the string [3]). Again he advanced, drawing his scimitar; the prince cut off his hand. Then he approached, desiring a pugilistic encounter. But the prince by his disc deprived his body of the head. Thereupon, in that very moment, the Royal Fortune of the Vidyādhara Asaṇivega, together with all the Vidyādharas, went over to Sanamkumāra. Thereupon, having killed Asaṇivega and being extolled by Candavega and the others, he descended

1) Garuḍa, the giant bird that serves as the vehicle of Vishṇu, is the implacable enemy of the Serpents, and Varuṇa is the god of the waters, or of the ocean.

2) This Mountain Missile — of course a magic weapon, as are also the rest — employed to check the Wind Missile, is perfectly natural, since the wind cannot prevail against a mountain. The student of Indian subjects need hardly be reminded of the well-known story of the mouse that was turned into a maiden and then could not find a husband mighty enough, because also the wind had to own his weakness, till at last she became a mouse again and married a young gallant of Mouseland. The mountain's calm repose in the midst of the storm is a favorite idea of Hindu Spruchpoesie.

3) Jīva, given by Skt. lexicographers, owes its origin to Prākrit, I think (jyā > jiyā > jīva).

from the air together with the Vidyādharas into a most magnificent palace [1]), and he was seen there by joyful Sunandā and Saṃjhāvalī and addressed by them: "Noble consort, welcome!" Thereupon, having gained the victory and gone to Mount Veyaḍḍha, surrounded by companies of many Vidyādharas [2]), and filling the ends of the world with the sound of auspicious festive instruments, they entered their own dwellings. And Saṇaṃkumāra was enthroned as king of all the fairies. Then they lived in great joy [3]).

"And one day Candavega humbly addressed the universal sovereign as follows: "Your majesty, the saint Accimāli announced to me: "Your hundred girls here and the eight girls of Bhāṇuvega the universal sovereign will marry, and he who is called Saṇaṃkumāra has been pointed out by the Jinas as the fourth universal monarch, and he will go to Lake Mānasa in only a month from now. When he steps out there from his bath the Yaksha named Asiyakkha, who is his enemy from a former birth, will see him, regarding him as come from viciousness. Why is he said to be his enemy from a former birth? [4]).

1) Lit., "a crest (a jewel) of a palace". Or perhaps, "Palastparadies", since vaḍiṃsaga has also the meaning of "paradise" (e.g. at Uvāsagadasāo § 80). Leumann in his Beziehungen der Jainalitteratur etc. p. 495 translates vaḍiṃsaga by "Palasthain". I do not know if vaḍiṃsaga means "palace" (Jacobi).

2) Lit. "surrounded by the company (or, companies) of many male and female fairies (Vidhyādhara)", "or, by many companies of fairies".

3) Or, "in continued joy (joy upon joy)". Expressions modelled on this type are very common in Prākrit and are also found in Pāli.

4) Or, "why is he his enemy from a former birth? It is being said:" So Jacobi, and probably this way of taking the words is to be preferred.

"There is a city, Kancaṇapura by name. There lived a king of the name of Vikkamajasa; five hundred were the ladies of his harem. There dwelt a great merchant, Nāgadatta by name. He had a wife, called Viṇhusirī, who surpassed even the fair women of the gods in the excellent qualities of beauty, bloom of youth, grace, and charm. She was seen by Vikkamajasa somewhere or other. Sick with love, he carried her off into his harem. Thereupon Nāgadatta in his separation from her lamented thus: "Alas, my moon-faced love! Where have you gone? Give me a view of you!" He became a madman, surrounded by children, and so spent his time. Thereupon that king Vikkamajasa, discarding the duties of kingship, not heeding the reproaches of the people, despising his seraglio of five hundred most beautiful young women, spent the time excessively addicted to the pleasures of love with this Viṇhusirī.

"One day these women of the harem, being treated with contempt by the king and overcome with jealousy, killed Viṇhusirī by the power of witchcraft [1]). Thereupon the king, sick with excessive grief for her death, his eyes filled with tears, became mad just as Nāgadatta [had done]. He did not allow the body of Viṇhusirī to be burnt [2]). Then the ministers, taking counsel together, tricked the king and took the body to the forest and cast it away. The king, not seeing it anymore, remained

1) Kammaṇa = Skt. kārmaṇa. PW² quotes only Rājatar. 7, 427 for this word, but it occurs also in Bhāminīvilāsa II (Çṛiṅgāravilāsa), 79 (ed. Sheshādri Iyar, Bombay); Hemacandra's Yogaçāstra I, 5, and in many other Jaina Sanskrit passages. It looks like the Sanskritising of a Prākrit word. Cp. kṛityā and German "einem etwas anthun."

2) Cp. the interesting Jātaka N°. 207 and Goethe's Wahlverwandtschaften toward the end).

three days without food or drink. The ministers thought: "If he does not see it, he will die", and led him into the forest. And the king saw the dead body, trickling with a mass of pus, swarming with hosts of wriggling, wiggling worms, its eyes torn out by the crows, hacked to pieces by the fierce beaks of the birds, emitting an ill-smelling odor. And seing this body the king at that very moment was overpowered by fear and he began to blame himself: "How! in that body for whose sake, O miserable soul, thou hast given up family, good character, noble birth, fame and shame, such a condition has set in!" Thereupon the king, entering the path of indifference to the world, gave up kingship, realm, city, harem, and the company of his relatives, etc., like a straw and renounced the world in the presence of the teacher Suvvaya. Thereupon, having perfected himself by various practices of austerity, such as fasting for one day and a half, for two days and a half, for three days and a half, and having mortified himself by starving to death he went to the Saṇaṃkumāra heaven. When his life there had come to an end he was born in Rayaṇapura as a merchant's son, Jiṇadhamma by name. And perfecting his mind by the words of the Jinas, discharging the twelvefold duty of a lay disciple[1]), which has its root in true faith, and delighting in the worship of the Jinas, he passed the time.

Now that Nāgadatta who died distṛessed by the separation from his beloved, bereft of sense, with body

1) As to the twelve vows of the lay devotee, see Uvāsagadasāo §§ 12 ff.; Vol. II, Appendices pp. 34 ff.; Aupapātikasūtra § 57; Bhandarkar, Report p. 114; Lecture on Jainism by Lala Benarsi Dass, p. 60.

wasted away by intense sorrowful reflection, wandered through many animal births and then was born in the town of Sīhaura as a Brahman's son, Aggisamma by name[1]). And in the course of time, taking the vow of a three-staved ascetic[2]), delighting in penances such as fasting for two months, etc., he came to Rayaṇapura. There reigned a king of the name of Harivāhaṇa, who was devoted to Brahmanic ascetics. He knew him when he arrived there, knew: "A great ascetic has come here". On the day when he broke his fast he was invited by the king and came to his dwelling. At this juncture the lay disciple Jiṇadhamma came there by chance. When the saint saw him he was filled with hatred engendered in another birth and said to the king, his eyes reddened with anger: "If you want me to eat, then let me eat hot rice boiled in milk from a dish placed on the great merchant's back". The king said: "I shall let you eat it on another man's back". Thereupon, in pursuance of the hatred engendered in another birth, the saint said to the king: "I shall not eat in another way". Then the king agreed from affection for him. But the great merchant bore properly the burning of the dish put on his back, thinking: "The fruit of a wicked action [done in a former existence] has thus

1) His many low births were brought about by his senseless love for his wife, for such a strong affection, according to the Hindu view, simply means an uncontrolled attachment to the sensual world. Cp. Jātakas N°. 34 and N°. 147.

2) Brahmanic ascetics carry three staves tied together. In Pāli they are therefore called tedaṇḍika. Auguttara-Nikāya III, p. 276; Jātaka II, p. 316, stanza 25, where the commentator says: kuṇḍikaṃ ṭhapanatthāya tidaṇḍaṃ gahetvā caranto.

come". Thereupon when the meal was finished, the dish was wrenched from his back together with blood, sinews, flesh, and fat[1]). Then he went home, honored the company of his own people, asked their forgiveness, worshipped the shrines, took monk's orders, left the city, and went to a mountain peak. Abstaining from food he remained there in the East for half a month in the kāyotsarga posture and in the same way in the South, West etc.[2]), always for half a month. Thereupon, his back being eaten away[3]) by vultures, crows, and jackals, and other animals he bore the pain properly; devoted entirely to worship[4]), he died, went to the Sohamma heaven and became Indra[5]). But the Brahmanic monk was born as his riding animal Erāvaṇa on account of that deed productive of servitude[6]). Falling thence

1) It would be better to separate-vasā from paṭṭhīo, although Jacobi's text is *possible*. The sense remains in both cases essentially the same.

2) Lit. "remained there in the eastern direction.... and in the same way also in the other directions".

3) Lit; "im Rücken angefressen von, etc."

4) Or, "to the (fivefold) formula of worship".

5) Cp. the tale of Avantisukhumāla in Pariçishṭaparvan IX, 132—162.

6) This is the meaning of ābhiogakamma, as clearly shown by Āvaçyaka-Erzählungen, ed. Leumann p. 47 (II, 78ª) and Pariçishṭaparvan III, 123—139, where note especially 139:

> Sollako 'py arjayāmāsa
> ciraṃ vañcanayā tayā
> vaḍavājīvavishayaṃ
> karmoccair ābhiyogikam.

Cp. III, 126 and Daçavaikālikasūtra IX. 2, 5 (Zeitschrift der deutsch. morgenländischen Gesellschaft Vol. 46, p. 635). It is but natural that such a sinner has to serve the being against which he sinned.

There is also a class of gods or genii called the ābhiogiya. They are the servants and slaves of the other gods (ābhiyogadevā hi devānām ājñākarinaḥ kiṃkaraprāyā dāsaprāyāç ca. Uttarajjh. p. 1103, ll. 7, 8). Cp. Aupapātikasūtra § 121 and Uttarajjh. XXXVI, 268:

and wandering through existences as man and animal Erāvaṇa [1]) was born as Asiyakkha the Yaksha. Indra too fell from his position and was born as the universal monarch Saṇaṃkumāra in Hatthināura. And this is the cause of that enmity" [2]).

Mantā jogaṃ kāum bhūīkammaṃ ca je pauñjanti
Sāyarasaiddhiheuṃ ābhiogaṃ bhāvaṇaṃ kuṇai.

"Those who practise sorcery by means of spell and who perform auspicious rites for the sake of happiness, pleasure, and abundance engage in abhiogabhāvanā". Mantā jogaṃ is = mantreṇa yogam, not mantrāyogam, as explained by the dīpikā, for that would be represented by mantāyogaṃ. Mantā is one of the instrumentals singul. of a- and ā- stems which end with ā and are frequently found in Prākrit and Pāli. Cp. the Veda. The commentator has also gone astray in his taking bhūti as meaning "ashes"; else his explanation is correct and seems to have been misunderstood by Jacobi. Bhūīkamma represents the Skt. bhūtikarman. Possibly the varia lectio bhūyakamma is not simply a mistake; for "necromancy, spirit-magic" would fit still better here. But see Aupapātikasūtra § 121.

Most probably the notion that the acts specified in stanzas 267 ff. (in Jacobi's translation 262 ff.) bear their respective names because they are productive of rebirth among the Kandarpa, Ābhiyogika, Kilvisha, Moha, and Asura gods is a secondary one. Kandarpa, "wantonness", abhiyoga, "service (servility)", kilvisha, "wickedness", moha, "folly", and asuratva, "devilishness" are natural characteristics of certain classes of men. And such men would, of course, remain true to their natures also in another life. Man is a little, flickering light in a dark room casting gigantic shadows into the far, dark beyond, and these shadows are his gods.

Observe, too, that Āsuratta in stanza 260 is in reality not asuratva (for that would become asuratta), but *ācuraktya, and it is connected with āsuratta = āçurakta, "easily inflamed", which occurs so often in Uvāgadasāo and elsewhere.

1) From Airāvaṇa, not from Airāvata. Cp. § 246.

2) Tales of hatred and of love extending through many births, through aeon upon aeon, are common, especially with the Jainas. Particularly interesting is the story of Pārçva's prior existences. Uttarajjh. pp. 682—88. [C. fol. 299*b* sqq.] Cp. Oswald und Klara of the great peasant poet Christian Wagner (Neue Dichtungen von Christian Wagner. Heilbronn 1897).

Here ends the muni's tale, and now Candavega, who has retold it, goes on speaking of his own affairs.

"Now when this had been announced by the sage I despatched Bhāṇuvega for the purpose of affording you shelter over night on your way, and after entering the city of Piyasaṃgamā you were induced to marry the eight daughters of Bhāṇuvega and abandoned for some reason in the very same place, for we thought, "Upon the accomplishment of your business we will render you our service". Forgive the offence that you have been abandoned in the wood. Therefore I request you: "Agree to marry my hundred daughters. May also these eight young wives of yours see the lotus face of their lord". When he had agreed with the words: "So be it", these maidens approached. With great pomp [1]) our noble consort married the hundred girls. Attended by his hundred and ten queens he enjoyed the objects of pleasure. Thus the time went by. But today our noble spouse commanded as follows: "Today we must go to that lake where I fought with the Yaksha". Thereupon, having come here we [2]) happened

1) Separate mahayā vibhūie, as also in line 39 mahayā vaḍayareṇa, and so wherever this mahayā occurs. It is = Skt. mahatā (the instrum. sg.). This form being very frequent and its original sense not being felt very keenly anymore it was also used with the feminine. An interesting instance is Uttarajjh. XVIII, 2:

Hayāṇie, gayāṇie,
rahāṇie taheva ya
payattāṇie mahayā
savvao parivārie.

"Surrounded on all sides by a great troop of horses and elephants and chariots and foot soldiers". Hayāṇī is = Skt. *hayānī, "a collection of horses" (the other words are to be explained accordingly). The commentary's hayānīka is impossible. This mahayā seems to have become also an adverb. In Uttarajjh. XVIII, 18 we read: mahayā saṃveganivveyaṃ samāvanno. I think, mahayā here means "very much, exceedingly".

2) According to Pischel majjha = amhaṃ or amhānaṃ has not been found in the literature. We have it here.

to see you on the occasion of the dramatic representation".

At this point Saṇaṁkumāra, who had slept well, advanced from the chamber of love's pleasures. And they went in a great throng [1]) to Mount Veyaḍḍha. And when Mahindasīha had got an opportunity, he requested him as follows: "Your mother and father pass their days in sorrow. Therefore do you to people like me a favor by seeing them". Immediately upon this request they went to Hatthināura in a great thronging crowd consisting of the companies of the Vidyādharas, who rode on elephants [2]), who had mounted various flying palace chariots, horses, elephants, and other means of conveyance, who wore brilliant costumes [3]), and who were adorned with ornaments. He gladdened his mother and father and the townspeople. Thereupon king Āsasena, together with all his counselors and subjects, installed Saṇaṁkumāra with great splendor in royal authority, appointed Mahindasīha commander of the army, and then performed his duty by embracing religious men-

1) Perhaps vyatikara (a mixture, blended mixture, blended mass, host, from kṛī) > vaḍiyara > vaḍayara (assimilation of vowels, helped along by the striving for distinguishing this word from vyatikara > vaiyara (from kṛī). [*Bhaḍavaḍayara* C. fol. 259*b*; 272*a*, written caḍayara both times].

2) So if we follow Jacobi's text and glossary. It would be strange, however, if we really had the elephants twice. I would rather take the compound to be = gatanishṭhita, "skilled in traveling". This adjective might be understood to qualify the fairies or, perhaps better, their vehicles. If we accept the reading of MS A the difficulty is done away with. Gayaṇaṭṭhiya = gaganasthita, "moving (lit., standing, being) in the air" qualifies the vimānas and probably also the horses, elephants etc. — Uttarajjh. p. 429, p. 429, l. 4 from bottom says: gamanasthita-vidyādharavimāna [C also reads gayaṇaṭṭhiya].

3) Or, "various costumes". Maybe the translation: "who were adorned with brilliant costumes and ornaments" would be better.

dicancy in the church of the founders of the true church [1]), at the feet of elders of the same faith [2]).

As for Saṇaṃkumāra, he administered the government of the realm full of courage, increasing in honor, treasure, military forces, and riches. And there appeared the fourteen "Jewels" [3]) beginning with the disc, and the nine "Treasures", and he worshipped them. Immediately after this, the way being shown to him by the Jewel of the Disc, he conquered Bhāraha in this order: Māgaha, Varadāma, Pabhāsa, Sindhu, Khaṇḍappavāya [4]) etc., and after a thousand years came to Gayapura.

Sakka saw by means of the superhuman knowledge Ohi: [5]) "Formerly he was a lord of Sohamma like me". In his love for his brother-Sakka [6]) he commanded Ve-

1) Or, "the Church of Piety". Primarily, dhammatittha means "the ford (across the saṃsāra) which is the true religion" (or whichever way we prefer to translate dhamma).

2) I do not see how tahāviha can mean "quidam" (Jacobi). At any rate, the usual signification of the word fits very well both here and on p. 1, l. 21.

3) Of the universal monarch. The fourteen jewels of the Jaina cakravartin are: 1) senāpati, 2) grihapati, 3) purohita, 4) gaja, 5) haya, 6) sūtradhāra, 7) strī, 8) cakra, 9) chattra, 10) carma. 11) maṇi, 12) kākiṇī 13) khaḍga, 14) daṇḍa. As to the "appearing of the jewels", cp. Milindapañho p. 213.

4) These are the first five khaṇḍas (parts) of Bhāraha or Bhārataland (roughly speaking, = India). The sixth is Timisagūha. — Uyavia (or, oyavia as corrected by Leumann in Wiener Zeitschrift für d. Kunde des Morgenl. VI, p. 44 note) clearly has the meaning "to reduce to subjection". The most common word in such a connection is sādhayati (Prākrit sāhei). The dīpikā has sādhitavān also here. The only derivation of the word that I can think of is: *avajayiya (present stem avajayati with ya suffix and epenthetic i) > oyaviya with the not unusual change of y to v, which here would be very welcome as a means of dissimilating at least one of the three y's. But I may be wrong. Cp. Kathākoça pp. 192, 241.

5) See Hoernle's Uvāsagadasāo, Vol. II, p. 48 note 132, and p. 44 of the Appendices.

6) Lit., "for his relative".

samaṇa:[1]) Do you perform the installation in regal power of Saṇaṃkumāra and bring him the pearl necklace, the garland of wood-flowers, the parasol, the crown, the pair of chowries[2]), the pair of ear-rings, the pair of garments, the throne, the pair of slippers, and the footstool here as a present and speak to him as follows: "Great king, Indra asks you how you do". And Vesamaṇa said; "So be it", took the present, and went to Gayapura. Also Rambhā and Tilottamā[3]) were sent by

1) Strange havoc the Jainas have made of Indian mythology and legendary lore. Vaiçravaṇa, the god of riches, with them has become a servant of Indra and an ideal of beauty (Uttarajjh. XXII, 41). And he has fared better than many other worthies of the land of Hindu fancy.

2) The yak tail fan, the sign of royalty so often mentioned. It was used also to adorn the heads of horses (Çakuntalā I, 8; Rajendra Lala Mitra, Indo-Aryans I, p. 337; Çiçupālavadha XVII, 36; etc.); of elephants (Çicupālav. XVIII, 34 [red chowries]; XVIII, 73 [white]; Gauḍavaha 267); to deck the warrior's chariot (Rāvaṇavaha XV, 49). Shields, too, sometimes were thus made rather gorgeous. See the picture of one in Indo-Aryans I, p. 328). No wonder that the yak took such good care of its tail (cp. my Kshemendra's Samayamatrikā, p. LI, note). According to a far-spread belief it also is able to kill its enemy by merely licking him with its tongue. This peculiarity it shares with the rhinoceros. Yule's Marco Polo[3] Vol. I, p. 277; II, p. 285, 290. Query, Do we have an allusion to this superstition in the difficult stanza N°. 682 of the Kuṭṭanīmatam and can prāṇahata there be intended for khaḍga (rhinoceros, but also sword, "killer" [prāṇahata = hataprāṇa, cp. Whitney's Sanskrit Grammar § 1314; or read prāṇahara?])? Or is prāṇahata some word for yak?

3) Two famous Apsarases or heavenly bayaderes. Rambhā according to Brahmanic mythology, is the wife of Nalakūbara, the son of Kubera or Vaiçravaṇa and a type of grace or personal charm (lalita) with the Jainas (Uttarajjh. XXII, 41). Rambhā was carried off by the demon king Rāvana, who was transported by her beauty. But this lawlessness of his brought a rather inconvenient curse upon his head, that is, inconvenient for Rāvaṇa. So we are told in the Rāmāyaṇa.

Indra got a thousand eyes when he looked on the loveliness of Tilottamā for the first time, and two eyes certainly were not enough to drink in such a sea of beauty. But the Hindu explanation of this remarkable occurrence is not the Darwinian one. See Kathāsaritsāgara, Taraṅga XVII, 137 ff; and Lanman's note in his Sanskrit Reader p. 330.

Sakka, who entrusted to them [1]) a present destined for the celebration of the great festival of coronation. And the universal sovereign was requested by Vesamaṇa: "We have been sent by Sakka for your coronation. Therefore agree to this". When the universal sovereign had consented, saying: "Yes", he conjured forth a floor [2]) consisting of jewels and extending for a yojana, on this the coronation tent made of jewels, in the middle of that a base and on this the throne. There the gods seated Saṇaṃkumāra and amid the sounds of singing blended with the shouts of "Victory, Victory!" they sprinkled him with water from the Ocean of Milk poured from pitchers made of jewels and gold, and Rambhā and Tilottamā were made to dance. Having decked him with all ornaments and introduced him with great profuseness of splendor [3]) into Gayapura, the company of the gods: Dhaṇaya and the rest went to the world of the gods. As for the universal sovereign, he spent the time enjoying the objects of pleasure.

1) Read samappiya (gerund) with the MSS.

2) Lit., "basis".

3) Vicchaḍḍa = viccharda, "scattering, emission, flood, mass, abundance, splendor" is very common in Prākrit. Pāiyalacchī 62 produces as synonyms: samiddhī, riddhī, vihava, sirī, sampattī. The scholiasts and commentators usually translate it by samūha. I see no reason why it should not be connected with the Skt. root chṛid (to throw, and from that the different meanings). Goldschmidt in his note to Rāvaṇavaha X, 49 (translation) declares: "Dass diese zwei Prākritwörter zusammengehören, ist ganz unwahrscheinlich". The passage that gave rise to his note he misunderstood. Vicchaḍḍia there means" ausgestreut." The moonlight scatters like powder over the lamps so that they may be extinguished and that the women, abandoning shame, may yield to the dalliance of love; but, of course, the obliging friend cannot accomplish her design. Cp. Meghadūta 67. With vicchaḍḍa cp. sarga, discharging, emission, gush, stream, troop".

And one day the Indra of Sohamma, seated on his throne in the assembly hall of Sohamma, was seeing the play Soyāmiṇī. At this juncture a god from the Isāṇa heaven, whose name was Saṃgama, came to the Indra of Sohamma. And by the brightness of his body the splendor of all the gods present in the assembly hall vanished; as the stars at the rising of the sun, so the immortals became lustreless. When he had gone the astonished immortals questioned the Indra of Sohamma as follows: "Why, O lord, has this god Saṃgama a splendor surpassing that of twelve sunrises?" Indra said: "In a former life he performed the penance called āyambilabaddhamāna" [1]). Then the gods again questioned

1) The commentators transcribe this word by āyāmamlavardhamānaka. The second part of the word seems tolerably clear. Vardhamānaka means "growing, increasing, something that goes on increasing". Jacobi's "Reihenfolge" answers the purpose quite well. The first part has caused much dubious thought. I do not know if anybody has yet offered a tenable explanation. There is another word derived from āyambila, viz. āyambiliya. The commentators render it by ācāmla. This term means the eating of dry food moistened or boiled in water, as Hoernle informs us. He is certainly entitled to the highest respect. But I do not undertake to say that he is right. Jaina commentators declare: Prākrit āyāma = ācāmla. For instance, Lakshmīvallabha at Uttarajjh. p. 1097, l. 8; 1098 ll. 2 ff. Now āyāma evidently is = ācāma, and that denotes "the water in which rice has been boiled". I think, the first part of the compound is certainly ācāma. The second may represent two words. 1) There is a Pāli word bilaṃ (which I derive from the root bil = bhid, in my opinion, also the root of bila, "hole, cave"). It means "part, bit, piece (for instance, piece of meat), lump" etc. Majjh.-Nik. I, p. 58; II, 178; Jātaka Vol. VI, p. 111, stanza 467; cp. p. 153, st. 716, 717. Angutt.-Nikāya III, p. 384; Vinaya Vol. I, p. 344. So we might assume: ācāmabila > ācāmbila > āyambila (see § 148). Ayambila would thus signify "Reiswasser mit Brocken". Of course, only a *few* lumps or bits of rice would be found in such ascetic's food. For this view of the compound I can quote a very good authority, viz. Aupapātikasūtra § 30, IV. There we have ten synonyms all expressive of poor food. No. 3 āyambilie is followed by āyāmasitthabhoī. This

Indra as follows: "Is there also another who is endowed with such splendor and beauty?" Indra said: "In Hatthināura, in the Kuru race, there is a universal sovereign, Saṇaṃkumāra by name, whose splendor and beauty surpasses even that of the gods". Thereupon the gods Vijaya and Vejayanta, not believing this, went in the form of Brahmans [1]). Thereupon, admitted by the door-

collocation favors my identification of the first part of the compound with ācāma. Ayāmasitthabhoī means "one who eats lumps of rice with the water in which rice has been boiled" and cannot mean anything essentially different from its synonym āyambilie. 2) Ācāmāmla > āyambila (one of the two syllables ām immediately following each other dropping out [a thing not rare in the Prākrits] and amla regularly changing to ambila as in Pāli). The term would thus mean "water in which rice has been boiled mixed with sour gruel (or, sour lumps of rice)". Kulmāsha, "sour gruel" commonly consists of the fermented juice of boiled rice. So the difference is not great, whether we accept the first or the second derivation. According to the commentary quoted by Leumann (Aupapātikas. sub āyambiliya) ācāmla is "sour rice gruel, etc." (odanakulmāshādi). If ācāmāmla is the real prototype, the āyāmāmla of the commentators is almost entirely correct; and also their ācāmla ceases to be a word invented ad hoc; for it would be the shortened form of ācāmāmla.

1) Similar stories we find also elsewhere. Especially interesting is Āvaçya-Erzählungen p. 34—p. 36. Viṇhu (Kaṇha, Vāsudeva, Kesava, i.e. Kṛishṇa, of whom the Jainas have a number of tales; see above all Zeitschrift der deutsch. morgenl. Gesellsch. 42 pp. 492 ff.) is extolled by Indra in the assembly of the gods as a man who only sees the good side in men and things. But:

Samaguṇadosā, dosekkadaṃsiṇo santi, dosaguṇavāmā,
Guṇadosaveiṇo; natthi je u geṇhanti guṇamettaṃ.

"There are those who are indifferent both to virtues and faults; such who hate both virtues and faults; and those who distinguish between virtues and faults. But men who pick out only the virtues (good qualities) do not exist".

Gauḍavaho 964.

So one of the gods, hearing Indra's words and considering this an impossible thing, transforms himself into the carcass of a dog with most beautiful teeth lying on the roadside in an advanced stage of putrefaction. Vāsudeva with his retinue passes by. They all hold their

keeper [1]), they entered into the presence of the king. And they saw the king engaged in the occupation of anointing himself with perfume and oil. They were astonished to see a perfection of beauty and other excellences even greater than the splendor of beauty described by Indra. And they were asked by the king: "Why have you come here?" They said: "Your beauty is being praised in the three worlds; from curiosity to see it [we have come]". And again the king proud of his extreme beauty, addressed them: "Hear, hear, O Brahmans! how could you have seen my beauty! Wait a little while till I enter the hall of audience". "Yes", said the Brahmans and went out. But the universal sovereign quickly bathed, and, having put on ornaments, finery, and an elegant dress he sat down on the throne. The Brahmans were called. When they saw his body they were sad. And they said: "Alas, that the beauty, grace, and youthful bloom of men should be seen one moment and then vanish!" Hearing this the universal monarch said: "Hear! why do you, utterly plunged in

noses and go out of their way to escape from the stench. Vāsudeva quietly gazes on the dog and remarks: "How brilliantly white his teeth shine!"

This tale as told of Jesus and his apostles has become well known through Goethe's notes to his Westöstlicher Divan. There he gives the story as found in Nisāmi (Noten und Abhandlungen. Allgemeines. Sämtliche Werke mit Einleitungen von K. Goedecke, Stuttgart 1881. Bd. II, p. 328).

One is also reminded of the book of Job by such tales (conversation in heaven — diesbelief — trial of the good). Anent this matter cp. Indische Studien XV, 410—417. But I do not believe that the Hebrew story and the Hindu legends are connected by any nexus causalis. The idea is natural enough, so that it can have sprung up independently in different lands and times.

1) Lit., "having doors opened by the door-keeper".

sorrow, find fault with my body?" They said: "Great king, the beauty, youthful bloom, and splendor of the gods remain from the first moment till only six months of their life are left; then they diminish. Those of men, on the other hand, increase till the middle of life has come; thereupon they wane. But a miracle is seen in regard to the brilliancy of your beauty and youthful bloom, for even now it has vanished in a moment like the friendship of a villain". The king said: "How do you know?" They told him the matter, beginning with the praises of Indra. And astonished he looked at his two arms, bedecked with armlets, and saw that they were dim, and he noticed that his breast also, adorned with the pearl necklace, was wan. And seeing this he reflected: "Alas for the instability of the saṃsāra! Alas for the vanity of the body! Even in such a short time beauty, youthful bloom, and splendor have disappeared. Therefore attachment to existence is not meet. Ignorance is the infatuation with the body, foolishness the pride of beauty and youth, madness the enjoyment of the objects of pleasure, a disease brought about by magical influence the possession of anything [whatsoever] [1]. Therefore I shall leave these behind and work my welfare in the other world. Having thus reflected, he installed his son in the government of the realm.

"You, prudent man, have imitated the conduct of your own ancestor, the great king Bharaha, whose fame is proclaimed in the three worlds".

1) According to Jacobi gaho ceva pariggaho would mean: "Property is theft". But we have here no anticipation of Proudhon's celebrated dictum. See Monier-Williams sub graha. The things men possess in reality possess their so-called owners like demons.

Having extolled him in this and other ways the gods departed.

But the universal sovereign, leaving all he possessed like a straw clinging to him[1]), renounced the world at the feet of the teacher Rāya. All his "Jewels", beginning with the "Jewel of a Woman", his other beautiful wives, the gods that served him, the great kings, the "Treasures" all of them; in short, all the people inhabiting his whole royal capital followed him on his way for six months, but they are said not to have been looked at by him even with a lion's glance. Thereupon, having fasted for two days and a half, he entered his begging district and at once was given millet porridge with goat's buttermilk[2]). Having eaten this, he again fasted for two days and a half. From this time on he had, in consequence of the detrimental effects of this [manner of life], scab, fever, cough, asthma, bulimy[3]), pain in the eyes, bellyache; these seven dreadful diseases he bore fitly for seven hundred years. Then performing frightful penances, painful penances, gruesome penances, he acquired all the perfections: the ability to cure by simple touch, to cure with his spittle, to cure with the drops spirting from his mouth while speaking, to cure

1) Jacobi attributes the meaning "sick, weak, frail, perishable" to paḍilagga. Such a use of the word is unknown to me. In our tales, I think, it does not occur. Still Jacobi may be right after all.

2) Kūra according to commentators is = odana, porridge (see e.g. Uvāsagadasāo § 35 and comm.). The dīpikā (Uttarajjh. p. 531, last line) says: Gocarapravishṭasya prathamam eva ajñātakraṃ tasya gṛihasthena dattam. Chaliyā therefore is chagalikā > chayaliyā > chaliyā. See § 149. Saccavai "to-see" I take = satyāpayati. English Cp. "to realise".

3) I see now that my conjecture that bhattacchanda means too intense a craving for food, morbid appetite has Leumann's authority to support it. See Kathākoça p. 237.

with his filth, to cure with everything, etc. But even then he did not apply any remedy to his body. Again he was praised by Indra. "Ah, the firmness of the saint Saṇaṃkumāra! Although harassed with diseases he applies no remedy against them". Not believing this, the same gods approached him in the guise of Çabara physicians. And they said. "Reverend sir, we'll remove your diseases". The holy man remained silent. When they said it again and again the saint answered: "Do you put an end[1]) to the disease of the body, or to the disease of karma?" They said: "To the disease of the body". Then the reverend man rubbed his finger with his spittle[2]), made it bright as gold, and showed it to them, and he said: "I myself do away with other

1) The roots sphiṭ and sphuṭ go together and are only different forms of "split". The p.p.p. phiḍia occurs very often especially in the Setubandha (meaning "escaped, run away" etc.). Pāiyalacchī 191 offers as synonyms: bhaṭṭha, cukka, paribhūya, ahilia, parūhūya. Cp. Hāla; Uttarajjh. XX, 30. In pheḍei vāhiṃ we have the original meaning still quite palpably preserved (cp. our "to break up" in a simular use). In Weber's Indische Studien XV, p. 385 we read:

Jo na vi dukkhaṃ patto, jo na vi ḍukkhassa pheḍaṇasamattho,
Jo na vi dukkhiye dukkhio, kaha tassa kahijjai dukkhaṃ?

"How could one's sorrow be told to him who neither himself has ever suffered sorrow, nor is capable of assuaging sorrow, nor sorrows with the sorrowing?

Parallel is Skt. sphoṭayati vedanām, sphoṭayati vivādam, "to appease (do away with) pain, — a quarrel". Vetālapañcaviṃç. ed. Uhle p. 35, l. 36; p. 38, l. 39; p. 54, l. 25. Cp. also sampheṭa and samphoṭa, "battle".

2) Niṭṭhuhaṇa is = nishṭubhana. See § 120. And not only stubh, I think, but also stu means first "ausstossen". That original meaning is preserved in stoma, "mass, heap, multitude" — the same development that we have in vicchaḍḍa = samūha and in sarga. Cp. sku, "stossen, to poke, stir" and Pāli oṭṭhubhati (Majjh.-Nik. I, p. 127). Another case of collateral roots, the one beginning with ksh, the other with st, is to be seen in Pāli cheva = theva (root kship = stip). Cheva occurs, for instance, in Jātaka, Vol. V, p. 137, l. 16.

diseases; if you are able to do away with the saṃsāra, then do away with it". The two gods were astonished in their minds; praised him with these words: "You are the supreme physician to do away with the disease of the saṃsāra"; announced to him what had passed in the presence of Indra; made a low obeisance to him in their own divine forms, and went to their own abode.

And the holy man went to the peak of Mount Sumeya after he had occupied the station of a prince and of a ruler of the district for fifty thousand years in each instance and that of a universal sovereign for a lakh of years and after he had observed çramanaship for a lakh of years. There on a rock he died after confessing himself and fasting for a month. He was born again in the Saṇaṃkumārakappa. Falling from there, he will attain final emancipation in the land of Mahāvideha.

UDĀYAṆA.

UDĀYAṆA[1]).

In that period, at that time, there was in a city in the countries of Sindhu and Sovira, called Vīyabhaya, a king, Udāyaṇa by name, and a queen Pabhāvaī. Her eldest son, Abhii by name, was crown prince and vice-regent. The king's own sister's son was called Kesi. This king Udāyaṇa lived exercising the sovereignty over sixteen countries, beginning with Sindhu-Sovīra, three hundred and sixty-three[2]) cities, beginning with Vīyabhaya, ten kings who were crowned and on whom had been bestowed white chowries and fans, Mahaseṇa being the first of them, and over other princes and chiefs. And thus it was so far.

Now in that period, at that time, there dwelt in the city of Çampā a goldsmith, Kumāranandi by name, who was continually lusting after women. Whereever he saw a beautiful girl or heard of one, then and there he gave five hundred gold pieces for her and married her. And in this way he brought together[3]) five hundred. Then, being of a jealous disposition, he built a palace resting

1) A Sanskrit version of this tale, which is partly written in the Ardhamāgadhī dialect is found in the Uttarajjhāyaṇa, pp. 553 ff. Cp. also Bhandarkar's Report p. 142.

Concerning hotthā see § 517.

2) See Pischel's Grammar p. 409, correction to § 447. The ṭīkā reads: triçatatrishashṭinagarāṇām. Uttarajjh. p. 553, l. 5 from bottom.

3) Lit., "lumped, heaped together".

on one pillar[1]) and dallied with these wives. And his friend, Nāila by name, was a Jaina lay disciple.

And one day the Vāṇamantara goddesses resident in the island of Pancasela at the command of the lord of the gods set out on a pilgrimage to the excellent island of Nandīsara. And their husband had been the ruler of Pancasela, Vijjumāli by name; he had now fallen [from his position][2]). They reflected: "Whom shall we entice [3]) to be our husband?" Presently[4]), while going on, they saw Kumāranandi in Campā dallying in the company of five hundred women. They thought: "He is eager for women; him let us seduce". Then he said: "Who are you?" They said: "We are goddesses, named Hāsā and Pahāsā". Infatuated he looked upon them. They said: "If you care for us, then go to the island of Pancaselaga". Having said this they flew up and departed. Infatuated with them, he paid gold in the king's court and had the drum brought out [i. e. had a drum beaten to attract attention and then publicly announced:] "He who takes Kumāranandi to Pancaselaga, to him he gives a crore of money". The drum was stopped by an old man. A ship was prepared and loaded with provisions for the voyage. The old man gave that money to his sons and put to sea on board the vessel together with Kumāranandi. When they had

1) Such palaces we find also in the Jātaka book; e.g., in vol. IV, pp. 79, 153.

2) That is, the store of his "merit" being exhausted his life as lord of the Vāṇamantara gods on the Island of Pançasela came to an end and he entered some lower form of existence.

3) Vuggāhei, lit. "to take out of the way, verführen".

4) See § 184.

sailed a great distance on the ocean, the old man said: "Do you see anything?" He answered: "I see something black"[1]). The old man said: "That is a fig-tree growing on the coast of the sea at the foot of a mountain. Below that the ship will sail along; then do you be on the alert and cling to the fig-tree[2]). Then the Bhāruṇḍa birds[3]) from Pancasela will come. A pair of them has three legs. Thereupon, when they have fallen asleep, do you cling to the leg in the middle, yourself being bound to it by your garment. Then they will take you to Pancasela. But if you do not cling to the fig-tree the ship will enter the submarine fire; so you will perish there"[4]). Thus he clung [to the tree] and was taken [to Pancasela] by the birds. Then he was seen by these Vāṇamantara goddesses. And he was shown their splendor. They seized him, took him along, and said, "With this body [of yours] you cannot enjoy us at all. Enter the fire and do the other things that are necessary, so that you may become the ruler of Pan-

1) Lit., "Do you behold (observe) anything?" He said: "Something black is seen (appears)."

2) In regard to the optative see Pischel § 459. He is undoubtedly on the right track in taking this formation to be a yā-aptative, and if we had only Prākrit to account for, no objection could be raised. But the Pāli endings are eyyāmi, eyyāsi, eyyāti, eyyāma, eyyātha, eyyuṃ. The ā clearly shows that also here the specific optative element yā is used. But Pāli does not change i to e before yy. So I think, we find here another of the double formations so numerous in the Prākrits, i.e., the e-optative and the yā-optative combined. Vaṭṭejjāsi therefore would answer to * varteyāsi (> vatteyyāsi, Pāli).

3) Fabulous gigantic birds — emblems of heedfulness (appamāda) with the Jainas. Kalpasūtra I, 118 (p. 62, 3d line from bottom); Uttarajjh. III, 6.

4) Pavisihitti (i. e. pavisihī tti) of the MSS is all right. Ti is inserted before the end of the quotation quite frequently in our tales.

casela" [1]). How then shall I go?" They carried him along in the hollow of their hands and left him in the public garden [of his native city]. Then the people came and asked him: "What marvel have you seen there?" [2]). He said:

"I have seen, heard, experienced what happened in the island of Pancasela. Alas! alas! gazelle-eyed, moon-faced Hāsā and Pahāsā!"

And with this purpose [in mind] he began to attend to the fire [3]), And his friend prevented him: "Listen, friend. This act, which befits the herd of contemptible fellows, is not meet for you. Therefore, illustrious sir:

"Do not on account of empty pleasure and happiness lose the life of a man which is hard to obtain [4]). Does anybody buy a quartz for the price of a lapis lazuli"?

"And another thing. Even if you are desirous of pleasures, do you nevertheless engage in the practice of the true religion. For:

1) Hojjāmi is intelligible. Translate: "Do the entering into the fire and the other things, thinking: So that I may become the ruler of Pancasela". But in all probability we have to read hojjāsi. S and m are very often confounded in the Devanāgarī alphabet, and such mistakes are very natural. [C, in fact, reads hojjāsi.]

Burning one's body in order to get a heavenly body occurs in a number of Hindu tales. See my Daçakumāracaritam pp. 138, 165; Weber's Indische Studien XV, pp. 370, 364 sqq.

2) Or, "How? Have you seen a marvel there?"

3) That is, made preparations to enter the fire.

4) A favorite idea of the Jainas. Cp. the durlabhānuprekshā, Bhandarkar, Report p. 113. According to the doctrine of the Jainas only a man and not even a god can attain moksha or final emancipation from the round of existences. Quite different is the Buddhist view.

> "The religion taught by the Jinas gives riches to those who desire riches, brings about all pleasures for those who desire pleasures, and is the cause of attaining heaven and final beatitude".

Though thus held back by his friend, he died a death by fire [1]) and became the ruler of Pancasela.

But a disgust of life came upon the faithful disciple and thinking: "Why should I delay who know that men suffer [2]) for the sake of the objects of enjoyment?" he renounced the world. When he died he was born in the Accuya heaven. By the superhuman knowledge Ohi he saw him [3]). One day when he [4]) was running away on a pilgrimage to the excellent island of Nandīsara a drum hung around his neck. Then he went

1) Ingiṇī in the sense in which we seem to have it here is a word unknown to me. Angāra becomes iṅgāla (in Pāli even inghāla and inghela. Therīgāthā 386). So perhaps the development is this: aṅgārinī > iṅgālinī > iṅglinī > ingiṇī. I take aṅgāriṇī (scil. karshū) in the sense of agnikuṇḍa. See Weber's Indische Studien XV, pp. 364 ff.; 372 for this agnikuṇḍa. It is very unlikely, if not impossible that ingiṇī had the meaning so common in Jaina writings. According to that it denotes one of the three orthodox ways of starving onesself to death. They are: Ingiṇīmaraṇa, bhaktaparijñā — (or, — pratyākhyāna —) maraṇa, pādopagamana. The modus procedendi of the first is this: One makes a circle, steps inside this, without ever leaving it anymore, and fasts. He himself must perform the necessary movements of his body, as turning over, etc., and may not allow another to do this for him (whereas one who seeks death by bhaktaparijñāmaraṇa may move his body himself or may have it moved by another). Thus he continues till life departs. Pādopagamana is a wrong Skt. translation of pāyovagamaṇa = prāyopagamana.

2) Or, "are defiled". Kilissai, as with the Buddhists, may have both meanings. Defilement and suffering mean the same thing, the former inevitably produces the latter.

3) That is, the former lay disciple Nāila now a god in the Accuya heaven, saw his former friend Kumāranandi, now ruler of Pancasela.

4) I. e. the whilom Kumāranandi.

to Nandīsara sounding it [1]). The faithful disciple came; he saw him [2]). Not being able to bear his splendor he fled. He withdrew his splendor and said: "Hear! do you know me?" He said: "Who does not know Indra and the other gods?" Then he showed his [former] form of the lay disciple. And he was made to know him. Then his soul was thoroughly stirred. And he said: "Instruct me. What shall I do now?" He said: "Make an image of the lord Vaddhamāṇa [3]). From that, then, the germ of the true faith will spring for you. And it is said:

> "Whosoever causes to be made the images of the Jinas, who have conquered love, and hate, and delusion, obtains in another birth the jewel of the most excellent religion which brings forth happiness.

1) The Sanskrit version is more intelligible: "One day all the princes of the gods started for a pilgrimage to Nandīçvara. That god, the former lay disciple, also started with the ruler of the Acyuta heaven. Then there hung a drum around the neck of that god, Vidyumālin by name, the lord of Pañcaçaila, and could not be taken off (read: uttāritum). Hāsā and Prahāsā said: "This is the law and custom for the one who dwells in the Island of Nandīçvara that the (then) god Vidyumālin, sounding the drum, goes there at the head of the gods when they have set out for a pilgrimage to Nandīçvara Island. Therefore, do you not be cast down. Do you together with us two, who are singing songs, go to Nandīçvara Island, sounding the drum." Then doing so he started, bound for Nandīçvara. The lay disciple god, seeing him sound the drum in distress, observing him by means of the mystic application of his mental sight (upayoga, see Cowell and Gough's Sarvadarçanasaṃgraha p. 49) said etc."

2) I. e., the present ruler of Pancasela saw the resplendent god, his former friend.

3) The last of the Tīrthaṃkara, the founder (or, reformer) of the Jaina sect, commonly called Mahāvīra. Vaddhamāṇa or Vardhamāna was his secular name, the name his parents gave him, just as Gautama Buddha was Prince Siddhārtha before the Great Renunciation.

"And another saying:

"Poverty, misfortune, an inferior birth, an inferior body, an inferior intellect, an inferior station, contempt, disease, and sorrow do not fall to the lot of those who have images of the Jinas made".

Then getting gosīsa sandal wood from the great Himavat[1]), he fashioned there an image and put it[2]) into a wooden box. At that time he saw a ship driven about by a raging storm in the middle of the sea for six months. Then he calmed the storm. He gave the chest to the sea-faring merchants. And he said: "In it is the image of the supreme god of the gods[3]). Therefore open the chest in his name". Saying: "Yes", the merchants consented. They crossed the sea and came to Vīyabhaya. There king Udāyaṇa was devoted to Brahmanic ascetics.

1) The Himālaya.

2) Chubh = khubh is also found in Pāli. Of the simple verb I only mention the form chuddha in the 41st stanza of the Dhammapadam. It is not = kshudra, as usually explained, but = kshubdha, "cast away". So also in Jātaka V, p. 302, stanza 37 (= chaḍḍito accord. to comm.); Therīgāthā 468, where the readings are chuṭṭho and cuddho and where the commentary also explains by chaḍḍito; Buddhavaṃsa II, 97 (pushed forth, thrust —, moved forth).

3) The Jainas are atheists — originally. They are even forbidden to say: "The god rains," a phrase that the likewise atheistic Buddhists use freely. But man needs gods. The phrase: "Jina (Mahāvīra) is god" was soon taken in the crudest sense. And there are many other gods whom the Jainas worship, although these are styled "untrue gods", as distinguished from the "true god" (satyadeva). Uttarajjh. p. 550, ll. 3 and 4 from bottom. It need hardly be pointed out that the so-called gods of the many heavens of the Jainas are beings similar to the gods of the Buddhists — simply greater, mightier, happier, than men, but much inferior to the saint. And the trumpets that made the walls of the celestial Jericho fall to pieces and that made all the glory of the gods living therein vanish into nothing were sounded already in the days of the Veda. Cp. the vigorous and interesting protest against the charge that the Jainas are atheists in Benarsi Dass' Lecture p. 57, 58.

They showed him the box. They related the words of the god to him. He assembled a company of people numbering many sasarakkhas [1]), Brahmans etc. In the name of Rudra, Govinda, and other gods they wielded the axe. This is the way it was. Some said: "Brahma is the supreme god of gods, for this four-faced one brings about the final beatitude of the whole world and he is the revealer of the Veda". Others said: "Vishṇu is the highest, for he pervades the universe and destroys the demons who work the world harm; and at the time of the universal destruction he preserves the world in his belly". Others declared: "Çiva is the superior god, for it is he who causes creation and destruction and who is not born from a womb; parts and parcels of him are Brahma and Vishṇu". Amid vain imaginings of such like sort the axe was wielded; but it rebounded [2]).

At this juncture the chief queen of king Udāyaṇa,

1) Sasarakkha baffles me. The word is frequent in the Jaina books, but in another meaning than the one required here. Is it = *çvasaraksha, "one who guards himself from the breath [of others]", lest he be defiled? That is what Brahmanic ascetics did, as humorously described by Kshemendra in the first canto of his Kalāvilāsa; and the Jātaka contains many a story illustrative of such or similar dread of the high caste people. The word hardly refers to the Yoga practices in which the regulation of the breath holds so important a place. At any rate, it seems to denote Brahmanic ascetics. This sasarakkha, in all probability, ironically includes also the ordinary meaning of sasarakkha (= sarajaska).

2) Upphiḍai does not mean "zersplittern", but "aufspringen" (perhaps in both senses of the word, here in the sense of "to jump up"), just as phiḍ means "abspringen, (bhraṃç), entspringen (to escape)" etc. Cp. vipaṭati = palāyate, German "er reisst aus", Çiçupālavadha XIX, 56; upphiḍai = utpatati, Hāla 171; upphiḍa, "jumping up", Āvaçyaka-Erzählungen p. 7, the 4th stanza of the small print; upphiḍai, "to jump up, to caper", Uttarajjh. XXVII 5. German spalten, abspringen, springen aptly illustrates the development of the meaning of the root (sphiṭ).

the daughter of king Ceḍaga, the Jaina lay disciple Pabhāvaī, came there. Having performed worship she said:

> "The Arhat, who is free from love, hatred and delusion, who knows everything, who is endowed with the eight miraculous powers, who wears the form of the supreme god of gods, may he grant me a sight of himself".

She had the axe wielded. When the stroke fell the chest was opened. Straightway they saw the image of lord Vaddhamāṇa, complete in every limb, bedecked with an unfading garland of flowers. Pabhāvaī was extremely rejoiced. The religion of the Jina was established [1]. And she recited:

> "Hail, hail to thee, knower of all things, lovely to behold, thou who art never to be born again, heart's joy of the pious people, miraculous jewel that yields the world all its wishes, teacher of the universe, Victor, Hero, spotless one!"

And in the harem there was built a sanctuary. Sambhāvaī, after taking a bath, worshipped three times a day [2]. One day the queen danced, the king played the vīṇā. He did not see the head of the queen [3]. He took alarm. The plectrum of the vīṇā dropped from his hand. She was in a rage and said: "Why have you spoilt the dance?" When she insisted, he told her [the reason].

1) Or, "was glorified, (or, spread)".
2) In the morning, at noon, and in the evening.
3) This is a very bad omen and indicates her approaching death. Cp. Uttarajjh. p. 556, l. 8.

She said: "What of life! I have faithfully discharged the duty of a lay disciple[1]) for a long time".

One day when she had bathed, she said to a servant girl: "Bring me my clothes". She brought her the red garments. In a rage she struck her with the mirror, saying: "You enter the chamber of the Jina and give me the red garments!" The servant girl died. Then the queen thought: "I have broken my vow. So what is the use of life?" She asked the king: "I want to abstain from food". When she insisted he consented with these words: "Only if you convert me"[2]). The queen died by refusing food and was born in the world of the gods.

Devadattā, a hunchbacked slave girl, attended upon the image of the Jina. The god[3]) tried to convert Udāyaṇa, but he was not converted. He was devoted to Brahman ascetics. Then the god assumed the form of a Brahman ascetic. He came with ambrosial fruits in his hands. The king tasted them. He asked: "Whence are these fruits?" He answered: "Near the city there is our hermitage, [there they grow]"[4]). There he went together with him. Brahman ascetics of frightful appearance began to beat him. Fleeing, he saw Jaina monks in a thicket of the wood. He sought their protection[5]).

1) Lit., "Stainless has may lȧy devotee's law been kept."

2) He means, If by your meritorious fasting and death you become a god you are to visit me and convert me. Cp. Zeitschrift der deutschen morgenl. Gesellschaft (abbrev. ZDMG), Vol. 42, p. 503, ll. 35 ff.; p. 496, ll. 12—20; Kathākoça p. 42. The Sanskrit version accordingly has: yadi tvaṃ devībhūtvā māṃ pratibodhayasi. Uttarajjh. p. 556, l. 2 from bottom.

3) That is, the king's former queen.

4) The ṭīkā's words are: Etannagarābharṇe 'smadāçramo 'sti. Tatraitāni phalāni santi. Uttarajjh. p. 557, l. 2. But perhaps we ought to read āsame nevertheless.

5) For uvallīṇa = upalīna (or, upālīna) see § 196.

They comforted him with the words: "Do not fear". The Brahman ascetics turned back. The Jaina monks instructed him:

> "The true religion is the refuge of beings in the ocean of existence; and he whose aim is the true religion by enquiring tries to find [1]) god, the true religion, and the teacher".
>
> "God, i. e. the Jina, is free from the eighteen faults [2]); the true religion is accompanied by perfect compassion; and the good teacher is he who practises strict chastity and refrains from all worldly undertakings and possessions" [3]).

By instruction of this nature he became converted and embraced the faith of the Jinas. The god displayed his real self. And having firmly established him in the Law the immortal left. Straightway the king found himself in his hall of audience. Thus he became a believer [4]).

Now a lay devotee from Gandhāra, who had worshipped the places where the Jinas were born and all the other places [that had any important connection with them], and who heard that there were golden images [of the Jinas] on Mount Veyaḍḍha, was engaged in fasting [with

1) Parikkhae = parīkshate here seems to mean "forschen nach" (Jacobi "prüfen"), to enquire into. Faith in the true Deva, in the Guru, and in Dharma is required of the lay disciple by the first vow of the first Pratimā. Benarsi Dass p. 59.

2) The eighteen faults (dosha) are enumerated in Sarvadarçanasaṃgraha, p. 62 (I always quote the English translation).

3) That is, the saint, the true monk (sādhu).

4) A pia fraus as a means of converting some sinner is rather a favorite both with Buddhistic and with Jaina story tellers.

this resolution:] "I shall either die or I shall see them". A deity showed them to him. And highly gratified the deity gave him of its own accord magic pills that granted all wishes[1]). Returning thence, he heard that there was an image of the Jina made of gosīsa sandal wood in the city of Vīyabhaya. He went to worship it, and did worship it. While he stayed[2]) there he was waited upon by Devadattā. And, pleased with her, he gave her these pills. And he renounced the world.

One day she ate one pill with this wish: "May my body become like gold". Thereupon she became a woman of the most radiant beauty and of a hue like molten gold; "Suvaṇṇaguliyā[3]) became her name". Again she reflected: "I'll enjoy the objects of enjoyment. As regards this king now, he is my father; and the others are simply soldiers"[4]). Then she selected Pajjoya. Bearing him in mind she swallowed a pill. A deity announced to him: "A woman of such and such beauty is she". He sent a messenger to Suvaṇṇaguliyā. She said: "I will first see you". He came with [his elephant] Nalagiri during the night, was seen and liked. She said: "If you

1) Lit. "pills of all wishes". The expression looks rather suspicious. One is tempted to emendate to guliyāṇa and to translate: A hundred pills that granted all wishes" (saya = çata). Cp. the proverbial kāmiyaghaṭa, the wish-yielding pot in the Kālakācāryakathānakam (ZDMG. Vol. 34,) p. 270, l. 29 (= kāmakumbha Uttarajjh. p. 216) So perhaps kāmiyaguliyāṇa would be still better. But I hate to change the reading and as MS A ommits guliyā it may originally be a gloss explaining the rather obscure savvakāmiya. [C really reads guliyāṇa].

2) Lit., "clung there, stuck there". Jacobi takes paḍilagga to mean "sick"; and the dīpika favors his interpretation, for it tells us: Daivāt tasyātisāraroga utpannaḥ. Kubjayā dāsyā praticaritaḥ etc. Uttarajjh. p. 557, ll. 8, 9.

3) "Gold Pill".

4) Or, "his soldiers".

take the image along, then I shall go"[1]). Now, as there was no image fit to be placed in its place, he stayed over night and then went back. He made another image of the Jina and returned. Having placed Jiyantasāmi[2]) in that place, he took Suvaṇṇaguliyā and went to Ujjeṇī. There Nalagiri dropped urine and excrements. At that smell the elephants became mad. And in that direction the smell went; they[3]) looked forthwith, they saw the footprints of Nalagiri. They asked: "For what reason has he come?" Just then they missed[4]) the female servant. The king said: "The servant girl has of course been carried off. Look for the image". They reported: "Chief of men[5]), it is still there". Then the king came at the time of worshipping and he saw that the flowers had faded. When he inspected [the image] he knew: "It is an imitation; the image has been taken away". Thereupon he sent a messenger to Pajjoya: "I care nothing for the servant girl. Send me the image". He did not give it.

Then, in the month of Jeṭṭha, Udāyaṇa hurriedly took the field together with the ten kings [his vassals]. And in crossing the desert the army began to die of thirst. They reported it to the king. Thereupon he thought of Pabhāvaī and she came instantly. She created three lotus lakes, in the front, in the rear, and in the

1) She is like Rachel who stole the Teraphim of her father. Genesis 31, 19 ff.

2) "The Victorious Lord", Jina.

3) The people of king Udāyaṇa. "In that direction" means toward the place where the elephants and the king's people were.

4) Lit., "In the meanwhile the female servant was not seen".

5) I read naravara (MSS naravaraṃ). Cp. Erz. p. 40, ll. 8, 11; p. 73, l. 14. If we follow Jacobi we have to translate: "It is simply (lit., only. = kevalaṃ) still there."

middle[1]). Then refreshed and cheered up, he marched to Ujjeṇī. And the king said: "Why should the people be killed? Let there be a fight between you and me on horseback, in chariots, on elephants, or on foot, just as *you* please". Pajjoya answered: "Let us fight in chariots". Then he came with Nalagiri caparisoned for the fight, and the king in a chariot. Then the king said: "You are not true to [your] agreement. But nevertheless there is no escape for you". Then he drove the chariot about in a circle. The elephant followed it with impetuosity. And whatever foot the elephant lifted up, at that Udāyaṇa discharged his arrows till the elephant dropped. When Pajjoya descended he was bound (captured by Udāyaṇa). A brand was made on his forehead, reading: "Husband of a slave girl". And after that king Udāyaṇa hastened back to his own town. The image was unwilling. On the way he was stopped by the rain and encamped. Then the ten kings in fear of an attack made ramparts of earth and encamped. And whatever the king ate, of that they also gave to Pajjoya.

Before long the charioteer, on account of it being Pajjusan, asked Pajjoya: "What do you want to eat today?" He thought: "I am going to be killed". Then he asked: "Why am I asked today?" He said: "Today is Pajjusan; the king is fasting. "He said: "I too am fasting. I too have suppressed the workings of delusion. Only I did not know that it is Pajjusan today". It was reported to the king[2]). "I know that he is a rogue; but while he is a captive[3]) my Pajjusan, even, does not become

1) Lit., "for the front, for the rear, and for the middle".
2) Read ranno with the MSS and put a period after kahiyaṃ.
3) § 595.

pure and auspicious". Then he released and pardoned him. And he invested him with a golden turban in order to cover those letters. And that realm was given to him. From that time on kings were invested with the turban; before this they were invested with the diadem [1]). When the rainy season was passed the king marched on. The band of merchants that had come there remained on the spot. Then that became [the city of] Dasapura [2]).

Thereafter that king Udāyaṇa once upon a time was staying in the chamber of fasting, engaged in fasting, alone, without a single companion, attending properly to the fortnightly fast. Thereupon when he was keeping vigil at the time of midnight the following thought [3])

1) Cp. Jātaka Vol. VI, pp. 369, 370 and Kathāsaritsāgara XIII.

2) It was a common thing for merchants in Ancient India to accompany the march of an army. Cicupālavadha V, 24.

3) Ajjhatthia, "thought, idea" seems to have grown out of the phrase that occurs so often in Jaina books: ayaṃ eyārūve (imeyārūve) ajjhatthie cimtie patthie manogae saṃkappe samuppajjitthā, which Jacobi translates: The following personal, reflectional, desirable idea occurred, etc. (Sacred Books of the East (SBE) XXII, p. 249). Hoernle renders: "The following inward, musing, hidden reflection" etc. (Uvāsagadasāo § 66; patthie is missing here). Ajjhatthiya is uniformly explained by adhyātmika. In Pāli we often find ajjhattika. Phonetically ajjhatthiya may, after all, be adhyātmika. It is one of the many instances in which Jinistic and Buddhistic terminologies meet. But by a perverse craving for distinctiveness, intelligible in two sects of the same kith and kin, a difference is brought about no matter how. Thus in a phrase frequently employed in Pāli books and Jaina writings we have dhamaṇisanthata in Pāli, but dhamaṇisaṃtaya in Prākrit (see e.g. Uvāsagadasāo § 72; Uttarajjh. II, 2). Both seem to represent the Skt. dhamanisantata. Still Pāli saṃthita may stand for *saṃstrita = saṃstīrṇa. If ajjattha = adhyātma, found sometimes, be correct this form would exhibit "Untreten des Hauches" and by the influence of this type our ajjhatthiya would naturally develop. Now patthiya in the Jaina phrase can hardly be prārthita (as Jacobi takes it). That would match the other synonyms very poorly, and we have the same locution where the idea is by no means "desirable". But perhaps that does not count for much. It seems not unlikely that patthiya is

arose in him: "Blessed indeed are those villages and towns where the monk Vīra dwells and preaches the Law. Blessed indeed are those princes and other men who hear from the lips of Mahāvīra the Law that is proclaimed by the Kevalis. Thus they embrace the five lesser vows and the seven commandments, the twelve-fold religious duty of the lay disciple; thus they become men of bald heads, leave the house, and enter upon the houseless state. So if indeed the monk, the reverend Mahāvīra, while continually wandering about should come here to Vīyabhaya, then indeed I too would, in the presence of the Blessed One, become a man with a bald head, leave the house, and enter upon the houseless state"[1]). Thereupon the Blessed One, knowing such

prasthita, "set forth, arisen". If that were so, Hoernle's derivation of ajjhatthiya from adhyāsthita would gain in probability. I do not think, however, that his "abiding within" is correct. Neither the natural meaning of adhyāsthita, nor the context, which does *not* "require synonyms expressive of deep inward musing" call for such an interpretation. German "obliegen" would come nearest. So the phrase seems to be one of those tautological accumulations of words so rife in Jaina books and the literal translation would be: "There occurred to him this following thought, engaged in, thought, arisen, passing in his mind".

I add another strange case of "distinctiveness". In Prākrit we have thīṇagiddhī, one of the nine faith-obstructing karman. See Uttarajjh. XXXIII, 5, 6. That seems a palpable perversion of a Buddhistic term. The Pāli thīnamiddha is perfectly natural, especially if middha should be = *migdha (from migh, mih) and connected with megha and with mihikā, mist, fog, snow, frost, Cp. Prākrit mahiyā and Pāli mahikā, mahiyā, mist, fog (Milindapañho pp. 273, 299; Sumangalavil. I, 141; Cullavagga XII, 1, 3; Angutt.-Nik, II, p. 53). But the Jaina explanation of thīnagiddhī wears a queer look and is not in harmony with the other darçanāvaraṇa. For the commentator's explanations are correct. The first four are: sleep, dozing, deep sleep, very decided dozing (that seems better for the fourth than the dīpikā's explanation). Payalā, Pāli pacalāyikā, pacalāyati (Jātaka J, p, 384; Angutt.-Nik. III, p. 343), Skt. pracalāyati means "nodding".

1) Set phrases and descriptions occur on almost every page of the

thought of Udāyaṇa, left Campā; where the city of Vīyabhaya is, where is the public garden Migavaṇa, there he sojourned. Then the community came out, and Udāyaṇa. Thereupon Udāyaṇa, having heard the Law from the lips of Mahavīra and being rejoiced and delighted, spake thus: Presently I shall install my eldest son in kingship. Thereupon I shall renounce the world in your presence". The Lord said: "At your pleasure! Do not make any delay" [1]). Then Udāyaṇa mounted the Pearl of Elephants kept for his personal use and came to his own house.

Thereupon a thought of the following nature occured to Udāyaṇa: "If I renounce the world after appointing prince Abhii to royal power, then Abhii will become infatuated with royal power and royal dominion *down to* the country [2]) and with the enjoyment of human pleasures and will stray to and fro in the beginning-

Jaina canon. Usually only the beginning and the end of such a wearisome passage is given with the word jāva "down to" (or, vaṇṇao, "description"). In the present instance I have inserted the necessary words since they precede in the text only two or three lines above. In the sequel I shall simply translate what we have in the Prākrit.

The Jaina monks are called "men of bald heads" because they pull out their hair.

1) The oft-recurring expression: Ahāsuhaṃ, mā paḍibandhaṃ karehi has given rise to some discussion. See Hoernle's Uvāsagadasāo, Vol. II Appendices pp. 30 f.; Wiener Zeitschrift für die Kunde des Morgenlands III, pp. 347 ff. Leumann is right. Only, his translation sounds rather awkward. Ahāsuhaṃ corresponds to our "as you like, as you please, all right". I see now that my translation is confirmed by Uttarajjh p. 604, l. 6, where we find: jahāsuhaṃ = yathā bhavate abhirucitam, and by p. 545, ll. 3 and 4: "Bhavad-antikaṃ pravrajishyāmi" (says king Padmottara). Guruṇā bhaṇitaṃ: "Mā vilambaṃ kuru". [C. fol. 260 a we read mā vilambaṃ kuṇasu] — Cp. § 335.

2) The missing words are: (bale ca) vāhaṇe ca kose ca koṭṭhāgāre ca" (the army and) the vehicles and the treasury and the storehouses" (see, for instance, Nirayāvaliyāsuttaṃ §§ 14, 17).

less, endless tanglewood of the saṃsāra. Therefore it is evidently better that I renounce the world after appointing my sister's son Prince Kesi to royal power" [1]). Having meditated thus, on an auspicious lunar day, and on an auspicious half-lunar day, and in an auspicious hour, he called his servants together and spake thus: "Quickly [2]) bring about the royal coronation of prince Kesi". Thereupon prince Kesi was sprinkled [with the water of royal consecration] amid great splendor, became king, and lived governing the realm [3]). Thereupon king Udāyaṇa took his farewell of king Kesi: "I, indeed, O beloved of the gods, renounce the world, as I am appalled with fear of the saṃsāra". Thereupon king Kesi summoned the servants and spake thus: "Quickly prepare for king Udāyaṇa a sumptuous, worthy consecration for the renunciation of the world". Thereupon being consecrated with great magnificence he mounted a litter, went to the presence of the Blessed One, became a monk, and spent his time in performing fasts of one day and a half, of two days and a half, of three days and a half, of four days and a half, of five days and a half, of a month, of a half-month, and many other works of penance.

And one day a sickness came upon him, since he [always] partook of the meanest and vilest food. The physicians said to him: "Make a meal with sour milk". For his reverence was engaged in observing a vow. One day he went to Vīyabhaya. There reigned his

1) Concerning the infinitives with the ending ttae see § 578.
2) § 68.
3) Jāva I left out.

sister's son, king Kesi, whom he himself had established, in kingship. The ministers of state said to prince Kesi: "Subdued by hardships [1]), he seeks the royal power". He said: "I will give it to him". They said: "That is not the way of a king". They persuaded him after a long time; he consented. "What shall be done?" "Let poison be given to him. Give him pautta [2]) with sour milk by the hand of a herdswoman in the house". It was given to him, but a deity snatched it away and said: "Great saint, poison has been given to you. Abstain from the sour milk". He abstained from it. His malady began to increase. Again he took it. And again the deity took it away. A third time it was given to him, and that too was taken away. And the deity roamed about behind him. One day it was given to him, while the deity was paying no attention. Again he was forbidden by the deity while he ate.

Thereupon this wandering monk Udāyaṇa, having through many years fulfilled the course of a religious mendicant and omitting sixty meals in abstaining from food, reached that goal for whose sake the state of a naked monk, the state of a bald monk is entered upon *down to* he became freed from sorrow [3]).

And a potter had afforded him shelter [4]). When he

1) See Hoernle's Uvāsagadasāo II, p. 84, note 222; Uttarajj. II.

2) This word is not clear to me. It seems to mean poison, or a kind of poison, and my conjecture is supported by Lakshmīvallabha; for Uttarajjh. p. 560, ll. 9, 10 we read: "Tatas tair ekasyāḥ paçupālyā grihe vishamiçritaṃ dadhi kāritam".

3) Concerning this passage, which again strongly reminds us of the Pāli books, see Aupapātikasūtra § 116.

4) Sejjāyara is always transcribed by çayyātara, evidently one of the wrong translations so frequent with the Jainas. Naturally it would seem to represent çayyākara. It is used of one who houses a monk.

died, a deity let a shower of dust fall. And then the Siṇavallī, considering that he [the potter] was guiltless, built a town, called according to his name "Kumbhakāravekkha" [1]). She carried him off and placed him there. And the whole town of Vīyabhaya was buried by the dust. Even to this day it lies buried.

Thereupon, forsooth, at the time, at the hour of midnight there occured this thought to prince Abhii: "I am Udāyaṇa's eldest son, the child of Pabhāvaī; not appointing me to kingship, but appointing Kesi to kingship, he renounced the world". Being overpowered by this human sorrow he went out of Vīyabhaya, repaired to [king] Koṇiya in Campā, and was provided with abundant objects of pleasure. This Abhii was a Jaina lay disciple, knew animate and inanimate beings [2]), and continually nursed a hatred against king Udāyaṇa. Thereupon when prince Abhii had through many years fulfilled the course of a Jaina lay disciple and in self-mortification which lasted half a month had omitted thirty meals, he died, having neither confessed himselt nor repented of this matter [3]); and was born again as

1) "Potters Regard", I think; vekkha fr. avekshā (cp. in our tales vatthā = avasthā). Siṇavallī, "White Creeper" is to all appearance a feminine deity or genius, perhaps the Sanskrit Sinīvalī (see Monier-Williams sub voce). An interesting bit of popular etymology if my conjecture be correct. Another one is Veṇudeva = Vainateya (Garuḍa). Jacobi discusses this word in SBE. Vol. 45, p. 290, note. But his etymological suggestion is impossible. The development of Vainateya to Veṇudeva has other parallels as regards the changes in the consonants and the u has come in by an attempt at folk-etymology. For "Reed god" conveyed *some* sense at least.

2) The Jaina must have a full knowledge of this matter so that he may not injure or kill any living being while unaware of its real nature.

3) Thāṇa more litterally means case (here "a case of sin", a common use). This meaning is frequently found also in Pāli. The eighteen "cases

a demon prince. One paliovama [1]) will he remain such; in Mahāvideha he will attain final emancipation.

of sin" are enumerated in Aupapātikasūtra § 56, ZDMG. 46, pp. 62 ff. (stanzas 7—69).

1) See Hoernle's Uvāsagadasāo II, p. 40, note 111; Wilson's Essays and Lectures Vol. I, p. 308, and the other works quoted by Hoernle in the appendices p. 27. The idea is similar to the Buddhistic conception of a kalpa: From one of the great lakes (Anotatta, etc.), at the end of every hundred years one drop of water is taken out on the tip of a blade of grass. When in this manner the lake has been made shallow for seven times then a Great Kalpa draws to its close (e.g. Petavatthu IV, 3, 33, comm.; Sumangalavil. I, p. 164). Similes of this kind are current among us with reference to the idea of eternity.

THE FOUR PRATYEKABUDDHAS.

KARAKAṆḌU.

THE FOUR PRATYKABUDDHAS [1].

Karakaṇḍu in Kalinga, Dummuha in Pancāla,
King Nami in Videha, and in Gandhāra Naggai.
A bull, a banner of Indra, a bracelet, and a blossoming mango tree respectively caused the spiritual awakening of Karakaṇḍu, Dummuha, Nami, and the king of Gandhāra.

1) The following four tales are found also in the Uttarajjhayaṇa, p. 254 sqq. The story how these four kings became Pratyekabuddhas (or men who have attained illumination, but do not preach the Gospel to others) is another instance of the Buddhists and the Jainas having a tale in common. See Jātaka N°. 408 and Vol. VI, pp. 44 sqq. (cp. N°. 330). As Jātaka N°. 408 is translated I need not give the contents. The differences are interesting; the names especially instructive. For Karakaṇḍu we have Karaṇḍu in the Jātaka, but also the variants Karaṇḍako, Karakaṇḍa, and Karakaṃdaṃko (for Karakaṇḍako). As three of these kings bear names that seem to be nicknames our king of Kalinga cannot claim a prerogative; and our story expressly tells us the very same thing. The greatest probability of originality is for Karakaṇḍaka). Good MS. authority can be adduced for this form in Pāli, and the Jaina Karakaṇḍu is Apabhraṃça for Karakaṇḍa. "König Handstummel" or "Stummelhand" sounds well enough, too. The king of the Gandhāras, Nagnajit by name (Pāli Naggaji, Prākrit Naggai), is well known. Nimi appears as the name of several kings of Videha. The Jātaka form is therefore correct and Nami of the Jainas secondary. The same is true of Dummukho. For Durmukha is mentioned elsewhere as a prince of the Pañcālas, and our own tale has preserved Dummuha as a variant. "King Evil-Face (Ugly-Face, Evil-Mouth)" is quite befitting. So the names speak for the priority, or at least a greater originality, of the Buddhistic versions. Of course, I do not desire to say that the Buddhists *invented* these tales, nor do I want to deny that certain details in the Jaina forms may be more original than those in the Buddhistic ones. Both sects drew from a vast stock of stories which were common property.

Most interesting are the popular etymologies connected with the names in our four tales and the bits of legends to which they gave rise.

Karakaṇḍu [1]).

Here Karakaṇḍu. In the city of Campā there reigned a king, Dahivāhaṇa. His queen was Paumavaī, the daughter of Ceḍaga. One day this longing of a pregnant woman came upon her: "How can I divert myself riding through the parks and groves on the most excellent back of an elephant, attired in the costume of the king, having the royal parasol held over me by the great king?" [2]) She became sick [3]) and was questioned by the king. She told him matters as they were. Then the king and she mounted his Elephant of Victory, the king held the royal parasol, she went to the park. It was then the beginning of the rainy season. When the elephant was touched by the odour of the fragrant smelling earth he remembered the woods. And the elephant started toward the woods and went out of the path. The people could not keep up with him. The two entered the woods. The king saw a fig-tree. He said to the queen: "He will pass under that fig-tree;

1) Cp. Kathākoça pp. 115, 125.

2) Ahaṃ puṃveshadharā bhartrā dhṛitātapatrā etc. Uttarajjh. p. 254, l. 9.

3) Or, following Jacobi, "depressed". I have translated in accordance with Skt. avarugṇa, which sometimes has the meaning represented by my rendering. Cp. roga, lit., breaking", i. e. disease and German Gebreste, Gebrechen. Perhaps "sickly" would have been better. Nirayāvaliyāsuttam § 7 tells us: Cellaṇī devī..... sukkā, bukkhā, nimmaṃsā, ulaggā, ulaggasarīrā, nitteyā etc. "Queen C." (who too had an unsatisfied longing of a pregnant woman) "became withered, famished (in appearance), fleshless, wasted (abgefallen), of wasted body, lustreless, etc." We have to read uluggā (oluggā), it seems. But may be ulaggā (olaggā), "hanging down" means "drooping". In Pāli it signifies "clinging, fastened, hesitating" (Cariyāpiṭaka I, 7; Theragāthā 356). The dīpikā gives: sā kṛiçāngī babhūva.

then you are to take hold[1]) of a bough". She promised, but could not take hold. The king was prompt: he seized the bough. Joyless he descended, and perplexed as to what to do he went to Campā.

And this Paumavaī was carried into a desolate wood. When the elephant was thirsty he saw a lake which had a very great basin[2]). Then he descended to it and amused himself. But she softly dismounted from the elephant and ascended from the pond. She did not know the directions, affrighted with fear she looked at the wood on all sides. Then overpowered with distress, she began to weep: "Alas for the issue of one's acts [in a former existence], since all unexpectedly I have fallen into such a disaster! Now what shall I do? What refuge is there for me?" In a moment she gathered strength of mind and reflected: „One does'nt know something might happen in this dreadful wood swarming with many, many vicious wild beasts. Therefore I shall be careful". Thereupon she made the fourfold refuge[3]) her protection, repented of her sins, asked the forgiviness of the whole host of living beings, and engaged in abstinence from delicate food[4]).

1) Laggai may either be *lagyati, or *lagnati (denom. from lagna). Cp. § 488.

2) § 595.

3) That is, the arhats, the siddhas, the sādhus, the çuddhadharma (the Arhats, the beatified souls, the saintly monks, the pure Law).

4) Sākāra in Skt. means also "beautiful". Cp. German "ansehnlich". The "involuntary humour" of the passage is delightful. Nevertheless I think now that neither my translation nor that of Jacobi is liable to be correct. The grammatical construction presupposed in such an interpretation would be unusual, but not impossible. But the sequel clearly shows that she refrained entirely from eating. "She engaged in determined abstinence from food", appears to be the nearest approach to the

"If any carelessness be mine with regard to this body and this time, I have now [1]) renounced food, the clinging to the world, and the body.

Then the fivefold formula of worship [2]) is my refuge, for *that* brings wellfare in this world and the next. And it is said:

"Dangers from disease, water, fire, robbers, lions, elephants, fights, and poisonous snakes vanish instantly by the supreme charm which consists of the formula of worship [3]).

words of the original, especially if we think of the *two* ways in which "determined" may be understood. German "bestimmt" would be good too; "definitiv" perhaps less so. "Absolute" would be tolerably serviceable. Sākāra primarily means "having a definite form". But compare sāgāraṃ blattaṃ paccakkhāittā in line 9 on p. 43. The two expressions "have all the seeming" of being identical in meaning. [Cp. Appendix].

1) More literally, "of late", "for some time back". Carime samayammi corresponds exactly to German "in letzter Zeit". My interpretation of uvahi differs from that of Jacobi. In the sense adopted in my rendering the word occurs for instance in Āyāraṃgasuttaṃ 1, 4, 1, § 2. This use of the term is also found in Pāli. Majjh.-Nik. I, p. 435; 453; 454; Udānaṃ II, 4; Theragāthā 152, 840. Jacobi's view is also supported by Pāli; for there upadhi occasionally signifies "form, Gebilde" (Majjh.-Nik. I, pp. 162, 167). Prākrit uvahi is also used for "deceit" and frequently for "equipment, articles for use, property". In the this sense of "parigraha" it would fit in our passage too.

2) Cp. Namo arihantāṇaṃ! Namo siddhāṇaṃ! Namo āyariyāṇaṃ! Namo uvajjhāyāṇaṃ! Namo loe savvasāhūṇaṃ!

Eso paṃcanamokkāro
savvapāvappaṇāsaṇo
maṃgalāṇaṃ ca savvesiṃ
paḍhamaṃ havai maṃgalaṃ.

"Reverence to the Arhats! Reverence to the Liberated Ones (den Seligvollendeten)! Reverence to the Masters! Reverence to the teachers! Reverence to all saintly monks in the world!

This fivefold formula of worship destroys all sin (evil) and is the chief maṅgala (thing bringing good luck) of all maṅgalas".

Beginning of the Kalpasūtra.

3) § 251.

"And no danger from female imp, vampire, goblin, or Lamia prevails against it. And by the power of the formula of worship all calamities vanish [1]).

Thus it is:

"The assault of the elephant, "the eight fetters of karma" [2]) on those in whose innermost hearts continually abides the lion "formula of worship", is frustrated".

Then remembering the formula of worship she pushed ahead in one direction. When she had gone far, she saw an ascetic. To his feet she went. She saluted him. He asked her: "Whence have you come here, good lady?" Then she related: "I am the daughter of Ceḍaga and have just now been brought here by an elephant." And that ascetic was one of Ceḍaga's own subjects. He comforted her: "Do not fear", and he said to her: "Do not grieve. Just such is this unsubstantial saṃsāra, the cause of union and separation, full of birth, death, disease, and sorrow". With the fruits of the forest he made her sustain life against her own will, took her to his hermitage [3]), and said to her: "From here on, the ground is tilled with the plough; we do not set foot

1) Dāiṇī Skt. ḍākinī, is very inadequately rendered by Jacobi's "Hexe". See PW. sub voce. Their sucking the blood of men is also mentioned in Kuṭṭanīmatam 316. For rikkha we have to read rakkha (with MS B) = rakshas. In translating māri I followed Tawney. See Kathākoça, index sub Lamia.

2) As to the eight karman, see Weber's Bhagavatī p. 166; Wilson l. c. p. 316; Bhandarkar, l. c. p. 97 note (cp. p. 93, note *); Colebrooke, Essays[2] Vol. II, pp. 408, 409; Sarvadarçanasaṁgraha p. 55; Uvāsagadasāo § 218; Uttarajjh. XXXIII.

3) Lit. "settlement", German Siedelung. The dīpikā reads svāçramam.

on it[1]). This is the territory of Dantapura; and Dantavakkha is king here. Therefore go you fearless into this town; from there again set forth most cheerfully — to Campa." The ascetic returned. The other entered Dantapura. She went enquiring for a Jaina convent of nuns[2]). She saluted the lady superior. She was questioned: "Whence comes the lady disciple?" She told how matters stood. Crying bitterly, she was comforted a little by the superioress. "Illustrious lady, do not give way to distress of mind. The development of one's fate cannot be averted. For:

> "As we know, it tears apart even what is united, and some things it unites although they are separated. Extremely dexterous is this fate in working weal and woe for beings.

"And:

> "There is no happiness in the saṃsāra, where greatness is seen one moment and disappears the next, where various pleasures and sorrows change in a moment, where union and separation are only matters of a moment.
>
> "Because this saṃsāra is a storehouse of mani-

1) Because tilling the ground injures so many living beings, and especially "earth-bodies" (or "earth-lives"); for according to the Jainas living beings or souls in the world of birth and death are of two kinds: movable and immovable. The immovable are: Earth Souls, Water Souls, Fire Souls, Wind Souls, Plants. The Jaina monk may only walk on well trodden paths and dare not go across a field. Cp. the Īryasamiti.

For susattheṇa the dīpikā has susārthena.

2) This seems to be the meaning of sāhuṇīmūla here (establishment of nuns, place where they are "rooted"). Or should we, after all, simply translate: "the feet of Jaina nuns (of a Jaina nun)"? The dīpikā favors my conjecture. I find there: Sādhūpaçraye jagāma, "she went to a cloister". Uttarajjh. p. 255, l. 2 fr. bottom.

fold sorrows, just for that reason wise men [1]) here betake themselves to the path of final beatitude".

Being comforted in such and similar manner she was stirred to the depths of her soul and renounced the world on the spot in their convent. And although she was asked at her consecration, she did not tell of her pregnancy, for fear that they might not grant [her ordination]. Later, when the matter was found out she told the truth to the abbess. Being kept in concealment she gave birth to a child and exposed it in the cemetery, together with a ring bearing a name [2]) and a jewel of a blanket. And afterwards the child was taken by the guardian of the cemetery and handed over to his wife. They named the boy Avakiṇṇaya [3]). And this noble lady [4]) became a friend of this Caṇḍāla woman [5]). And this noble lady was questioned by the nuns: "Where is your child?" She said: "It was still-born and therefore left [in the cemetery] by me." The boy grew up there. He played with the boys. He said to the children [6]) there: "I am your king; pay me taxes." He was seized with the dry scab. He said to them: "Scratch me". Then they gave him the name

1) Or, "firm men".

2) The name of the child's father. Pitṛnāmamudrāṅkitaṃ ca kṛtvā. Uttarajjh. p. 256, l. 2.

3) "Castaway", that is, "Foundling".

4) Jaina nuns are often so termed.

5) Lit., "formed a friendship with this Caṇḍāla woman".

6) Ḍimbharūpa is used by Jaina writers also in Skt. Cp. German "Weibsbild, Mannsbild", which words have no derogatory tinge in the mouths of the people, at least not in Southern Germany, but simply mean "woman" and "man". In Pāli I find gorūpa, "bull, bullock" (Milindap. p. 396), = ox, blockhead, fool in Sumaṅgalavilāsinī I, 254. [Cp. ḍikkarūva (ḍekkarūva) = ḍimbharūva C. fol. 218*a* and dāsarūva "slave" C. fol. 71*b*].

of Karakaṇḍu [1]). And he was very fond of this nun. And she gave him sweetmeats or whatever delicate [2]) alms she obtained.

When he had grown up he guarded the cemetery. For some reason two ascetics passed by there [3]). At once they saw in one place a stick in a coppice.

1) "Tax-itch" (itching for taxes), a fine name for a king, especially for an Eastern ruler and above all for a monarch in India. For the revenues which the Hindu sovereigns extorted from their poor subjects were enormous. A number of Jātakas, for instance, introduce us to such vampires in the robes of royalty; not to speak at all of occasional and incidental flash-lights. Thus Jataka N°. 240 gives us a very graphic sketch of King Mahāpiṅgala of Kāsiland. The story is to be found in my book Kāvyasaṁgraha, pp. 38 sqq. We read:

> Wie man quetscht des Zuckerrohres
> Stengel in der Zuckerpresse,
> Also presste er die Leute,
> Presste sie mit Steuern, Sporteln,
> Zöllen, Strafen und Gewaltthat.

And Jātaka N°. 520 (Vol. V, p. 98 ff.) tells of King Pañcāla and how he oppressed his people so unbearably that they locked up their houses, barricaded the doors with briars and thorn-bushes torn up and piled up against them, and fled into the woods.

Kaṇḍū, "an itching for" is good Sanskrit (especially used in the erotic sense). Less probable seems the rendering: "Tax-scratch", although it is not at all out of the way. The words little Karakaṇḍu always used were "Taxes!" and "Scratch!" (i. e. scratch me). These two the children joined to form his nickname. "Karakaṇḍu" admits of different interpretations, and so it is no wonder that falk-etymology took hold of the name.

2) I derive laddha from *çlagdha, lit. "praised". Çlāgh usually becomes silāh in Prākrit. But that would not bar out a form like the one supposed by me. Cp. laṇha from çlakshṇa; and form sneha we have siṇeha and ṇeha. But perhaps we ought to read bhikkhāladdha, for the dīpikā has bhikshālabdha. Uttarajjh. p. 256, l. 7. On the other hand, it is possible that they simply did not understand laddha; and it is a matter of course, I think, that the nun did not give the boy all the food she obtained by begging. The little fellow would not even have cared for some of the things she received, although his foster-parents most probably were very poor.

3) Or, "who came there".

One of them knew the signs of sticks [1]) as follows:

A stick with one joint they praise; those with two joints cause quarrel; those with three joints are fraught with profit; those with four joints entail death.

A staff that is five-jointed wards off quarrel on the way; a six-jointed one is disease; a seven-jointed, health.

A stick that has a base of four finger's breadth and rises half a finger's breadth and has seven joints wards off mad elephants [2]).

A staff of eight joints is failure, one of nine productive of fame, but one of ten joints truly [3]) is all prosperity.

A stick that is crooked, worm-eaten, and spotted [4]), and bunchy [5]) and burned and dried up at the top is to be carefully avoided.

1) The Jaina monk is forbidden to make his living by this science. Uttarajjh. XV, 7.

2) This stanza is rather obscure to me. I suppose that the MSS. read addhangula-, which Jacobi in the corrections at the end of the book changes to aṭṭhangula. But even a staff of twelve angula, that is, of eight inches is impossible. That would hardly do for a cudgel. Laṭṭhī may mean "cudgel". But, to all appearance, staffs are the theme of our stanzas. So I take it that the knots of the staff rise for half a finger's breadth. Still that is not the natural import of the expression. But a stick of eight inches in length cannot have seven knots or joints (parvan).

3) Tahiya = Skt. tathya, not = tasmin (Jacobi).

4) I take cittalayā = citralakā (cittra + la + ka); cp. egavaṇṇa in stanza 6.

5) Pollaya (or pollara, which comes to the same thing) I derive from *pūlyaka (pūlyara), from pūla, "bunch"; or we may assume a word pulyaka, from pula. The word would thus mean "knotted, gnarled, covered with excrescences". Polla = rikta, antaḥsushira, used of the hand, I find in Uttarajjh. XX, 42. According to that we should rather translate "hollow". But being hollow would hardly be considered such a great

Having massive joints, shining with color, and of one color — a staff provided with such marks is to be considered an excellent staff".

Thereupon he said: "He who will take this staff will be king. But one must wait for it till it grows four inches more; then it is serviceable". This was heard by that Caṇḍāla lad and by a Brahman [1]). Then that Brahman dug out the four inches of the staff that had not yet shot up [2]) [out of the ground] and cut the staff. And that lad saw him and snatched it away from him [3]). He was taken before the court by that Brahman. He said: "Give me my stick". He answered: "It has grown on my cemetery; therefore I'll not give it". The Brahman said: "Take another". He did not want to. The boy did not give it. The boy was asked by them [4]): "Why do you not give it?" And he said: "By the power of this stick I shall be king". Then the people of the court laughed and said: "When you do come to be king, then you shall give this Brahman a village". He agreed. The Brahman spoke to other Brahmans as follows: "Let us kill him and take the

defect in a cane. Polla may mean the "bunched hand" or the fist, German "die geballte Hand (or, Faust)".

1) I do not see how dhijjāiya can be = dvijāti(ka). Dvijāti corresponds to Prākrit duāi (Çauraseni duādi. See Vikramorvaçīyam III, between stanzas 6, and 7, p. 78 in Shankar Paṇḍit's second edition; and § 436); Perhaps it represents dhigjātika, "one of the fie-people (einer vom Pfuigeschlecht)", alluding to the caste pride of the Brahmans, who felt contaminated by contact with others and loathed them. Of course, this name would be susceptible of a different and very spiteful sense. Cp. sasarakkha.

2) Lit., "stretched, extended".

3) Uddālei may easily be the causative of ud + dal with a peculiar development of meaning.

4) The judges.

stick". That was heard by his father. The three [1]) fled and straightway went to Kancaṇapura. There the king had died sonless. The deputed [2]) horse came to Karakaṇḍu's feet while he slept outside [of the city], circumambulated him with its right side turned toward him, and stood still. In the meanwhile the people of the city saw with great respect that he was endowed with the marks [of a king], the cry of "Victory"! was raised, and the drum of rejoicing beaten. But he got up yawning. With perfect composure he sat on the horse and was taken into the city [3]). "He is a Caṇḍāla", said the Brahmans and would not grant him entrance. Then he seized the jewel of a staff. It began to blaze. They were terrified. Then he made the Caṇḍālas of Vāḍahāṇa Brahmans. And the saying arose:

> By king Karakaṇḍu, the son of Dadhivāhana, the Caṇḍālas who lived in Vāṭadhāna were made Brahmans.

And they too disregarded the name given him at home, Avakiṇṇaga, and established the name given him by the Caṇḍāla boys, Karakaṇḍu.

1) That is, the boy and his reputed father and mother.

2) Ahiyāsiya in this and the more common meaning of "to bear" is = Pāli adhivāseti. It litterally signifies "wohnen lassen", If one bears hardships etc. he suffers them to rest on him. If one is made to "dwell" in an office etc. we call that "einsetzen", to install, depute etc., as the case may demand.

3) Cp. my translation of the Daçakumāracaritam p. 94, note (but instead of "Berührungswagen" I now give "Staatswagen" [= pushyaratha] for phussaratho); Wide Awake Stories pp. 140, 426 (king chosen by sacred elephant); Folk Tales of Bengal p. 99 ff.; Steel, Tales of the Punjab pp. 181, 387; Pariçishṭaparvan VI, 231 ff. (interesting and extremely similar to the story of Mūladeva in our collection); Kathākoça pp. 4, 128, 155; Tawney's Prabandhacintāmaṇi p. 181; Indische Studien XV, 359 (where we find the

Then that Brahman came: "Give me the village". "Take the one that pleases you". He said: "My home is in Campā; therefore give it to me in her territory". Then he gave him a letter to Dahivāhaṇa: "Give [1]) this Brahman a village. I shall give you any village or city that pleases you". He was enraged: "The wicked Caṇḍāla does not know his own self". The messenger returned and reported this. Karakaṇḍu was incensed. He besieged Campā; fighting was going on. Then the nun heard of it. Saying: "Let there be no destruction of people", she took leave of the abbess and went to the city. She took Karakaṇḍu aside [2]) and disclosed the secret to him: "He is your father". He questioned his mother and his father [3]). They told him the real state of affairs. From pride he did not march away. Then she repaired to [the city of] Campā, went into the king's house; she was recognized, the female servants fell down at her feet and wept. The king too heard of it; he too came, greeted her respectfully, gave her a seat, and enquired about her child. She said: "It is he by whom the city is besieged". Delighted, he went out and had a meeting with him. Giving him both the kingdoms

correct translation pañca divyāni adhivāsitāni); also Knowles, Folk-Tales of Kashmir pp. 158, 159, 169, 309, 17; Paramatthadīpanī III, p. 73 ff.

1) The Optative dijje is difficult. It could be taken as a passive optative (dijje = vaṭṭe, § 459; from passive dijjaï, § 545). The accusative as depending on a passive would be possible, but in prose extremely improbable. So it seems we have to assume a mongrel form — dejjā (or dejja, either precative, § 466, or optative of present, § 474) > dijjā (dijja) > dijje ("Angleichung an" vaṭṭe).

2) Hardly "herauskommen lassen" Jacobi).

3) Of course, his *supposed* father and mother, the Caṇḍālas who had reared him.

Dahivāhaṇa renounced the world. And Karakaṇḍu became a mighty monarch.

Now he was very fond of herds of cattle. He acquired many herds of cattle. In the meanwhile, at the time of autumn, he saw a bull calf, strong-limbed and white. He said: "Do not milk the mother of this one. When he has grown, then let him drink the milk of other cows". The cowherds promised. When his horns had come out and he had become a powerful bull [1]), the king saw him. He became solely intent on fighting. Again in the course of time the king came and saw a big-bodied old bull that was being harassed on all sides by the young bulls. He asked the cowherds: "Where is that bull?" They pointed him out in such a condition. And they said:

> "This very same bull here, by the sound of whose lowing [2]) in the middle of the yard of the cowpen even all the proud, overbearing bulls with very sharp horns were subdued, now suffers being harassed on all sides by the young bulls; as his pride has departed on account of old age, his eyes drip, and his distorted lip quivers".

When the king saw him in such a plight he fell into despondency. He pondered on transitoriness: "Alas, this bull who was such a splendid fellow has now come to this! So all objects in the saṃsāra are short-

1) Lit., "a shoulder-bull". The shoulder is the strong part of the body, used in carrying by men, in pulling by bullocks etc. The same idiom we have in Jātaka Vol. III, p. 114, l. 8: saṃjātakkhandha, having inborn strength" (= mahabbala) and in Uttarajjh. XI, 19: jāyakkhandha (jātaskhandha), which has the same sense.

2) Cp. Skt. ṭhetkṛita.

lived. For thus it is: "Wealth, which is indeed the basis of enjoyment and the cause of great delusion, is impermanent. And it has been said:

„Perishable by its very nature is wealth, evanescent as the rainbow, unstable as the streak of lightning, like unto dust that clings to the feet.

"Riches the thieves rob, the princes snatch away, the Vantara demons hide, the kinsmen seize [1]).

"Fire burns every thing, a deluge of water destroys it, and angry Yama [the god of death] is engaged in carrying off all.

"Likewise union with beloved people, the cause ot supreme joy, is transitory. How so?

"As many birds meet in the evening on a tree, as travelers, who come from other countries, [meet] in a traveler's lodging house and in the morning all go away, every one in a different direction, so also the many beings that have come together in one family home, at the time of the blow [2]) of death, all go in different directions, accompanied by their karma, to births as men, gods, animals, and other beings.

"A man strolls along the streets of the city, wanton and heedless, engaged in crushing and pushing, surrounded by many men.

"That same resplendent man, who perishes in a

1) To the Vyantara gods belong: piçāca, bhūta, yaksha, rākshasa, kiṃnara, kiṃpurusha, mahoraga, gandharva. Weber, Bhagavatī p. 159, note 1); Uttarajjh. XXXVIII, 208 (in Jacobi's translation, 206).

2) Praghāta, not prabhāta (Jacobi, by some lapsus calami). "The dawn of death" would sound very strange.

moment, is soon dried up by old age and disease, that thus make him a goblin [1]).

1) Or, "likewise make him a goblin". These Apabhraṃça verses do not need the emendations of Jacobi. But seperate jaṇa from khayabhanguraṃ and instead of the latter read with MS. B khaṇabhanguraṃ. The root in sosijjai (pass. of causative) is çush. Karantau = karantakas, the present participle with ka. Joyaṇa = dyotana. Jaṇa in line 39 is a common form of the accusative sing, in Apabhraṃça (§ 364). I hardly think that such forms are simply the stems, as Pischel seems to say. A stem is not a self-existent thing in the living language. The endings s and m of the nom. and acc. are dropped (a phenomenon similar to the Latin servo = servos (i. e. servus) and servom (i. e. servum) of the book language). The Apabhraṃça nom. and acc. plur. jaṇa might either be analogy with the singular, or shortened from jaṇā. The genitive sg. jaṇa could perhaps stand for jan-as = marut-as with the s dropped as in the nom. sg. and plur. If the genitive plur. may be janām = marutām (cp. the Vedic forms), why should not janas = marutas develop? The adverb to may also represent such a a genitive (and ablative), i. e. *tas = tasya, tasmāt. In the gen. plur. I assume: janām > jaṇam > jaṇa (anusvāra dropped as in acc. sg. and in other dialects frequently in gen. pl. ending with āṇaṃ). But my view may be wrong or at least susceptible to modification.

Rakkhaṃ = rakshas. The usual form in Apobhraṃça would be rakkhu. But we have bhanguraṃ in the preceding line too. The Prākrits clearly influenced one another. If we have Apabhr. forms in Māhārāshṭrī, why should the forms of Māhārāshṭrī (and of other dialects) be impossible in Apabhraṃça? Such a bit of choicer dialect imparts a certain dignity to Apabhramça stanzas. That would be the Hindu idea. Kharaum is an infinitive used in the sense of a gerund (§ 576, 577), formed from the present stem with the retention of a. It seems to preserve the older form, or rather collateral form of the root kṛi, "to make", that is, the form skṛ (which we have in Skt. after certain prefixes). But probably we ought to emendate it to kariuṃ or kareuṃ.

Moḍātoḍi(m) of B is to be preferred. It represents moḍi + toḍi. Cp. khaṇḍākhaṇḍi = khaṇḍi + khaṇḍi p. 22, l. 7; ghuṇāghuṇi = ghuṇi + ghuṇi p. 12, l. 11; koḍākoḍi = koḍi + koḍi, Weber's Bhagavatī pp. 261, 262. Cp. Tawney's Prabandhacintāmaṇi pp. 102—103. Query, Is there a connection between such forms and Vedic indrāsomā, agnāvishṇū? See moḍei in the vocabulary and cp. balamoḍi (for instance in Hāla and Setubandha. Toḍi is from tud; see § 258. But I suspect that we should rather translate moḍātoḍi(ṃ) karantau by "having joyful music made" (lit., "producing the musical notes moḍi [Skt. moṭakī] and toḍi [Skt. toḍī]"), That seems better both as regards the sense and as regards the forms of the two words. "Crushing and pushing" would, of course, be in order as indicating the careless animal spirit of the man. But the

"Likewise:

"In the womb, during birth, in childhood, in youth, in old age — in all states living beings go to pieces like earthenware vessels."

Reflecting in such and similar manner he experienced the spiritual awakening; he became a Pratyekabuddha. Having torn out his hair in five handfuls [1]), and having been presented by a deity with the distinguishing tokens of a monk, he wandered about. And the saying arose:

Having seen the white, noble bull with wellformed horns in the middle of the cowpen, the king of Kalinga saw prosperity and ruin and perceived the true religion [2]).

whole is rather a picture of the glitter, pomp and heedless pleasure indulged in by the natural man, which all however have to end in the hideousness of old age. The ugly appearance of goblins is naturally not rarely referred to in Hindu literature.

Difficult are the accusatives in line 30. They may be taken in an anacoluthic way. The author first has the active in mind: "Old age and disease dry him up". A parallel case would be Jātaka III, p. 186, st. 53: Na me sutaṃ vā diṭṭhaṃ vā bhasantiṃ mānusiṃ migiṃ, "no human, speaking deer has been seen by me". Or the accusatives could go with kharauṃ (kareuṃ): "By old age and disease, which thus (likewise) make this same.... man a goblin, he is dried up". One could also preserve the reading janakkhaya and translate: "The decay (ruin) of mortals (that is, the decay that all men must suffer) will by means of old age and disease soon dry up that same resplendent, perishable one, thus (likewise) making him a goblin". Janakkhaya would be an ordinary Apabhraṃça form of the nom. sg. For the use of the passive sosijjai in the active meaning see § 550. [Cp. Appendix].

1) The Jaina ascetics tear out their hair. "Five handfuls" is the most orthodox way. See my Daçakumāracaritam p. 215, note 1); Therīgathā p. 186; Prabodhacandrodaya (ed. Vasudevaçarman. Bombay 1898) p. 99 (3d act); pp. 114 ff.; esp. p. 126 (III, 23); Kalpasūtra I, 116, 157, 173, 211; III, 57 and cp. note; Aupapātikasūtra § 116; Āyārangasutt. II, 15, § 22 (p. 129); Uttarajjh. XXII, 24; pp. 308, 516, 567, 687; Kathākoça pp. 13, 85 and note; Pariçishtaparvan VIII, 76; XI, 146; Paramatthadīpanī pp. 101, 105, 107; etc. ad infinitum.

2) Samikkha is hardly an imperfect, = *samīkshat, but most probably = samīkshya (gerund), the sentence thus having not finite verb.

DOMUHA.

DOMUHA.

Now the life of Domuha. There is here in India a town, Kampilla by name. There reigned a king, Jaya by name, sprung from the race of the Hari dynasty. His wife was called Guṇamālā. And enjoying the glory of royalty together with her, this king spent the time.

One day when he was in the open hall of audience he asked an ambassador: "What have I not that other kings have?" The ambassador said: "Your majesty, you have no hall of paintings". Thereupon the king commanded the architects: "Quickly build a hall of paintings". Immediately after this order they set about it. When the workmen dug up the ground there, on the fifth day they found a great diadem made of all varieties of precious stones, flaming in splendor like fire; and, rejoiced, they gave notice of it to king Jaya. And he, with a gladdened heart, had it raised from the hole in the earth, amid shouts of exultation. He presented the architects and other men with befitting raiment and other things. In a short time the hall of paintings with its high peaks was finished [1]). On an auspicious day the [first] entrance into the hall of paintings was celebrated. Amid the sound of festive

1) Nimmāya = *nirmāta (Skt. nirmita). — As to the very interesting Brahmanic ceremonies of consecrating a new house, see Majjh.-Nik. I, 34 ff.; Angutt.-Nik. Vol. II, p. 207; Sāmkh. Gṛihyas. 5, 5, 7; Hillebrandt, Rituallitteratur (in Bühler's Grundriss) pp. 2, 126.

drums the king put the diadem on his head. By its magic power the king became two-faced. The name of Domuha [1] was given him by the people.

Some time went by. And seven sons were born to this king. Guṇamālā was unhappy because she had no daughter. And she vowed an oblation to the Yaksha called Mayaṇa. One day a daughter who had been announced by a dream, in which the queen dreamed that she had received a cluster of blossoms from the tree Parijāta[2]), was born of her. And she had the festival of her birthday celebrated. She gave the oblation to the Yaksha. And she named her Mayaṇamanjarī. And in the course of time the child became a young woman.

Now there was king Pajjoya the Terrible in Ujjeṇī. A messenger reported to him: "The king has become two-faced". Pajjoya said: "How?" The messenger said: "He has such a diadem; if one puts it on he gets two faces". A strong desire for the diadem arose in Pajjoya. He despatched a messenger to king Domuha: "Send me this pearl of a diadem. But if you do not send it, prepare for battle". King Domuha said to the messenger of Pajjoya: "If you give me what I ask, then I, for my part, will give the diadem". The messenger said: "What do you ask?" The king said:

"Give me the elephant Nalagiri and also the

2) "Two-Face" Curious are both the development durmukha > dummukha > dummuha > dommuha > domuha (because dommuha was unintelligible) and the story which was called forth by a wrong etymology..

3) The tree of paradise seems to be meant, not a coral tree (Erythrina Indica).

excellent chariot Aggībhīru and your spouse, Queen Sivā, and the writer [1]) Lohajangha".

These were the most precious things of Pajjoya's realm. The messenger went back to Ujjeṇī. He announced Domuha's answer to Pajjoya. Pajjoya was extremely exasperated; he set out with an army consisting of the four parts [i.e. elephants, chariots, cavalry, and infantry] — two lakks of elephants, two thousand chariots, fifty thousand horse, and seven crores of soldiers on foot. And by dint of incessant marches he came to the boundary of the Pancāla country. The other, too, king Domuha, departed [2]) from the city fully equipped with a fourfold army. He advanced against Pajjoya. On the frontier of the Pancāla territory the Garuda battle array was formed by Pajjoya, the Ocean battle-array by Domuha. Thereupon the two armies

1) Lehāriya is not quite clear to me. I follow Jacobi. The word may be looked upon as having developed from lekha + kāri(n) + ka (cp. § 167). The dīpikā has dūta, "envoy, embassador" (Uttarajjh. p. 259, l. 4 from bottom).

2) Nīharai cannot be niḥsarati. Why should it not represent nirharati? Cp. hinausziehen, herausziehen = "to pull or take out" and "to march out". A goodly number of verbs that are used only in the transitive sense in Skt., but in the intransitive (or both intr. and tr.) in Prākrit, might be collected. Goldschmidt gives nīharai = nirhradati in his Rāvaṇavaha, which is also impossible. Even the meaning does not tally. Rāvaṇ. XI, 122 has to be translated: "Having the sound of weeping issuing from" etc. The same holds good with XII, 7. Especially interesting is IX, 24. The correct German rendering of that passage would run: "Wo Löwen, an deren Klauen die Perlen (aus den von ihnen zerrissenen Elefantenstirnerhöhungen) hängen, auf den Häuptern der Elefanten sitzend, ausreiten". Freiligrath's celebrated "Löwenritt" in Old India already! Cp. also Skt. viharasi, "to roam about", and especially mṛigayāṃ viharati = mṛigayāṃ niryāti etc. and migavaṃ uvaniggae = mṛigayām upanirgata, Uttarajjh. XXVIII, 1 (where the commentary wrongly derives migavā from mṛigavyā). [C. fol. 254*b* uvahiya = upahṛita drawn nigh, approached].

closed in fight. By the power of the pearl of a diadem king Domuha was invincible. Pajjoya's army was defeated. Pajjoya was captured and brought into the town. An anklet was put on his foot. There the time passed pleasantly for king Pajjoya.

One day he saw Mayaṇamanjarī. He became ardently enamored. Thereupon the night wore[1]) away most dismally for him, who was burning with the fire of love and was merged in the torment of anxious thought. And at the break of day he went into the hall of audience. King Domuha saw that this face and body were faded and he enquired about his health[2]). He gave no answer. And he was questioned more urgently by the king, who suspected something. Thereupon Pajjoya heaved a long sigh and said:

> "One who is in the power of love, O chief ot men, one consumed by disease, and likewise a madman, an angry man, and one dying — all these leave shame far behind. So if you desire my welfare give me to wife this Mayaṇamanjarī, your own daughter, O chief of men; if you don't, I shall enter the fire".

Then Domuha, perceiving his resolution, gave her to him in marriage. On an auspicious day and in an auspicious hour the nuptial rite was performed. Pajjoya was detained a few days, dismissed with honor, and went to Ujjeṇī.

One day the great festival of Indra arrived. King

1) *Vyavalīta > volīya > voliya. Cp. § 79 sqq.

2) Lit., "the getting along of his body".

Domuha commanded the people of the city: "Raise the banner of Indra"[1]). Then amid loud and auspicious cries of joy the standard of Indra was raised, flagged with white banners[2]), adorned with a great multitude of rattles[3]) and little bells, covered with suspended beautiful wreaths and garlands[4]), decorated with a string of jewels, decked with a pendant mass of various fruits. Then the nautch girls danced, poetic compositions written by good poets were sung, the multitude of men danced, juggler's tricks that bewildered the eyes were seen, and betel and other things were given to the juggler; a great deal of camphor, saffron, and water was thrown[5]), great gifts were given, drums and other instruments were sounded. Thus seven days passed in great joy. The day of the full moon came. King Domuha worshipped the banner of Indra amid great profuseness of display with flowers, garments, and other things. Amid the loud din of musical instruments it fell to the ground on the next day. The king saw that it dropped into filth, urine and ill-smelling stuff and that it was despoiled by the people. Seeing this he thought: "Out on all magnificence, for it is evanescent as the streak of

1) Cp. Bharatīyanāṭyaçāstra I, 53 ff.; Oman, Indian Life pp. 66, 73 ff.

2) Less likely, "with a white banner".

3) I follow Jacobi's suggestion. But it would have been safer to translate "wooden spoons (ladless)" since we know only of this meaning of the word. Perhaps ḍoya connects with dru, wood, any wooden implement. I do not know why wooden spoons should have been fastened to the Indraketu.

4) Or malladāma is = Kranzgebinde, Kranzgewinde.

5) Or, "a great deal of water mixed with camphor and saffron was thrown". Cp. the note to stanzas 732—737 of my Damodaragupta's Kuṭṭanīmatam (p. 120, note 1) and Rosen, Die Indrasabhā des Amānat p. 37 note 1; p. 40, note 2; p. 60.

lightning and disgusting in the end". Thinking thus his soul awoke; he became a Pratyekabuddha. Tearing out his hair in five handfuls he renounced the world. And it is said:

> Beholding how the same banner of Indra that was beautifully adorned [1] fell and was stripped bare, the king of Pancāla saw prosperity and disaster and perceived the true religion.

1) Lit. "Which banner of Indra was a beautifully adorned thing seeing that etc." Such a use of the neuter is very common in Prākrit poetry. Cp. the well-known Homeric *οὐκ ἀγαθὸν πολυκοιρανίη*. Another possibility, though perhaps a less probable one, I indicate by the literal English rendering: "What was the banner of Indra. seeing that drop well adorned", etc.

NAMI.

NAMĪ [1]).

Now the life of Nami. There was here in the land of Bhāraha, in the country of Avanti, a city, Sudaṃsaṇa by name, and a king, Maṇiraha by name. And his own brother Jugabāhu was his crown prince and viceregent. Jugabāhu had a wife of incomparable beauty and grace, Mayaṇarehā by name. And she was an extremely excellent lay disciple. Her son, endowed with all good qualities, was called Cadajasa.

One day Maṇiraha saw Mayaṇarehā, became enamored [2]), and began to reflect: How now can a union of myself with her come about? But I shall rather first make love to her; afterwards, when I have found out her disposition of mind, I shall exert myself in the proper way. Having deliberated thus, he made love to her. He sent her flowers, saffron, betel, raiment, ornaments, and other things. And no other thought, no evil thought, came into her heart. In this way the time went by.

And one day Maṇiraha said to Mayaṇarehā: "Fair

1) Cp. Kathākoça pp. 14 ff.; 18 ff.

2) Ajjhovavanna is not adhyupapanna, as given by Jacobi and the commentators, but = Pāli ajjhopanna (Skt. adhyavapanna), which is found, for instance, in Majjh.-Nik. I, pp. 162, 173, 369; Grimblot, Sept Suttas p. 249; Angutt.-Nik. II, IV, 6; II, v, 7. It means "auf etwas hingesunken, clinging to, attached to, overwhelmed, carried away by" etc. Cp. Āyāraṃgasuttaṃ I, 1, 7, § 6; Āvaçyakaerzählungen p. 26, l. 24; p. 30, l. 7 below. Very common is also uvaveya = upeta. The repetition of va is curious.

lady, if you take, me for your man [1]) I shall make you queen of the whole kingdom". She said: "You, who are neither a hermaphrodite nor a woman [2]), have become a man by reason of your works in a former birth even without being taken for that by me [3]). But as regards queenship of the kingdom, who now can take that away from me who bear the name of your brother's, the crown prince's, wife? And another thing: Those who are noble men regard the misfortune of dying a great deal, but they do nothing that is detrimental to them in this world or in the next world [4]). For:

> "By injuring living beings, falsehood, taking the property of others, and intercourse with the wife of another man living beings go to hell.

"Therefore, great king, the case being such, relinquish your evil thought and embrace good conduct". Hearing this he was silent. And he thought: As long as Jugabāhu lives she will not desire another man. Therefore let us kill him quietly [5]). Then I shall seize her by violence. There is no other means. Thus the time went by.

1) The original, which bears a number of different interpretations, is hard to render. German: "Nimm mich als Mann" brings out the pun, at least partly. For we could also translate: "If you acknowledge me as a male (if you prove my virility by intercourse with me)"; or, "if you know me (by actual experience) etc."; or, "if you consent to me (accept me, approach me) etc." Of course, the first meaning is, "if you accept me as your husband" (or rather, "your paramour)".

2) Lit., "deprived of the state of a hermaphrodite or of a woman".

3) Or, "even without my consent (agreeing to it)" (of course, a pun).

4) Or, "incompatible with this world and the next", which ultimately amounts to the same thing.

5) Lit., "with assurance, fearlessly". Less likely, "by means of confidence, using our confidential intimacy as a means".

Once upon a time Mayaṇarehā saw the moon in a dream and told her husband. He said to her: "Fair lady, you will have a son who will be the moon of the heavens, called "circle of the whole earth"". Thereupon a child was conceived in her womb. And in the third month this longing of a pregnant woman came upon her: "If I only could do worship to the Jinas and saints and could always hear the discourses of the founders of the Faith!" Thereupon when her longing had been satisfied in accordance with her wish, she carried the child in her womb with perfect ease.

One day in the month of spring Jugabāhu, together with Mayaṇarehā, went to the park in order to disport himself. While he was elate with eating, drinking, and enjoying himself, the lord of day passed beyond the mountain of sunset; the expanse of the earth was covered by a mass of darkness. Thereupon Jugabāhu remained right there in the public garden. Maṇiraha thought: "This is a favorable opportunity. In the first place, Jugabāhu stays in the park outside of the city; in the second, he has few companions; in the third, it is night; in the fourth, the wood is obscured by a mass of darkness. Therefore I shall go and kill him. Then I shall make merry with Mayaṇarehā without misgiving". Reflecting thus, he took a scimitar and went to the park. Having indulged in the dalliance of love's pleasure Jugabāhu went to sleep in a bower of plantains. Men sat down on all four sides. And Maṇiraha said to them: "Where is Jugabāhu?" They told him. He entered the plantain bower saying: "I have come out of anxiety lest some enemy might overcome him in the night"[1]). Jugabāhu rose hurriedly. He made [the king] a low obeisance. Maṇiraha said: "Get up[2]): let us go to the city. Why should you stay here over night?"[3]) Then Jugabāhu prepared to start out[4]). In the meanwhile Maṇiraha, not considering what is allowed to be done and what is not allowed to be done, disregarding the censure of the people, abandoning all fear of another world, with a confident heart, stabbed him violently in the neck with his sharp sword. Overpowered by the pain of the deep wound and having his eyes closed, Jugabāhu dropped to the ground. Mayaṇarehā screamed: "Alas, a crime! a crime!" Then the men came running with swords uplifted. And they said: "What is this?" Maṇiraha prated: "On account of my heedlessness the sword fell from my hand. Away with fear, O beautiful woman"! Then the men knew that it was the deed of Maṇiraha and took Maṇiraha by force to the city. They announced to Candajasa what had happened to Jugabāhu. Lamenting most piteously, he came to the park, taking a number of medical men with him. The medical men dressed the wound. After a short while the power of speech was lost, his two eyes were closed, his limbs had become motionless, his body turned white, for a stream of blood had flowed out. Thereupon Mayaṇarehā, knowing him in the state

1) Lit. "out of the anxiety: Let not some dangerous enemy attack him (do him harm) in the night".

2) Or, "bestir yourself".

3) Lit., "enough of staying here over night!"

4) Pahuvai may be = pradhāvati, formed according to the sixt class (*pradhuváti). Observe the differentiation: pahāvai, "to run forward", but pahuvai "(to run forward), to set out, to go, to come, to arrive". Cp. dhuvai § 482.

of dying, bent down to Jugabāhu's ear [1]) and began to speak sweetly and softly to her husband: "Illustrious sir, concentrate your mind, do not harbor any hatred toward anybody [2]), and develop charity for all beings, go for protection to the fourfold refuge, repent of your misdeeds, bear properly this calamity, which has come by the power of your own acts. And it is said:

> "Whatever deed a living being does in this existence or in another existence, [the consequences of] that it must feel; the other is only the instrumental cause [3]).

"Therefore receive the viaticum for the next world. And also:

> "Betake yourself to him who knows all things — to god; believe the highest truths, [4]), during the

1) Lit., "standing over the root of the ear of Jugabāhu".

2) Paosa, padosa (and Pāli dosa) not = pradvesha (dvesha), but = pradosha. Cp. German "böse" = "bad" and "angry" (with one), filled with hatred. I am gratified to see that Pischel gives the same derivation (§ 129). The language itself clearly points in the same direction; notice the frequently recurring phrase maṇaṃ padosae and Uttarajjh. XXXIII, 33:

> Emeva rūvammi gao paosaṃ
> uvei duhohaparaṃparāo;
> paduṭṭhacitto ya ciṇāi kammaṃ
> jaṃ se puṇo duhaṃ vivāge.

"In the same way he who yields to hatred for things perceived by the eye falls into series upon series of floods of sorrow; and he whose soul is filled with hatred accumulates karman which in its ripening again means sorrow (or, is productive of sorrow) for him". In the Therīgāthā st. 413 we find dussate (dushyate), "to conceive hatred, bös werden".

3) The same stanza, with some unessential variations, we have in the Jaina legend of the fall of Dvāravatī, Zeitschrift der deutsch-morgenländisch. Gesellschaft Vol. 42, p. 502, ll. 10, 11. In the translation (p. 516) Jacobi has misunderstood the last pāda.

4) Savvaṇṇū acc. plur. honoris causa (plur. majest.). The all-knowing one, the god, is the Jina. But may be we have to join savaṇṇūdevaṃ, "betake yourself to the all-knowing god". Less probable would be the

whole of life [1]) betake yourself to the saintly Jaina monks as teachers, who are treasures of excellences.

"Refrain from killing living beings, from untruth, from [taking] the property of others, from sexual intercourse, and from earthly possessions in the thrice threefold way [2]), as long as you live [3]).

rendering: "Betake yourself to the all-knowing ones; believe the highest truths to be god". If I mistake not, this would be good Buddhistic doctrine, but not in the Jaina vein. Cp. Benarsi Dass l. c. p. 59 (bottom of page).

It seems to me that the trinity here alluded to, and on p. 31, ll. 20—24. that is, the Jina, the dhamma, and the community of saints, *in re* corresponds much better to the celebrated Buddhistic triratna: Buddha, Dharma, Saṅgha than the triratna of the Jainas: correct knowledge, correct faith, correct life. We seem to have here another of those almost frantic efforts at creating differences out of entirely identical or almost identical things. The Jainas outdo their rivals. The Buddhists have one triratna, the Jainas two, although one is not so termed. Probably they had originally the same triratna as the Buddhists, which they kept; but the name they transferred to another thing. Jinism may be even older than Buddhism — and we know that it is — but its sacred books are younger than the Pāli canon and some other Buddhistic works; and why should the Jaina faith not have undergone some changes in order to cope more successfully with its enemy? The Hindus were always prone to making modifications in their creeds for such purposes. Of course, *both* sects may have borrowed their triratnas, just as they have adopted so many other things. See also Benarsi Dass l. c. pp. 7—36.

By tatta = tattva possibly the "truths" (or "categories") in the technical sense are meant. They are also called tathya (Prākrit tahiya), paramārtha, padārtha, bhāva etc. Their number varies. Bhandarkar, Report p. 106 gives seven, Uttarajjh. XXVIII, 14, nine. Cp. Benarsi Dass pp. 55, 56. Also the five (six) "realities", or substrata of individual life, viz. dhamma, adhamma, āgāsa (ākāça), jīva, poggala, or matter (and kāla) are styled tattva.

1) Skt. yāvajjīvam.

2) Most probably this translation is not literally correct. But it does full justice to the sense. The expression seems to be on a par with suhaṃ suhena and means "threefold with threefold". I think, it refers to 1) thought, words, acts; 2) doing, causing to be done, consenting to a thing being done. Combine these and you get nine. But according to Jacobi we have in the second place: past, present, future. SBE. XXII p. 202.

3) Skt. *yāvad jīvāya. Yavād + dativ is found also in Skt., although

"Repent properly also of the eighteen cases of sin, ponder on the nature of existence, remember in your mind the formula of worship.

"For:

"If he whose ten vital airs depart at the end, while they have become one[1]) with the formula of worship, does not reach final emancipation, he certainly becomes a Vemāṇiya god.

"Likewise give up all clinging to wordly objects; for:

"Neither a father, nor a mother, nor a son, nor brothers, nor friends, nor relatives, nor heaps of wealth are a refuge in the saṃsāra, that is full of pain.

The Law *alone* expounded by the prince of Jinas, the treasure[2]) of happiness, is in this world the refuge of living beings that are tormented by the pain of birth, old age, and death"[3]).

not in this phrase, which is usually jāvajjīvam (= jā-jīvam, i. e. *yād jīvaṃ, above).

1) Lit., "become the same, identical, identified".

2) Jacobi takes nihāṇa here and on page 58, l. 3 in the sense of "cause". How the word can have that meaning I fail to see. At any rate, the natural and ordinary sense fits better both here and on p. 58. Cp. p. 36, l. 10: bahuvihadukkhāṇa esa bhaṇḍāro.

3) With these stanzas cp. the third stanza on p. 46 of Erz. (savve jāyā etc.) and with all three of them my Daçakumāracaritam p. 110, note; p. 362; Pariçishṭaparvan III, 149—184; Jacobi's introduction to same, p. 35; Hemacandra's Yogaçāstra IV, 67; Bhandarkar, Report p. 113 (ekatvānuprekshā); SBE. Vol. 45, p. 349; Kshemendra's Daçāvatāracaritam IX, 35; Āyāraṃgasuttaṃ I, 3, 3, § 4; I, 7, 6, § 1; Kathākoça p. 20; Hebbels Tagebücher (ed. Werner) I, 88; Werke (ed. Werner) VII, p. 44; Hugo von Hofmansthal, Ballade des äussern Lebens; Volter Kilpi, Bathseba, Davidin puheluja itsensä kanssa p. 219; Maupassant passim and many others; Benarsi Dass pp. 64, 65; and esp. Uttarajjh. XIII, 21—26. Appamāya in stanza 26 of the passage quoted last, which is discussed by Leumann in Wiener Zeitschrift f. d. Kunde des Morgen-

All this was received by Jugabāhu with hands folded in the manner of a bud against his head. In a short while he died, bent on a good resolve.

Thereupon Candajasa fell to wailing. Mayaṇarehā thought: "Shame upon my beauty, the root of such a misfortune! Now this evildoer will certainly destroy my virtue, although I do not desire it. Therefore enough of staying here! I shall go to some other country and carry out what is to be done for the other world. Else this wicked man will bring about the destruction of my son too". Deliberating thus, she departed from the park, her mind distressed with deep sorrow, at the time of midnight, while the hearts of Candajasa and the others were bewildered with sorrow. She went toward the East and came into a great forest. The night passed while she wandered on. At midday she reached a lotus pond. With the fruits of the woods she sustained life. Rejecting delicate fare [1]), wearied with the fatigue of the journey, she went to sleep in a bower of plantains. The night overtook her. The tigers growled, the lions roared, the boars grunted, the jackals howled gruesomely. While she, frightened [2]) by the sounds of numerous wild beasts, gave herself

landes, V, 137, I consider to be = alpamātra. That chimes in with the Buddhistic version. Cp. Uttarajjh. XVI, 12 (aimāya — atimātra); XVI, 8 (aimāyāe = atimātrayā) and § 87.

1) Possibly sāgāra means (having a definite shape, hence) determined formed, prepared, cooked, (Jacobi "zubereitet"), Cp. note on Erz. 35 l. 116.

2) Jacobi's derivation of vitattha from vitrasta, which I have followed in my translation, is perhaps not altogether impossible, but certainly very suspicious. Maybe vitattha is = *vitasta from vitas, to throw" and means "distracted, bewildered, agitated". Cp. vi + asta and vi + kshipta, both used in the sense of "distracted, bewildered".

up entirely to thinking of the formula of adoration, at midnight an excessive pain in her belly came on. With great difficulty she gave birth to a boy, who was endowed with all the marks [of a great future]. And at the break of day she wrapped him in a pearl of a blanket, hung a seal jewel marked with the name of Jugabāhu on his neck, and went to the excellent lake. When she had washed her clothes she stepped down into the lake in order to bathe. At this point a water elephant, like unto the God of Death, rushed up with extreme impetuosity from the middle of the water. He seized her with his trunk and tossed her up into the air. By the dispensation of fate she was seen by a fairy youth who had set out for the island of Nandīsara. In consideration of her beauty she was caught by him when she dropped, and weeping piteously she was taken to Mount Veyaḍḍha. And weeping she said to him: "Listen, noble sir; to night I have borne a boy in the middle of the wood. Leaving him in a bower of plantains I descended into the lake, was flung up by a water-elephant, and caught by you. Therefore this boy will be killed by some being living in the woods; or, destitute of food, he may die of his own accord. Therefore, O great man, do me a kindness by restoring my offspring to me. Do not be heedless, bring me my boy, or take me thither". The Vidyādhara youth said: "If you accept me as your husband, then I will do your bidding. And another thing: In the country of Gandhāra, in the city of Rayaṇavāha there is a king of the Vidyādharas, Maṇicūḍa by name; Kamalavaī is his wife. Their son Maṇippabha am I.

After exercising the sovereignty over the two mountain chains [1]), Maṇicūḍa became disgusted with the enjoyment of the objects of desire, appointed me to kingship, and received consecration as a monk in the presence of a perambulating ascetic. And wandering about, in course of time he had come here on the day just passed. Now he has gone to Nandīsara in order to worship the shrines. On my way to him I saw you. Therefore, beautiful lady, I shall install you as queen of all the female fairies; accept me as your lover. And another thing: Your son was seen by the lord of Mahilā, who had been carried away by a horse and who was wandering in the woods, and was given to his queen. And she tends him as if he were her own son. This I have known, investigating the matter by means of the great magical science Pannattī. It is exactly so. Therefore, lovely lady, drop your anxiety, lean on fortitude, be of a serene mind, enjoy the glory of youth together with me". Hearing this Mayaṇarehā thought: "Alas for the issue of my deeds, since various calamities are my lot! So what is to be done here? And a living being devoured by love considers not what is to be done and what is not to be done; regards neither good nor bad; knows not what is at war with the other world; minds not the dispraise of the people. Therefore matters being thus, I have to guard my virtue by some procrastinating". Having reflected thus, she said to the Vidyādhara: "Good sir, take me to Nandīsara; there I shall certainly do your pleasure".

1) Cp. Zeitschrift der deutschen morgenländischen Gesellschaft Vol. 33, 558 and Erz. p. 14 l. 11.

Thereupon, with a rejoiced mind, he created by magic a fine palace chariot that moved through the heavens. Mounting Mayaṇarehā on this, he went to the island of Nandīsara. And there are fifty-two temples of the Jinas. And it is said:

> On the four Anjana mountains, on the sixteen Sandamuhi crags, on the thirty-two Raibara peaks, in the interior of the island of Nandīsara, there are fifty-two pure temples of the Jinas one hundred yojanas long, fifty yojanas wide, seventy yojanas high [1]).

Thereupon Maṇippabhā and Mayṇarehā descended from the sky-traversing palace chariot and worshipped the images that bear the names of Usabha, Vaddhamāna, Candāṇana, and Variseṇa. And they made a low obeisance to Maṇicūḍa the perambulating saint. They sat down near him. That holy man was possessed of the [first] four stages of knowledge [2]). Knowing [by his superhuman insight] the story of Mayaṇarehā he calmed Maṇippabha by a religious discourse. Maṇippabha asked Mayaṇarehā's forgiveness and said to her: „From this day forth you are my sister. Tell me now what I can do for you". She said: "You have done everything by showing me this holy place Nandīsara". And she asked the saint: "Holy sir, tell me tidings of my son". The saint said: "Listen! In India, in Eastern Videha,

1) Concerning the yojana see note 5 in my Two Twice-Told Tales (The University of Chicago Press).

2) With the exclusion of kevalam. For the five kinds or stages of knowledge see Kathākoça pp. XIII; Sarvadarçanasaṃgraha p. 47; Bhandarkar, Report p. 106; Uvāsagadasāo Vol. II, p. 48, note 132; Appendices p. 44; Uttarajjh. XXVIII; Leumann, Beziehungen der Jaina-Litteratur p. 510.

in the country [1]) of Pukkhalāvaī, there is a city, Maṇitoraṇa by name. And there was a universal sovereign, called Amiyajasa. He had two sons of Pupphavaī his wife: Pupphasiha and Rayaṇasiha. And they, having exercised kingly power for 840,000 years of former, ages [2]), were terrified by the sorrows of the saṃsāra and renounced the world at the feet of a perambulating monk. Having properly engaged in religious mendicancy for 160,000 years of former ages and their life being spent, they were born again in the Accua-Kappa as Indasamāṇiya gods, destined to live as such for twenty two sāgarovamas [3]). And after enjoying there the happiness of the gods and falling thence, they were born in the part of India named Dhāiyasaṇḍa as sons of Samuddadattā, the queen of the addhacakkavaṭṭi [4]) Harisepa; the one was called Sāgaradeva, the other Sāgaradatta. And knowing the splendor of royalty to be unsubstantial, they renounced the world in the presence of the blessed twelfth teacher of the three worlds, i. e., of Daḍhasuvvaya. On the third day they were killed by a stroke of lightning and reborn in the Mahāsukka heaven, destined to live there for seventeen sāgarovamas. Enjoying there the happiness of the gods they spent the time. One day they went to glorify as Kevali the twenty-second Blessed One [5]). And there they asked the Blessed One: "Where shall we be reborn, having fallen

1) Cp. Pāli vijita, "realm".

2) SBE. Vol. 45, p. 16, note.

3) As to the different classes of gods, see Weber's Bhagavati pp. 210 ff.; Uttarajjh. XXXVI, 203 sqq.

4) "Half-Universal-Sovereign".

5) I think that the twenty second Jina is meant. For the Jainas assume that there have lived 24 "Founders of the Faith" or Jinas. The

from our position?" The Blessed One said: "One of you will be the son of king Jayaseṇa in the city of Mahilā here in India, but the other will be the son of Mayaṇarehā, the wife of king Jugabāhu in Sudaṃsaṇa town; and you will in reality be father and son". Having heard this they went to their heaven. There one of them fell first, was conceived in the womb of Vaṇamālā, the queen of king Jayaseṇa in the city of Mahilā, in the country of Videha, and was born in the course of time. They gave him the name of Paumaraha. And when he had reached puberty, his father made over the kingdom to him and embraced the life of a religious mendicant. And that Paumaraha became the lord of great kings. His wife is named Pupphamālā. And while he administered the government of the realm the time went by. The other god, falling from his station when his life had worn away, was born as your son. And that Paumaraha was carried away and taken into the woods by a horse trained in the inverse way. And straying about there he saw your son this morning, and, by reason of the love sprung up in a previous existence, he took him with extremely gladdened heart. And in the meantime the army came, following the track of the great king. Thereupon he ascended an elephant and went to his city. He handed the boy over to Pupphamāmālā. The birth-festival was celebrated. There he grows up, encompassed by love".

last of these was Mahāvīra. When a man reaches kevalam (absolute knowledge and perfection) the gods are often said to come and do homage to the saint. Especially Jinas are so honored. To the Buddhistic parallels attention need hardly be called. On such and similar occasions the throne of Sakka (and of other deities) first begins to tremble, whereas with the Buddhists Sakka's throne becomes warm.

While the reverend man was recounting this there came an air-traversing palace chariot, having pillars made of jewels, pendent strings of pearls, hosts of big pearls [1]), placed on its doors, and pinnacles made of crystal, resounding with a multitude of bells, deafening the quarters of the sky with the din of musical instruments and accompanied by the cries of "Victory! Victory!" which were shouted by the women of immortals. Out of it stepped a god who wore a diadem of resplendent jewels and a pair of moving ear-rings consisting of precious stones, and whose breast glittered with a shining necklace. He walked thrice around Mayaṇarehā with his right side turned towards her, and then fell at her feet. After that he made a low obeisance to both the feet of the saint and sat down on the ground. Then the Vidyādhāra, seing this disrespectful demeanor to the monk, said:

"The immortals and the best of men have expounded the conduct of kings; where *they* offend, there one cannot speak of the fault of others.

"Why did you, O god, first make a low obeisance

1) Jacobi's vocabulary points to "host of stars". That would sound as grandly as "The Prince with the moon on his forehead and stars on the palms of his hands" (Folk-Tales of Bengal pp. 236 ff.). But it would hardly be correct. In the sixth Canto of the Rāvaṇavaha, in st. 4, we meet with tārekkāvalī, "a string of big pearls"; but the first member of the compound may be tāra as K takes it. In ZDMG. Vol. 34, p. 263, l. 36 the words occur: varathavaimiyakuladevapaṃtīu vva sutārā ya rayaṇīu tti, which mean: "the nights are brilliant with stars as the rows of family idols which have been fashioned by clever carpenters are well adorned with big pearls" (Jacobi's translation I consider to be wrong). But here again the gender remains doubtful. Sanskrit dictionaries give only the masculine in this meaning, but that is not all decisive even for Skt.; and far less for Prākrit.

to this woman, passing by this firm [1]) monk, who is free from anger and from the other blemishes, who has killed the five senses, for whom delusion has vanished, who possesses most excellent knowledge and insight [1]), who is endowed with ascetism and self-control, and by the mere sight of whom the floods of darkness are removed"?

The immortal said: "Prince of the Vidyāharas, what you have said is wrong. Only [2]) hear the reason for this. There was a king Maṇiraha in the town of Sudaṃsaṇa. His own brother was Jugabāhu. And Jugabāhu, on account of a certain enmity dating from a previous existence, was struck in the neck with a sword by his own brother Maṇiraha, when he had gone to the park in the month of spring. When his vital breaths were on the point of departing, this Mayaṇarehā made him cease from the pursuance of hatred by means of a discourse on the religion of the Jinas; having experienced the development of true faith, etc., he died and was born in the fifth heaven as an Indasāmāṇiya god, destined to live as such for ten sagarovamas. And I am he. And she is my teacher of religion, for by her I have been made to grasp the Law of the Jinas, which has true faith for its root. And it is said:

"He who establishes one in pure religion, be he ascetic or householder, becomes for him the teacher of religion, because he imparts religion to him [3]).

1) Or "wise". Or, "who possesses the insight of superior knowledge (or, the excellent insight of knowledge)". Hardly, "possesses superior (right) knowledge and faith (doctrine)".

2) Or, "forthwith"; navaraṃ = kevalam is very common in Prākrit.

3) Cp. Prabandhacintāmaṇi translated by Tawney p. 83.

"Therefore she has been greeted by me first. And it s said:

"Those who impart the true faith it is difficult to requite in many existences even by a thousand crores of services that are endowed with all excellences".

Having heard this the Vidyādhara thought: "Ah, the power of the Jinas' Law of Piety! And also:

"Living beings incur sufferings in the endless saṃsāra as long as they do not diligently comply with the Law proclaimed by the excellent Jinas".

And the god said to Mayaṇarehā: "Fellow-believer, tell me, what happiness dear to you shall I bring about?" She said: "In reality you are not able to bring about the happiness dear to me; for the happiness of final emancipation, which is exempt from birth, old age, death, disease, and sorrow, *that* is dear to me. Nevertheless, best of the gods, take me to Mahilā. After seeing the face of my son there I shall work out my welfare in the other world." Thereupon she was *instantly* taken to Mahilā by the immortal. There is the place where Naminātha and Mallinātha, the teachers of the three worlds, were born, renounced the world, and attained supreme knowledge. Therefore they descended. From devotion to the establishers of the Faith they first worshipped the sacred things in the temple of the princes of the Jinas. And they saw nuns in a convent, went and made a low obeisance to them. They sat down before the nuns. They [1]) propounded the Law of Truth:

1) Of course, the nuns are intended by "they".

"When one has obtained existence as man and has known the fruit of piety and impiety, he should strive strenuously in the Law of Piety, which secures every bliss".

In this manner they went on. At the end of their religious discourse the god said to Mayaṇarehā: "Let us go to the king's palace. I will show you your son." She said: "Away with love, which only increases the saṃsāra! And also:

"All beings have become my own people, and all have become strange people to me. What delusion about relatives could there be for the solitary man here!" [1])

"I shall take upon me the life of a religious mendicant. Therefore do you according to your pleasure". And he made a low obeisance to the nuns and to Mayaṇarehā and went to his heaven. And she received ordination in the presence of these nuns. Taking the name of Suvvayā, she lived engaged in the self-denial of asceticism.

Now that boy lived at perfect ease in the dwelling of king Paumaraha. The kings who were that king's adversaries humbled themselves before him. Thereupon the king gave the boy the name of Nami [2]), which arose from his exellences. Thereupon he grew up hap-

1) That is, man who stands so all alone in the world as a single individual, shut off from other beings, who again are self-centred entities and unfathomable mysteries. See the note on Erz. p. 42, ll. 34—37. At the same time the word denotes the ascetic, who has cut himself loose from all ties. — Ekeka (Prākrit egega), "all alone, solitary" we have, for instance, in Jātaka III, p. 378, ll. 5, 6.

2) "The Humbler". To a similar cause Mahāvīra owes his name Vardhamāna and Buddha Gautama his name Siddhārtha.

pily, surrounded by five nurses [1]). When he was eight years old he had grasped the whole substance of the arts and sciences [2]) as soon as they were shown to him. In course of time he became a young man. He was married to one thousand and eight maidens who were sprung from the Ikkhāga race and the lustre of whose beauty was surpassed [only] by that of the women of the immortals [3]). Like the ruler of the gods he passed the time in enjoying the pleasures of the senses with these wives. But king Paumaraha, knowing the vanity of the world of living beings, appointed prince Nami to lordship over the country of Videha, acquired the splendor of self-denial, gained the insight of supreme knowledge, and thus stood at the head of the three worlds [4]). King Nami spent the time in maintaining the majesty of kingship.

1) The five kinds of nurses are: khīradhāī (wet-nurse), majjaṇadhāī ("bathing-nurse"), maṇḍaṇadhāī (adorning-nurse"), aṃkadhāī (nurse for holding the child on her lap), kīlāvaṇadhāi (nurse for playing with the child). Aupapātikasūtra § [105], p. 76. Cp. Divyāvadāna p. 3 etc.

2) Lit., "he had grasped the whole extent of the matter of the arts and sciences".

3) Cp. the phrase that is frequently used in the Jātaka, for instance on p. 249 of the third volume: atikantā manussaṃ vaṇṇaṃ apattā devavaṇṇaṃ. — In line 29 C rade uvabhuñjamāṇo, which is better.

4) Perhaps tiloyamatthaya has also a more technical meaning and is equivalent to logagga. Logagga, "the top, the highest point of the world" is often = moksha, nirvāṇa; for instance in Uttarajjh. XXIX, 38; XXIV, 84 (where Jacobi wrongly translates: "in view of all"). Cp. XXXVI, 57, 64. In the two passages quoted last we are told that the Siddhas (die Seligvollendeten) "dwell in the highest world" (loyagge paiṭṭhiya). Cp. Aupapātikas, § 130. A description of this place is found in Uttarajjh. XXXVI, 58 ff.; Aupapātikas. § 163 sq. Paumaraha obtained kevalam and thus had "stepped upon the summit of the three worlds", in every sense that this expression may convey. Cp. the Dhammapadam's beautiful stanzas of the man who has reached the terraced hights far above the maddening crowd. — See also Tattvārtha X, 5 (ZDMG. 60, p. 543).

Now that Maṇiraha had been bitten that very night by a snake, had died, and had been born as a hell-being in the fourth hell land. Thereupon Candajasa was established as king by the vassals and the counsellors. And the obsequial ceremonies for the two brothers were performed. And Candajasa maintained the majesty of kingship.

And one day a white elephant belonging to king Nami, the chief elephant of the whole realm, broke the post to which he was fastened, and set out toward the Vindhya forest. And he passed the neighborhood of Sudaṃsaṇa town. And when king Candajasa had gone to the riding-ground for horsemen the elephant was seen by his people and reported to the king. The elephant was seized by him and brought into the city, and he stayed there. Spies knew of it and reported to king Nami as follows: "The white elephant is seized by Candajasa; your majesty will decide." King Nami sent an envoy to Candajasa with the following message: "This white elephant is my property: send him to me!" The envoy went and announced the words of Nami to Candajasa. Candajasa said: "The jewels of no man are inscribed with the letters [of his name]; *he* who is superior in strength — *his* they are. And also:

> Who gives the earth? By whom is it given? To whom has it come by birth-right? To whom is it tied? In this world it is enjoyed by the princes of men who have the essential thing—courage" [1]).

1) Cp. vīrabhajyā vasuṃdharā. Pariçishṭaparvan VIII, 248 (virabhojjā puhavaī. Appendix to same, p. 15). The earth is the kings wife. "To enjoy" has therefore also an erotic meaning.

Thereupon the envoy returned to Mahilā, unregarded and unhonored. He reported Candajasa's words to the prince. Nami was enraged and with his whole army marched upon Candajasa [1]). Now Candajasa found out that king Nami was approaching, and fully equipped with an army he issued forth with face turned toward him, but was checked by an evil omen. Thereupon his counsellors said to Candajasa: "Shut the city gates for the present and remain. When we know what is befitting the time, we will again bestir ourselves" [2]). Thereupon the king did so, saying: "Yes". And the king Nami came and besieged the city on all four sides.

Through the rumor of the people, which went from mouth to mouth, the reverend lady Suvvayā heard of this and she thought: "Let them not travel the downward road by working the ruin of the country. Therefore I shall go and pacify the two". Upon obtaining the permission of the prioress she went to Sudaṃsaṇapura together with [certain] nuns [3]). The reverend lady saw king Nami. He gave her the principal seat. Having made her a low obeisance Nami sat down on the ground. The reverend lady preached the Law of Piety established by the princes of the Jinas, which produces every bliss. And at the end of her religious discourse she said: "Great king, vain is the splendor of royalty, frightful in its consequences the pleasure of the senses; the perpetrators of evil and forbidden things will in-

1) A word seems to have dropped out. Perhaps it was io (ita, p.p.p. of i), which could easily disappear on account of the io (adv. itas) following it.

2) Ceṭṭhai here = Skt. ceshṭate.

3) A nun may not travel alone. Kalpasūtra ed. Schubring (Leipzig 1905) 5, 15–18 (p. 33).

evitably have to live in hells that are full of extreme pain. Therefore, the case being such, turn back from this war. And another thing: What kind of war is war waged with one's elder brother?" Nami said: "How is he my elder brother?" The reverend lady laid his own history just as it was before him together with convincing proofs. Nevertheless from pride he did not leave off. Thereupon she entered the city by a postern gate and went to the royal palace. Entering, she was recognized by the female attendants. King Candajasa heard of it through the company of the women of his harem [1]). He too came and fell at the feet of the reverend lady, his eyes streaming with a flood of tears. He sat down on the ground. And Candajasa said: "Reverend lady, why did you take this vow which is so exceedingly hard to keep?" The reverend lady told him her tale. Candajasa said: "Where is now this own brother of mine?" The reverend lady said: "It is he by whom you are beleaguered". Then he issued out of his city, his heart bewildered by an abundance of joy. When Nami had seen his own brother draw nigh, he went to meet him and fell at his feet. His elder brother conducted him into the city with great delight. Candajasa installed Nami in the task of kingship; "Lord of the whole country of Avanti" was his title.

1) The passage in Jacobis text should read as follows: Candajasarāiṇā [vandiyā. dinnaṃ paramaṃ asaṇaṃ. uvaviṭṭho dharaṇivaṭṭhe rayā] nisuyaṃ anteurajaṇeṇa. As the bracketed words have evidently come in through a blunder (some gloss) I left them untranslated. They mean: "She was worshipped. A superior seat was given to her. The king sat down on the surface of the earth" (that is, on the ground, Erdboden). [Cp. Appendix].

Candajasa, for his part, embraced the life of a monk and wandered about at will.

Now king Nami, whose rule was extremely severe, exercised his lordship over the two realms with justice. A long time went by. One day there arose in the body of king Nami a fever that lasted for six months. He was given up by the physicians. And the queens, with bracelet-bedecked arms, rubbed sandal in order to anoint him with it. The palace was filled with the jingling, jangling sound of the bracelets [1]). The king said: "My ears are being pained", The queens took off all their bracelets, taking them off one by one; only one bracelet on each arm was left [2]). The king asked: "Why do the bracelets not clink and clank?" He was told how they were taken off. Being smitten with that pain, he turned his face toward the other world and reflected: "The harm is in the many, not in the solitary man" [3]). And it has been said:

> "Exactly as great as are the appurtenances and exactly as great as is the retinue, exactly so great is always the pain, but never the pleasure.

"Therefore if I am freed from this sickness, then I shall renounce the world". At that time it was the full

1) Lit., "with the jingle-jangle-tinkle (or, tinkling) of the sound of the bracelets".

2) Woe would befall the woman, especially the married woman, who would not wear at least that one bracelet. Uttarajjh. p. 267, l. 5 correctly states: ekaikaṃ maṅgalāya rakshitam, "they kept one for good luck".

3) The dīpikā has the doggerel stanza:

Yathā saṃyogataḥ çubhā
açubhāḥ cabdā jāyante
tathā rāgādikā doshāḥ
saṃyogata eva bhavanti.
Uttarajjh. p. 267, l. 7.

moon of Kattiya. Thinking thus he fell asleep. When the morning dawned he dreamed dreams, [he saw] Seya on Mount Mandara and himself mounted [1]) on this king of elephants. Free from his malady, he was awakened by an instrument that sounded gladdening music [2]). Rejoiced and delighted he thought: "Ah, I have dreamed a capital dream!" And he reflected again: "Where have I seen such an excellent and noble mountain before?" He pondered; he remembered the birth: formerly after leading the life of a monk in a human existence he had been born in the heavenly abode Pupphuttara; there, in the condition of a god, he formerly came at the glorifications of the Jinas and on other occasions and saw Mount Mandara. He experienced spiritual awakening and became a religious mendicant [3]).

After hearing that many bracelets sounded and that *one* did not sound, king Nami, the lord of Mahilā, renounced the world.

1) But better cancel comma after pāsai and translate, "When the morning dawned he, in a dream, saw Seya" etc.

2) This is a good omen. According to the Hindu's belief music is auspicious and augurs fulfillment of one's wishes if heard at the moment when one's thoughts and desire are directed toward a certain object. Cp. Raghuvaṃça XVII, 11 and Shankar Pandit's note in his edition; also Vātsyāyana's Kāmasūtram übers. von R. Schmidt (1st edition) p. 245, bottom of page.

3) Cp. the beautiful Tale of the Monk in Uttarajjh. XX.

NAGGAI.

NAGGAI.

Again, the life of Naggai. There is here in the land of Bhāraha, in the country of Gandhāra, a town named Poṇḍavaddhaṇa. There was a king Sīharaha by name. One day two steeds arrived from the Northland as a present for him. In order to ride them about, the king mounted on one of them, a prince [1]) on the second. Thereupon the king with all his army issued forth from the city, came to the riding ground, and prepared to ride. And that horse was trained in the inverse manner. When the king pulled at the rein, it went only the faster. And while he kept pulling, it sped on and went twelve yojanas. It entered a great forest. And the king who had become wearied of the thing [2]), let the bridle go; at the very same moment [3]) the steed stood still. The king saw: "It is a horse trained in the inverse way". He dismounted, tied it to a tree, and commenced to wander about. He sustained life with fruits.

When he had ascended the top of a mountain in order to stay there over night he saw a palace of seven stories. He entered there and saw a maiden, endowed with the fresh bloom of youth, beauty, and grace. And she rose in zealous haste and gave the king a seat. The king sat down. An intense love sprang up between them.

1) Or, "a Rājput". The dīpikā simply says: aparo naraḥ.

2) Jacobi should have set down "überdrüssig" for this passage too.

3) Lit., "at these very steps" (that the horse was just then making).

And she was questioned by the king: "My good lady, who are you? And why do you stay alone in the wild-wood?" And she said: "Do you lean on fortitude and marry me here in the palace on the balcony prepared for the nuptial rite. Afterwards I will tell you my story at length". And with delighted mind the king entered that habitation. He saw there a sanctuary of the Jina and in front of that the balcony for the wedding. And having honored and worshipped the Jina he celebrated the Gandharva marriage[1]). They went to sleep in the bed-chamber. The night passed. At the break of day both adored the Jina. The king sat down on a throne; but she sat down on the other half of the seat. And she said: "Hear my story, best beloved.

"There is here in India a city named Khiipaiṭṭhiyaṃ. Jiyasattū was king there. Once the king commenced a hall of paintings and handed it over to the guild of painters in equal portions [*i. e.*, assigned the head of every family — professions being hereditary in India — an equal share of the work to be done][2]). Many painters painted. Also an old painter, Cittangaya by name, painted. A long time passed. And his young daughter, Kaṇaya-mañjarī by name, brought him his meals. One day she was on her way to her father with his dinner in her hands, when a horseman came along the king's highway,

1) The form of marriage peculiar to the Gandharvas (a kind of heavenly beings), "a marriage proceeding entirely from love without ceremonies and without consulting relatives". For vedi cp. Monier—Williams.

2) Uttarajjh. p. 268, l. 3 from below tells us: Tato nṛipatiç cittrakarān ākārya sabhagṛihabhittibhāgāh sarveshāṃ samāc citrayituṃ dattāḥ Sarve 'pi cittrakarāḥ svasvabhittibhāgān gāḍhodyamena citrayante. So citta-sabhā would seem to be a painted hall (the walls being decorated with paintings).

that was crowded with people, on his horse, making it run at full speed. And she fled in fear. Then after he had rushed by she went to her father. When Cittangaya saw that his meal had come, he went to ease nature. To while away time Kaṇayamañjarī painted there in colors, on the paved floor, a peacock's feather entirely true to nature.

"In the meanwhile King Jiyasattū came to the hall of paintings. Looking at the paintings he saw the peacock's feather on the paved floor, and thinking, "It's beautiful", he stretched out his hand to pick it up. He broke his nails, which were like pearl-oyster shells. Abashed he looked into space.

"Kaṇayamañjarī said with a laugh: "While I reflected, 'A chair doesn't stand on three legs', and sought the fourth foolish man, I have now found you as the fourth leg".

"The king said: "How is that? Tell me the whole matter as it is".

"She said laughing: "While I brought my father his meal a man rode a horse in hot haste on the king's highway. He had not a bit of pity, for old people, children, women, and all other weak people on the highway were trampled down. Therefore this horseman, being an arrant fool, is the chair's one leg. The second leg is the king, by whom the hall has been assigned [1]) to the painters in equal shares. In the individual families there are many painters. My father is, firstly, without a son; secondly, an old man; thirdly, poor. But although he is such, an equal portion [of the work]

1) Sīyala, Skt. cītala, "cold", seems to be used just as jaḍa for "cold, torpid, senseless, stupid", in Skt. — For virikka see § 566.

has been set down for him [which he cannot do under the circumstances]. The third leg is my father here, because while painting at this picture-gallery he has spent what he had earned before; now I bring him any food I get, and when it has come — he goes to ease nature! What a dull man he is!"

"The king said: "Why am I the fourth leg?"

"The other said: "Now, anyone knows at once [or, in the first place]: 'How should a peacock's feather come here indeed!' If it [the feather] had been brought here in some way or other, even then one would perceive it by the eye at once" [1]).

"The king said: "I am really a fool and as such the fourth leg of the chair". Hearing how [cleverly] she put her words together and seeing the loveliness of her body, he became enamored of her. But when Kaṇayamanjarī had given her father to eat she went home.

"By mouth of Sugutta, his prime minister, the king asked Cittangaya for Kaṇayamanjarī" [2]). He said: "We are poor. How could we celebrate the marriage and pay the king due honor!"

"This was told the king. He had Cittangaya's house filled with money, grain, gold, etc. On an auspicious lunar-day, in an auspicious hour, Kaṇayamanjarī was

1) Or, "by his intelligence". The literal translation would be: "It might have been brought here in some way or other [so one might object]. Even then one would perceive it, etc." The sense may be: Even if a man of sense had thought for a moment that the feather had been brought there, he would have rectified the mistake right away (i. e. would have perceived that it was no real feather). Or, "Even if the feather had been brought there, one (i. e., people) would have seen it right away (and picked it up, of course, not leaving it till the king came).

2) C correctly reads Kaṇayamanjariṃ.

married [by the king] in great splendor. A palace and a great multitude of female slaves were bestowed on her".

"Now the king had many queens; every one [of them] entered the king's sleeping apartment on the night when her turn came. And on that day the order was given that it was Kaṇayamanjarī's turn. Bedecked and adorned she went, together with her slave-girl Mayaṇiyā, and sat down upon a seat.

"In the meanwhile the king came. She rose to greet him and performed the other acts of politeness and modesty. The king lay down on the bed.

Before this time already Kaṇayamanjarī had said to Mayaṇiyā: "When the king has lain down you must ask me for a story in a way that the king hears it". Therefore Mayaṇiyā said at this appropriate moment: "Mistress, tell me a story while the king tarries [with us here"]. The other said: "The king must first sleep soundly, then I will tell one".

The king thought: "Now, what kind of a story will she tell? I too will hear it". So he pretended to be asleep. Mayaṇiyā said: "Mistress, the king is asleep; tell the story".

The other said: "Listen! There was in a city Vasantaura a merchant Varuṇa. He had a chapel built of one hand in size that was made all of one block of stone. Into this he put a certain idol of four hands". Mayaṇiyā said: "Mistress, how could there be room for an idol of four hands in a chapel of one hand in size?" The other said: "I am sleepy now; tomorrow I shall tell". "Thus let it be", said Mayaṇiyā, went out and went home. The king's curiosity was roused and he thought:

"What kind of thing is this?" She (Kaṇayamanjarī) also lay down to sleep.

When on the second day again the order was given that it was her turn, she was addressed in the same way by Mayaṇiyā: "Mistress, tell that half-told tale [to the end]". The other said: "Friend, that god is the Four-Armed One [1]), but this is not the size of his body [*i. e.*, what I said does not refer to the size of his body]. Thus far goes the story".

Mayaṇiyā said: "Tell me another".

Kaṇayamanjarī said: "Friend, there is a great forest. In it there stands a great red açoka tree with outspread boughs and branches. And it has no shade".

Mayaṇiyā said: "How could such an excellent tree have no shade?"

She said: "Tomorrow I'll tell; now I am overcome by sleep".

The third day again, out of curiosity, she was summoned. In the same manner she was questioned by Mayaṇiyā. She explained: "That tree's shade is below it" [2]).

Asked for another story, she narrated: "In a certain place there was a village magistrate. He had a big camel. And this roamed about at will. One day when it roamed about it saw a babbūla tree abounding in leaves, blossoms, and fruit. And toward that it stretched out its neck and could not reach it. And for the tree's sake it harassed itself a very long time. Then it stretched out its neck still a great deal more in all four directions.

1) Vishnu, who is represented with four arms and hands.

2) Therefore it *has* no shade. is not protected by shade; whereas Mayaṇiyā (and the king) took the painter's daughter to mean that the tree cast no shade.

When it could not reach [the tree] in any way, it was seized by anger. Therefore it discharged its urine and dung on the tree".

Mayaṇiyā said: "How could it discharge its urine and dung on the tree which it could not even reach with its mouth?"

The other said: "Tomorrow I'll tell".

In the same manner she declared on the following day: "That babbūla tree was down in the pit of a 'blind' well[1]); therefore the camel could not eat of it"[2]).

"In this way Kaṇayamanjarī befooled the king with such interesting stories for six months. Thereafter he became exceedingly enamored of her. Exclusively devoted to the pleasure of love with her alone, he passed the time".

Straightway her fellow-wives became enraged against her, sought for weak points in her, and conferred together: "She has bewitched the king by witchcraft, so that he has abandoned even his queens who were born in the highest families; in his passion for this artisan's daughter he considers neither excellences nor faults; pays no attention to the affairs of the kingdom; cares not that his wealth is being ruined by her juggler's tricks".

"Now Kaṇayamanjarī, day by day, entered one of the

1) Literally, "in the middle of a blind well-pit". A well dried up, overgrown with plants, and not used is meant. The metaphor may be the same as in the German, *blindes Fenster. blinde Thüre*; or the term may refer to the fact that such a well is hidden from view; or the word may be taken more literally. The shining water in the well is its pupil of the eye *(Augenstern)*. *Cf.* the interesting. oft-recurring passage, *Majjhima-Nikāya*, Vol. I, p. 80, where we have *udakatārakā*, *Wasserstern* = *Wasserspiegel* (of a well).

2) The Sanskrit version here adds six other stories, all of a similar nature. Three of them are well-known tales (Nos. 5, 6, 7). As they are neither in the Māhārāshṭrī text nor affect the matter in hand, I pass them by.

chambers in her palace at noon-time, all alone, cast off the garments and the finery that belonged to the king [*i. e.*, that the king had given her], and put on the ragged dress and the finery made of tin and lead that she had got from her father. And she admonished her own soul: "Do not be proud [1]), O soul, of [this] wealth, do not become conceited, forget not thyself! The king's is this wealth, thine are these clothes all beaten to pieces with the stick [2]) and this finery. So be of a calm mind, because for a long time thou didst not enjoy such splendor. Else the king might take thee by the neck and put thee out".

"Observing these her doings day by day, her fellow-wives said to the king: "Although you are destitute of love for us, nevertheless we will ward off misfortune from you; for: Woman's deity is her husband. This woman here, who is your sweetheart, works some incantation or evil spell. Being bewitched by her, you do not notice this mischief".

"The king said: "How is that?"

"They said: "At noon-time she goes into a chamber, shuts the door, and stands there mumbling something by herself, day by day, for some time. If you don't believe it, watch her [3]) yourself or [have it done] by a number of others".

1) Gūrava, fr. garu (not guru), "do not attach importance to, do not consider yourself an important personage on account of".

2) In the process of washing numberless times.

3) Or: "investigate the matter". Lit. "by some group of others". The text is hardly correct. Possibly the reading of A and of C is better. Attavaggeṇa could be taken in the sense of *ātmavyāgryeṇa — "investigate [the matter] through some one or by your own intentness

"And, having heard this, the king went himself. Standing at the door in order to watch Kaṇayamanjarī, who had entered the room, he saw the doings described already and heard how she instructed her own self. His heart was filled with joy. "O what prudence of hers! O what freedom from pride! O what discrimination! Therefore she is in every respect a treasure of all excellences; and these [her fellow-wives] are envious by reason of their being fellow-wives. For even excellence they deem a fault".

"And full of joy the king made her mistress of the whole kingdom and invested her with the turban [1]).

"Thus the time went by. One day the king and Kaṇayamanjarī embraced the law of lay devotees at the feet of the teacher Vimalacanda.

"And in the course of time Kaṇayamanjarī, after having been a goddess [2]), descended to a lower birth and was born as the daughter of Daḍhasatti, king of the Vidyādharas on Mount Veyaḍḍha, in the city of Toraṇāura. The name of Kaṇayamālā was given her. And in due course she reached the bloom of youth. One day she was carried off by a Vidyādhara, named Vāsava, whose heart had been ravished by her beauty. Calling forth by magic a palace on this mountain he

(by carefully attending to it yourself)". Vā (omitted by C) *possibly* emphatic, "just investigate".

1) I. e. he had her crowned as paṭṭarājñī — as his principal wife or queen consort.

2) The dīpikā reads: devītvaṃ prāpa, Uttarajjh. 274, l. 7; and devī jātā, p. 276, l. 6. But devīhouṃ = devībhūtvā could also mean: "having become a god". That would tally well with a number of stories, one of which we have met with already in our collection. The meaning is: In the course of time Kaṇayamanjarī died, was reborn in heaven, and her period of life there having come to an end, was born as the daughter of Daḍhasatti.

put her there. And he built this balcony for the nuptial ceremony: "I shall surely marry her here".

"In the interval Kaṇayamālā's eldest brother Kaṇayateya came. Fighting ablaze with the fire of anger, they both died from the blows they gave each other. Kanayamālā, for her part, wailing a very great deal in her grief for her brother, stayed in this palace, disconsolate and distressed.

"One day a god, named Vāṇamantara[1]), came here. He said to her with tender affection: "Child you are my daughter". While that god was speaking thus, the Vidyādhara Daḍhasatti arrived in order to search for his son and daughter. By magic Vantara made Kaṇayamālā take a different form. The bodies of Daḍhasatti's son, of his daughter, and of Vāsava were lying dead on the ground. Having seen them Daḍhasatti thought: "My son here has been destroyed by Vāsava, and Vāsava by Kaṇayateya, and Kaṇayamalā has been destroyed by Vāsava when he was on the point of being felled. Therefore out on the saṃsāra, that is full of many sorrows! Who that knows its nature[2]) delights in it?"

1) A strange proper name. For the Vāṇamantara or Vantara are a class of gods. It is possible however to understand the phrase thus: "one of the gods who are called Vāṇamantara" and to translate in the sequel "the Vaṇamantara", "the Vantara".

2) Sayaṇṇa I have taken to be = svakajña, "knowing the self, the real nature of a thing (or of things in general), wise". The commentators translate it by sakarṇa, and Hemacandra uses this word in Pariçishṭaparvan XIII, 120 in the sense of prajña. They may be right after all. In Jātaka II, p. 261 we read:

Bahūni narasīsāni
lomasāni brahāni ca
gīvāsu patimukkāni;
kocid ev' ettha kaṇṇavā.

"Many heads of men, hairy and big are put on necks; sometimes only

Thus he fell into a displeasure with the world and entered upon the life of a wandering ascetic. And Vantara withdrew his magic power. Daḍhasatti was respectfully greeted by Kaṇayamālā and the god. The monk said: "What sort of thing is this?" And Kaṇayamālā told him the story of her brother's death. The monk said: "I saw *three* dead bodies". The god said: "I exercised my magic power". "For what purpose?" The god said: "Hear the reason. In the city of Khiipaiṭṭhiya there was king, Jiyasattu by name. He married Cittangaya's, the painter's daughter, whose name was Kaṇayamanjarī. And she became a lay disciple. And this Cittangaya was piloted [1]) by her by means of the fivefold formula of veneration. Dying, he became a god, Vantara by name. And I am he. One day when I came here, I saw this Kaṇayamālā overwhelmed with grief. An extremely tender affection for her sprang up in me. And I thought: "Has she been a near relative of mine in a former exis-

there is one who has ears", i. e. knowledge, wisdom. "Kaṇṇavā = paññavā", says the commentator. So the translation: "Who that is wise delights", etc. might have been better.

1) Nijjāmiya Jacobi renders by "converted". This is a slip. Nijjāmaya means "pilot", just as Skt. niryāmaka, and Pāli niyyāmaka (Jātaka I, pp. 107 sq.; IV, pp. 137 sqq.; Milindapañho pp. 194, 378). In the Jaina books it is used for a "spiritual guide" (pilot across the saṃsāra). In Pariçishṭaparvan XIII, 87 young Āryarakshita meets the old Jaina teacher Bhadragupta, who is just preparing to starve himself to death and who requests him: "Mama niryāmako bhava", "be my spiritual pilot"; and Āryarakshita performed niryāmaṇā for him. In his introduction to the Pariçishṭaparvan Jacobi translates niryāmaka correctly. The painter's daughter had no need of *converting* her father. The cabbalistic formula is potent enough to ensure the sinner's welfare in the next world. Of course, I speak of the views, frequently perverted, that we find in these and in other popular tales.

tence?"[1]) I made use of the superhuman knowledge Ohi. I knew: "This is my daughter Kaṇayamanjarī. After her death she has become a Vidyādhara's daughter". At this point you came. I thought: "She will go away with her father!" Afraid of separation from her I turned her into a woman of a different appearance in order to delude you, and showed you the dead body of her. And you betook yourself to the life of a religious mendicant. Thereupon I was seized with distress, thinking: "This illustrious man has been deceived by me". So do you forgive this evil act". But the monk said: "You are my benefactor on account of being the cause that I grasped the Truth". And he flew up and roamed about in accordance with his desire.

"But when Kaṇayamālā mused on the story told by the god, recollection of her [previous] birth arose in her, she knew her former existence, knew "I am that Kaṇayamanjarī, and this father of mine has become a god". Thereupon she was filled with intense affection and said to the god: "Father, who will be my bridegroom?" The god found out by means of the superior insight Ohi and said: "Child, your husband in your former existence, king Jiyasattu, after being a god has become king Daḍhasiha's son, Sīharaha by name. He

1) The idea that relatives and all souls that belong together are drawn to each other by a gentle, but irresistible mystic force is frequently encountered in Hindu books; therefore Kirātarjunīya XI, 8 declares:

Avijñāte 'pi bandhau hi
balāt prahlādate manaḥ.

The doctrine of metempsychosis offers a natural explanation for our likes and dislikes, which often seem so wayward and unaccountable. Cp. my Daçakumāracaritam, pp. 301 and 302, note 5); Uttararāmacaritam V, 17, and esp. VI, 12; Mālatimādhava I, 27; Kirātārjun. XIII, 6; also Gottfried's Tristan ed. Bechstein 3238 ff. and note.

will be your husband". She said: "How[1]) will my union with him come about?" The god answered "He also will come here, carried away by a horse trained in the inverse manner. Therefore stay here happy and at ease. Do not yield to anxiety. I shall continually do your bidding". And the god remained right here in the palace. But Kaṇayamālā spent the time pleasantly with the gods. And she, my noble consort, am I. Yesterday that god went to Mount Meru in order to worship the shrines. Meanwhile[2]) you arrived here in the afternoon. And because I was longing excessively I did not wait for him to return thence, but myself made you marry me. Thus I have told you my own history, for which you had asked".

In Sīharaha too the recollection of his [previous] birth arose when he had heard this tale. At this juncture that god came, accompanied by a troop of gods. The king made a low obeisance; the god welcomed him with delight. Kaṇayamālā told the god the story of her own marriage; he was rejoiced. Amid proper conversation noon came; the king, together with his wife, ate that heavenly fare. Thus he remained there a month. And the king said to Kaṇayamālā: "My love, the host of adversaries in all probability oppresses my realm[3]). Therefore I am going. Give me leave". She said: "Best beloved, just as you command. But your town is far

1) Read kaham with the MSS. — Ābhogeuṇa possibly means "having made the matter the object of his turning to, of his efforts, i. e., having investigated it". Or from ābhoga = range?

2) Put the comma (or better, a period) after gao.

3) Or perhaps better: "The host of adversaries will oppress my realm (if I stay longer)".

away. So how could you go there traveling on foot? Therefore accept of me the magic spell Pannattī". The king accepted it. And he worked it after the fashion she told him. Bidding farewell to Kaṇayamālā he went to his own city. A great festival was celebrated in the city. The king was asked his adventures by his vassals and the others. He told them as they had happened. All were astonished. And they said:

> "Whereever the man of moral merit goes, to a foreign country, into the forest, or to the middle of the sea, there he is always happy. Therefore do you acquire [1]) moral merit".

Thus the time went by. On the fifth day the king went to that mountain [where Kaṇayamālā dwelt]. He stayed with Kanayamālā for some days. And the people said: "The king passes to the mountain". Thereupon in course of time, because he passed to the mountain, the king's name was fixed as "Naggai" [2]) by the people. Once Naggai had gone to the mountain. Vāṇamantara said to the king: "I have stayed here very long. Now an order from my lord has come. That must necessarily be executed. A long time will pass in it [i. e., in executing this order] [3]). And Kaṇayamālā here will feel unhappy in her separation from me. Therefore you must

1) Samajjinai with epenthetic vowel and according to 9th class. §§ 510 ff. But perhaps we should follow the reading of A, that is, should derive from sam + ud + jyā (= ji).

2) "He who goes to the mountain". Nagagati drops the second vowel and becomes Naggai — an interesting bit of popular etymology. The literal translation would be: therefore, "This is Naggai", thus [his] name was fixed by the people".

3) Or, "I shall have to tarry there a long time".

so act that she does not become lonesome". Having spoken thus the god departed. And the king thought: "There is no other means for the repose of her mind". So he had a charming city built on that mountain. And by enticement he brought many of his subjects there. He had temples of the Jinas erected. Their images were set up in them. And some time passed while he celebrated a great festival with religious processions[1]) and ruled the realm with justice.

One day when he went out with his train[2]) he saw a flowering mango tree. A cluster of blossoms was plucked by the king. In the same way by the army, which took[3]) clusters of flowers, leaves, shoots, and branches. Only the wood was left. When the king returned he asked: "Where is that mango tree?" The minister of state pointed it out. How has it got into such a condition?" He said: "You took one cluster of flowers, after that the whole army took [clusters] and thus made it so". He reflected: "Surely, as long as there is wealth, there is splendor; but all wealth is unstable". And thinking thus he experienced spiritual awakening.

But he, the king of Gandhāra, seeing in the
charming mango tree which was bright[4]) with

1) Or, "while he celebrated religious fairs and great festivals" (neutre dvandva compound).

2) Lit., "with his people", jaṇayuttam = janayuktam, if we accept the reading of B. The reading of the text would mean: "when he went out in a religious procession" (anuyātram in Skt.); or, "in a festive procession, marching along". It is an adverb formed with anu, not = anuyātrā, "Gefolge" (Jacobi).

3) Layanta from lā, "to take". The verb is frequently found in Prākrit. Perhaps layantena = lagan tena is more probable.

4) Or, "variegated". Probably better, "with clustered [samanjari] young shoots and flowers".

clusters of blossoms, young shoots, and flowers prosperity and disaster, perceived the Truth.

**
*

All four of them [1]) wandering about, went to the city of Khiipaiṭṭhiya [2]). There in a temple of four doors, Karakaṇḍu entered by the eastern door, Dummuha by the southern. "How can I manage never to avert my face from a monk?" So thought that Vāṇamantara and turned his face also to the south. Nami [entered] by the western [door]; there too he turned his face. Naggai by the northern; there too he turned his face.

Karakaṇḍu still had that scab from the days of his childhood. Therefore he took a little scraper and scraped his delicate ear. Thereupon he hid it [3]) somewhere. Dummuha saw that and said:

> "After giving up kingship and kingdom as well as town and harem, why do you engage in this hoarding?"

When Karakaṇḍu gave no answer, then Nami said:

> "While you employed in your paternal realm many men to perform services [4]) for you, you now, after rejecting their services, perform such services yourself!

1) That is, all the four Pratyekabuddhas: Karakaṇḍu, Domuha (or Dummuha), Naggai, and Nami, whose history the the preceding tales have recounted.

2) Khiipaiṭṭhiya represents Kshitipratishṭhika, I think. In Uttarajjh. p. 208, l. 9 we find Kshitipratishṭha.

3) The scraper.

4) Or, "execute [wordly] affairs" (and the same translation of kicca everywhere in the stanza). But the sense is in both cases essentially the same. Karakaṇḍu's "worldliness", of course, consists in the care he takes of the comfort of his body. Cp. Jātaka N°. 406.

Then the prince of Gandhāra said:

"If you have left everything behind and [now] as a fool exert yourself for existence, why do you reproach another, [reproach] those who themselves attend to all their needs?" [1])

Then Karakaṇḍu said:

"Restraining [people] from sin, do you please not speak of faults in monks who have chosen the path of final emancipation and live in chastity.

"And likewise there is the old saying:

"Whether one be wrathful or of a peaceable mind or administering poison, one should speak salutary words to him, words that are profitable to the idea one stands for" [2]).

1) I. e., people who do not practise asceticism, but follow their natural instincts. But attanīsesakārae perhaps should rather be translated: "those who have completely done away with Self (cp. niḥçesham karoti, "to destroy completely)". You have no right to lay down the law to others, to really perfect ascetics; for you are not emancipated from the world, you who pay so much attention to your body that you even carry a scraper with you all the time. You devote too much care to life (bhava) and thus you will bring about for yourself new existences (bhava) in the saṃsāra. Mokkha could possibly also be = mukhya, "you, a preeminent man". The stanza is rather obscure. But it seems tolerably clear that all three monks upbraid Karakaṇḍu.

2) This is a knotty stanza. Rūsao presents no great difficulty. Rūs is the common form of the root in Prākrit both in the verb and in the derivatives. Most probably the present rushyati > rūsai gave the start. Paro mā I write paromā = pra + roman. If the form be correct it is indeed "old" or "archaic" (ārsha). Cp. Vissakammā (from vicva + harman). We would expect paromo. Probably paromo was utterly unintelligible; so wiseacres corrected it to paro mā, which, by itself at least, was clear. Paroma I take to be = Pāli palloma. This word I always considered as equivalent to *praroma, *praloma. For the doubling of the l cp. Childers sub sakkāya and patikkūla and §§ 196, 90. It is a synonym of anuloma, the opposite of Pāli paṭiloma and viloma, and occurs, e.g., in Majjh.-Nik. I, 17; Dīghanikāya I, p. 96. Cp. Sumangalavilāsinī I, 266; Journal of the Pāli Text Society 1889 p. 206. If pratiloma means "wider-

They agreed to this instruction delivered by Karakaṇḍu and in course of time all four attained final emancipation.

haarig", praloma (praroma) literally means: "mithaarig, vorwärtshaarig" (pratiloma, "rückhaarig"). Cp. anuloma. The only other etymologies for which I could see some foundation are: 1) pannaloma > panloma > palloma. Pannaloma, "of a quiet soul" (lit., "on whose body the hairs have ceased from bristling") is frequently found in Pāli (for instance, in Majjh.-Nik. I, p. 450; Udānam II, 10 [p. 19]; Sumangalavil. I, 266, explaining palloma). It is not impossible, though not very probable perhaps, that pannaloma lived on in two forms, the original and the shortened one. But the second vowel of the word would naturally bear the accent and therefore would not drop. This is a very serious objection. 2) Pātaloma > pātloma > palloma, springing from the phrase lomaṃ pāteti (for which we would rather expect lomaṃ pādeti). Lomaṃ pāteti occurs in Majjh.-Nik. I, 442 and other passages. The most natural form would in that case be pātitaloma.

Pariyattao and visaṃ can stand for several prototypes. The most likely explanations seems to me: visham parivartakaḥ, "one who brings poison near", or "one who changes" (lit., "turns around", or "wraps up) poison", that is, who makes his enemy swallow it in a disguised form. Or could it represent vṛishaṃ parivartakaḥ, "one who destroys virtue (or, one's semen virile, by magic means)"?

Sapakkha = svapaksha, "ones party, side, position, theory, idea". With great diffidence I advance my translation of this stanza [and of stanzas 2 and 3. The Skt. gloss apparently takes these latter as spoken in *defence* of Karakaṇḍu. The end of stanza 2 would, in that case, have to be translated "perform services, trouble about affairs (faults, of others)". The second quarter of stanza 3 would accordingly mean, "and, O lord, strive as a preeminent man" (read mokkhe "for final emancipation"?) Ghaḍasī (garahasī) aorist 3d sg.?].

MULADEVA.

MULADEVA [1]).

There is a city, Ujjeṇi. And in that city arrived from Pāḍaliputta a Rājput, Mūladeva by name, skilled in all the arts, proficient in many sciences, of noble mind, grateful, a hero in the service of those who sought his protection, devoted to excellences, of pleasant speech, clever, endowed with beauty, grace and youth, who roamed through the land because he was addicted to a passion for gambling and was therefore despised by his parents. There changing his appearance and taking the form of a dwarf by the use of a magic pill, he astounded the people of the city by his brilliant [2]) tales, his proficiency in music and the other arts, and by many wondrous feats of various sorts. He became famous.

And there lived a peerless courtesan, Devadattā by name, proud on account of her beauty, grace, and accomplishments. And he heard: "She, being proud of herself, is not pleased with any common man". Thereupon from curiosity he stood near the house at the time of morning and in order to stir her emotions he commenced a song of the sweetest tone, charming with

1) About Mūladeva see Pavolini, Vicende del tipo di Mūladeva. Giornale della società Asiatica italiana IX, p. 175 sqq. Skt. versions of our tale are found in Uttarajjh. pp. 152—153 and pp. 181 sqq.

2) Or, "various".

its union of various sounds[1]), and sung in a voice that vibrated with many modulations. And Devadattā heard this and she thought: "Ah, a voice never heard before! Therefore this is some celestial, not a mere man". She had him sought out by her servant girls. They looked for him and saw Mūladeva in the shape of a dwarf. And they told her how matters were. She sent a humpbacked female servant, named Māhavā, to summon him. She went and civilly said to him: "Hear, O far-famed one! My mistress Devadattā requests: "Do me a favor; come into my house". And he said in his craftiness: "I do not care to hang about courtesans; for excellent men intercourse with prostitutes is a forbidden thing. And it is said:

> "Excellent men do not love the courtesan, her who has been rubbed and worn away by crores of various paramours, delights in liquor and meat and is extremely vile, tender in her speech, but wicked in her heart.
>
> "Cursed is the courtesan like a thorn[2]), she who like a flame of fire is only intent on burning, who like strong drink bewilders the mind, who like a knife cuts the body".

"Therefore I have no desire to go". But she won his heart by many phrases of a witty turn[3]), and with great importunity seized him by the hand and led him

1) Perhaps we have to read annannavaṇṇāsaṃveha —, "because the various (or, mutual i. e.. interlocking) sounds (or, syllables) were not merged in one another", but each was clearly enunciated. Saṃvedha I do not find in the dictionaries; but I have seen it in Bharatīyanāṭya-çāstra XI, 21 (where a variant reading has saṃçlesha).

2) This is a conjectural rendering. I can find çalikā nowhere.

3) Lit., "with many phrase-turns (phrase-witticism)". Jacobi takes it to mean "with many a manner of speech".

into the house. And going along he slapped that hunchback and made her straight by means of his cleverness in the arts and by the employment of magic science. Agitated with astonishment in her mind, she introduced him into the house. And Devadattā saw him in his form of a dwarf, but possessing peerless grace, and surprised she had a seat offered to him. And he sat down. Betel was given him, and Māhavā showed her own shape and told the story. They wondered very much; conversation commenced in sweet, clever phrases, and he won her heart. And it is said:

> The talk of the shrewd, which is conversant with propitiation, skillful in jesting, wantoning in a lovely voice[1]) — that is sorcery; and what of roots![2])

1) Dullaliya here is by no means "überdrüssig" (Jacobi). Its import is: "spoilt, wayward, capricious, yielding to every impulse". In Rāvaṇavaha XV, 54; Gauḍavaha 342, and in other passages it has the meaning "spoiled", just as Skt. durlalita. In Hāla 892 we find sarasakavvadullalio, "a spoiled connoisseur of impassioned poetry"; C fol. 36 *a* dullaliyagoṭṭhī. Most instructive is Gauḍavaha 47, where the scholiast correctly renders it by hevākin, "capricious, wantoning". Why the editor criticises this by a sic! I fail to see. German "verzärtelt" would be a good rendering. Hence also Skt. durlalita = atipriya, Mālatīmādh. VIII, 45; Çiçupālavadha XX, 78 (according to the scholiast = lolupa, but "verzärtelt, spoilt" would do too) and dullaliya = "delicate" C fol. 271*a*.

2) The belief that you can inflame man or woman with a most ardent love for your person by means of magic roots always held sway over the minds of the people both in India and in other countries, although a saying was current in India declaring: "The procuring of love by the might of charms and roots is called treachery against a husband". Prabandhacintāmani p. 191.

Mūlīhim is best taken as an instrum. plur. from mūlī (fem.). Mūlī and mūlikā, "healing root, magic root" is also found in Jaina Sanskrit. Uttarajjh. p. 343, l. 5 from bottom; p. 621, l. 1. Cp. mūlīkarman = mūlakarman, employment of roots for magic purposes". With the stanza cp. Kuṭṭanīmatam 48:

Idam eva samullapitaṃ, Līlāvati, vijitaparabhṛitadhvanitam
Tava niḥçeshabhujaṃgavyākarshaṇasiddhamantra uccaritaḥ.

At this point a vīṇā player came there. He played the vīṇā. Devadattā was pleased and said: "Bravo, lute-player, bravo! Brilliant is your art". Mūladeva said: "Ah, the people of Ujjeṇī are too clever; they know the difference between beautiful and bad!" Devadattā said: "Say, what is there defective?" He replied: "The bamboo rod [of the vīṇā] even is not clear and there is something wrong [1]) with the string". She said: "How do you know?" "I'll show you!" The vīṇā was handed to him; he drew out a little stone from the rod of the lute [2]) and a hair out of the string. Having put it in order [3]) he began to play. The hearts of Devadattā and of her attendants were overpowered. And in the neighborhood there was a female elephant that used to roar [4]) all the time; this too stood there swaying to and fro, with ears hanging down. Devadattā and the lute-player were exceedingly surprised. And they thought: "Ah, it is Vissakammā in disguise" [5]). She honored and dismissed the lute-player. Meal time came. Devadattā said: "Call the masseur, that we two may bathe". Mūladeva said: "Permit me, I myself shall perform the duty of anointing you". "Do you know that too?" "I don't know it well; but I have stood near those who knew". Campaka oil

1) Khūṇa, I think, is connected with the root kshi [collateral kshu]. The development of meaning from "worn away, feeble, wanting" to "defective, wrong" is natural. Cp. German fehlen. Khīṇa: khūṇa = hīna: hūṇa (hūṇa is not rare in Prākrit).

2) Note that the vīṇādaṇḍaka is proverbial for its crookedness. Jātaka II, 225, 226, st. 136; II, 252, l. 24.

3) Sam + ṛi forming the causative *samārayati > samārei. The differentiation from samarpayati in form and meaning is noteworthy.

4) Lit., "that had crying (trumpeting) for her character".

5) Lit., "Vissakammā having a disguised costume (or appearance)".

was brought. He began to anoint her. Her heart was enslaved. And she reflected: "Ah, the superabundance of acquirements! Ah, the incomparable touch of his hands! Therefore this must be a man endowed with supernatural powers who hides his real form. One of his figure does not naturally possess such eminence. Therefore I shall make him manifest his real shape". She fell at his feet and said to him: "Hear, illustrious sir! Just by your matchless qualities one knows you to be a most exalted man, affectionate toward those who resort to you and superior in gallantry [1]). Therefore show me your self. My heart is yearning mightily for the sight of you". And when she had urged him time and again, Mūladeva laughed a little and removed the pill that changed his appearance. He entered his own state and was seen shining in splendor like the lord of day, bewildering all the people with his beauty like the god of love, having a body that abounded in the fresh bloom of youth and in beauty [2]). Devadattā again fell at his feet, the hairs on her body bristling on account of joy. And she said: "It is a great kindness". She anointed him with her own hands. They both bathed and feasted in great magnificence; she made him put on [3]) divine garments; they sat in exquisite conversation. And she said: "Illustrious sir, my heart has not yet

1) Or, "kindness".

2) Concerning the magic pill that changes the form see my Daçakumāracaritam p. 83; Tawney's Kathākoça pp. 110, 114; Tawney's Kathāsaritsāgara II, p. 302; Prabandhacintāmaṇi pp. 105, 106 (here also a story which is very similar to Lessing's tale of the three rings and its application in Nathan der Weise).

3) Paridhāpita > paribāviya > pahirāviya (by metathesis). Cp. the wellknown Vāṇārasī = Vārāṇasī. But I am not sure of the etymology.

been moved to love by any other man except by you". Hence the following saying is true:

"Who is not seen with the eyes? With whom is there no talk? But manhood [1]) that delights the heart, that is rare.

"Therefore, to oblige me, you must come here all the time". Mūladeva said: "O woman pleased with excellent qualities, attachment to people like me who come from another country and are penniless, is not a splendid thing and does not endure. As a rule, too, everybody's love is dependent only on serviceability. So it is said

"The birds leave a tree whose fruit is spent, the cranes a dried-up lake; bees leave a faded flower, the deer a burned wood.

"Courtesans leave a man without money, servants a fallen king. Everybody is pleased if his own affairs are being promoted. [In reality] no one is dear to another".

She said: "One's own country, or another country — that is no reason for noble men. And it is said:

"Although separated from the ocean, the moon dwells on the head of Hara. Whereever the excellent go, there they receive the highest honor [2]).

"Likewise it is thus: Also wealth is vain; of it the wise do not think highly, but to excellent qualities only are they attached. Furthermore:

1) "Manhood" is misleading, but the nearest approach to the original I could find for māṇussaṃ. It is exactly the German "Menschentum".

2) Lit., "they are carried on the head". Hara or Çiva wears the moon for a diadem. The moon's original home (or birth-place) is the ocean. Cp. also my Daçakumāracaritam p. 222 (note) and with that Pariçishṭaparvan VI, 146; Lamprechts Alexanderlied ed. Kinzel 2675.

"A good man's speech is worth a thousand pieces, the favors[1]) flowing from his love are [worth] a hundred thousand, his affection itself surpasses a crore.

"Therefore by all means comply with my request". He consented. A union between them that teemed with love was the result.

One day Devadattā danced before the king; Mūladeva sounded the tabor. The king was highly gratified with her. He granted her a boon. She laid it up in store. And Mūladeva was excessively addicted to gambling; not even his clothes remained. And with conciliating words she said to him in a pleasant voice: "Best beloved, as the image of the deer[2]) is the blemish of the moon of the full-moon-night, so is the vice of gambling of you [who are] the abode of all virtues. And it is a hoard of many evils. For thus it is:

"My beloved, do not be devoted to gambling, which taints the family, is an enemy of truth, causes the people who are to be respected shame and sorrow, is an impediment to virtue and destructive of one's property; which precludes[3]) liberality and enjoyment and withers son, wife, father, and mother, in which one knows neither god nor teacher; in which there is neither good work nor

1) Niryātita, "given as a present"; see PW² and cp. Pāli niyyātana, "gift".

2) The spots of the moon have to the Hindu fancy the semblance of a deer (or of a hare).

3) Lit., "is deprived of."

crime, which torments the body, and is the path to hell[1]).

"Therefore give it up by all means". And on account of his excessive passion Mūladeva could not avoid it.

And a great merchant's rich[2]) son, Ayala by name, who had an army of friends, was deeply in love with Devadattā. He gave her what she desired and furnished her dresses, ornaments, etc. And he bore Mūladeva a grudge and sought vulnerable points in him. For fear of him Mūladeva did not go to her house without an opportunity. And her mother said to Devadattā: "Daughter, give up Mūladeva. There is no use in this handsome fellow who has no money. This illustrious, liberal Ayala sends you time and again a great multitude of things. Therefore make *him* your own with your whole soul. Two swords do not find room in one scabbard[3]); nor does any one eat the gleaned ear of corn without salt[4]). Therefore give this

1) Or, "to low (imfortunate) reincarnations". Kugai includes both translations. The stanza needs no emendation. Only for marajju we have to write ma rajju, as Jacobi has done on p. 158. See Pischel's Materialien zur Kenntnis des Apabhraṃça Nos. 365, 2); 384; 385 (here maṃ = ma); 387; 388; 422 4); 442. Rajya (imperat) > rajju. For sosaṇa B has mosaṇa (= moshaṇa), "robbing", which is not as good from the literary point of view. Regarding kalaṁkaṇa, "tainting" see § 602. Paṇāsana = pranāçana; saṃtāvana = saṃtāpana; tasmin > tassiṃ > tasiṃ > tahiṃ (exacly so Apabhraṃça *putrasmin > puttassiṃ > puttasiṃ > puttahiṃ (puttahĩ). Cp. the genitive sg. putrasya > puttassa > puttasa > puttaha (and perhaps puttasa > puttasu > puttahu) and the gen. plur. *putrāsām > puttāhaṃ (puttāhā̃). See §§ 263, 363 ff.; 425.

2) § 595.

3) Prativāra (from vṛ, "to cover") > paḍiyāra. Cp. vivṛ, "to draw out of the scabbard". — Savvappaṇayāe = sarvārpaṇatayā?

4) Sila = çila, lit., "ear-gleaning", metaphorically > gleaned ears. But perhaps çila is originally a concrete word and the Skt. meaning a derived one. Cp. Pariçishṭaparvan II, 13: Tad etad khalvalavaṇakubhojananibhaṃ

gambler [1]) the slip". She said: "I am not exclusively devoted to money, mother; my attachment is only for excellent qualities". Her mother said: "What kind of excellent qualities has this gambler?" She said: "Truly he is made up entirely of excellent qualities. For:

"He is steadfast, of a noble heart, an ocean of kindness, clever in the arts, of pleasant speech, grateful, devoted to excellences, conversant with distinction.

"Therefore I shall not give him up". Thereupon the mother undertook to instruct her by many similes: "When one asks for lac, he offers [2]) some without juice; when one desires a piece of sugar cane, he offers crushed [and pressed cane]; when one begs for flowers, he offers merely the stalks". And being pressed [for an explanation] she said: "As is that, so is this your best beloved. And still you do not give him up". Devadattā thought: "She is foolish; therefore she gives such illustrations".

Thereupon she said to her mother one day: "Mother, ask Ayala for sugar cane". And she told him. He had a wagon loaded with it and sent it. Devadattā said: "Am I a she-elephant that so much sugar cane of such a kind together with the leaves and the branches [3]) is

mama. The salt which should make the morsel (Devadattā) palatable to the eater (the lover, Ayala) is love; without that even the beautiful *hetaira* palls upon the sense. On the other hand, the remark very likely is intended by the bawd to mean this: You cannot serve both lovers; and as for living with your dear Mūladeva, that is nonsense, since he lacks the salt of human life — money; without that even love is an insipid thing.

1) Dyūtakārika > jūyaāriya > jūyāriya. Cp. § 167.

2) Cp. Pāli paṇāmeti.

3) Ḍālā is not connected with dal as Bühler thinks (Pāiyalacchī sub voce), but = Skt. çālā, "branch, bough". Cp. Skt. çāka = Pali ḍāka, Prākrit ḍāya (Āyāraṃgasuttaṃ II, 1, 5, § 5).

sent?" She said: "Daughter he is generous, forsooth; therefore he sent it thus. And he thought: "She will [be able to] give of it also to others"". The next day Devadattā said to Māhavī: "Friend, say to Mūladeva: "Devadattā has a craving for sugar cane; therefore send me some"". She went and told him. And he took two stalks of sugar cane; cutting them up[1]) he made of them little blocks[2]) of two inches in size, sprinkled them with four spices[3]), perfumed them a little with camphor, split them a trifle from the bottom end[4]), took two new receptacles[5]), filled them [with the pieces of sugar cane], shut them[6]), and sent them. And Mahavī went and delivered them. And Devadattā showed them to her mother. And she said: "See the difference between men, mother. Therefore I am enamored of these excellent qualities".

1) Cp. nicchoḍejjā Uvāsagadasāo § 200 (p. 117, l. 2) and Skt. choṭayasi.

2) Gaṇḍiyā is not and cannot be p.p.p. "durchduftet" (Jacobi), but = gaṇḍikā, a word that frequently occurs in Pāli in the meaning "block", especially in the compound dhammagaṇḍikā, "the executioner's block, Richtblock". Jātaka I, pp. 150, 151; IV, p. 176; III, 41, l. 14; V, 303, l. 24 and stanza 45; II, 124; Vinaya Vol. II, p. 172 (block, bar, ledge; fillet); II, p. 110. Cp. Skt. gaṇḍi, "the trunk of a tree from the root to the beginning of the branches". Gaṇḍiyā, "block" we have in Daçavaikālikasūtra VII, 28; gaṇḍī, "block" in Āyāraṃgasuttaṃ II, 4, 2, § 11.

3) This rendering is conjectural. Cp. caturūshaṇa.

4) Mūlāhi is ablative sg. of mūla. The bottom end of a piece of sugar cane is called mūla, the top end prānta. Pariçishtaparvan VII, 120. Less probable is the translation: "Mixed with mūla (asperagus racemosus, or some other root or plant).

5) Jacobi's mallaga = Jasminum sambac does not fit. The word corresponds to Skt. mallaka (cp. mallikā) and is frequently employed also in Pāli. See Childers and Therīgāthā 423; Angutt.-Nik. III, 99, 3; Vinaya Vol. I, p. 48. It means "receptacle, vessel" (in our text most probably a box).

6) Ḍhakkai = Pāli thaketi, Skt. sthagayati, "to cover, close, shut". It is probably a denominative from p.p.p. ḍhakka (possibly, though, = *sthakyati). See § 221.

Her mother thought: "She is infatuated beyond measure; she will not give him up of her own accord. Therefore I shall employ some scheme, that also this lover goes to foreign parts. Then it will be well". Having reflected thus, she said to Ayala: "Announce before her a pretended departure of yours for another village. Afterwards, when Mūladeva has entered the house, you may come with a sufficient number of men and dishonor him, so that he, being dishonored, may leave the country. So you may stay united [1]). I shall give you notice". And he consented. The next day he did exactly so. He departed under the false pretence [2]) of going to another village. And Mūladeva entered. Ayala was notified by her mother; he came with a great multitude of men, and Devadattā saw him come in. And she said to Mūladeva: "Such is his opportunity; and my mother has accepted the money sent by him. Therefore stay below the couch for a moment in the meanwhile". And he stayed below the couch. He was noticed by Ayala. Ayala sat down on the couch. And he said to her: "Get everything ready for the bath". Devadattā said: "Yes. Therefore get up, put the dress on [3]), that you may be anointed". Ayala said: "Today I have had a

1) That is, you and Devadattā then may live in love's union indisturbed. Or does the expression mean: "Therefore act in unison" (ceshṭate)?

2) Anent miha = misha see § 263. The reading of B nibha has the same meaning. There is a second, although remoter possibility of derivation: miha = *mitha, "conflict, conflict with the truth, lie, sham, semblance. Cp. mithuyā and mithyā.

3) Jacobi's "entkleiden" for niyaṃsai I consider to be a blunder. Naturally the word means just the reverse. Probably it seemed to Jacobi that the context required his rendering. But Ayala hardly did bathe stark naked before the people although he was in a house of ill-fame (as we would say). He wore the dress that was customary during that

dream, that, even dressed and with anointed limbs, I ascended this couch and bathed on it. Therefore make my dream come true". Devadattā said: "Will not the costly cotton things, the pillow, etc., be ruined?" He said: "I shall give you others that are more exquisite". Her mother said: "So be it". Thereupon, sitting right there he was anointed, rubbed, and bathed with warm water for washing. By that Mūladeva, who was lying below, was drenched. The men with weapons in their hands entered. The mother gave Ayala a sign. He seized Mūladeva by the hair and said: "Ho there! now see if there is any one [who will be] a refuge for you". And when Mūladeva looked about him he saw that he was enclosed by men who had sharp swords in their hands. And he thought: "I cannot escape from them and I have to pay him back his hostility. Now I am without weapons; so there is no chance for a manly deed". And he said: "Do what you please". Ayala thought: "He is known by his appearance already to be some excellent man. And misfortunes are easily incurred by great men in the saṃsāra. And it is said:

"Who is here always happy? whose bright lot [1])

procedure, and a Skt. word for it is varāçi. Taṃ kumāraṃ snapayituṃ varāçiṃ paryadhāpayat. Pariçishtaparvan I, p. 186. With our poṭṭī cp. poṭṭa in Karpūramañjarī I, 27. Bear in mind also that nivasana denotes an *undergarment*, and Wilson's Vishṇu Purāṇa III, 139 declares: "A man must neither bathe, nor sleep, nor rinse his mouth, whilst naked".

1) "As the moon passes by many a cloud and sheds her loveliness on all of them, but remains with none, so is woman and her love". Thus declares Pushkin in his "Gypsies"; and the Hindus have a host of sayings in prose and poetry which all dwell on woman's fickleness in love.

The MSS. reading is latthī. Las means "to shine, frolic, appear", etc. A word lasti > latthi, signifying "brightness, joy, good fortune" would not be an impossibility. But cch and tth are confused numberless times

is constant love? whose is there no tripping? say, who is not crushed by fate?"

And he said to Mūladeva: "Hear! after you have fallen into such a state I'll let you go now. Do just so to me too when by the power of destiny I shall at some time get into misfortune".

Thereupon Mūladeva went out of the town, sad and sombre. "See how I have been outwitted by him!" Thinking thus he bathed in a beautiful pond and he formed a resolution. He thought: "Let us go to a foreign country. Having gone there I shall find some means to retaliate on him". He set out toward Beṇṇāyaḍa. Traveling along through the midst of villages, cities, etc., he came to the edge of a forest twelve yojanas in extent. And he thought: "If I find another one traveling along even as companion in conversation merely, I shall cut through this forest pleasantly". After a short time there came a Ḍhakka [1]) Brahman of distinguished

in the Jaina books. So Jacobi's emendation most probably is perfectly in order, and in all likelihood the translation, "Whose good luck is constant love" would be open to no objection. Possible, though less probable, is the following translation of the second pāda: "For whom does Good Fortune cherish an abiding love (lit., make love firm; enduring)". Thirāi might be = sthirāyayati, as vimhāi is = vismāyayati ZDMG 34, p. 277, l. 25. See § 558, and for pimma § 90.

1) Also Pischel takes ḍhakka as (closed, close-fisted) niggardly, stingy", and he connects it with ḍhakkai (§ 221). This etymology is very captivating, and still I consider it wrong. I think that ṭakka, ṭhakka and ḍhakka cannot be torn apart and that these words denote a kind of people (tribe). See my Kshemendra's Samayamātṛikā, note to III, 33 (p. 33). And now Prof. Zachariae kindly refers me to Kern in Indische Studien, Vol. 14, p. 396. I see that this great scholar anticipated my remarks on ṭhakka and kerāṭika by many, many years. Internal evidence also speaks against the usual opinion. From a literary point of view it would be a most awkward thing if our tale introduced the "Niggardly Brahman" and spoke of him constantly in the way this is being done.

appearance and goodly to look upon and provided with a box [1]) containing provisions for the journey. And Mūladeva asked him: "Ho, doctor, do you have far to go?" He said: "On the other side of the forest there is a place, Vīranihāṇa by name: to that I shall go. But whither are you bound?" The other said: "To Beṇṇāyaḍa". The doctor said: "Then come, let us go ahead". Thereupon both started to go. And traveling along they saw a fine lake at the time of midday. The Ḍhakka said: "Hear, let us rest a moment". They went to the lake and washed their hands and feet. Mūladeva went into the shade of a tree [2]) that stood on the bank. The Ḍhakka untied his box of provisions and took out barley meal in a bowl. This he moistened with water and fell to eating. Mūladeva thought: "That is just like the Brahman caste, whose principal characteristic is hunger [3]). So he will give me of it afterwards". But when the doctor had eaten, he tied his box and started to go. Mūladeva started after him, thinking: "He will surely give me something in the afternoon". Then too he ate just in the same way; gave him nothing. He traveled on in the hope: "He will give me something tomorrow". And while they strode on night came. Thereupon they stepped out of the road [4]) and went to sleep under a fig tree.

1) "Knapsack" for thaiyā (Jacobi) seems a little too far removed from sthagikā, "a box (for betel)". The word probably connects with sthag, "to shut" (a meaning of the root that is very common in Pāli and Prākrit).

2) Or, "shadow of trees".

3) Lit., "Just of such kind is the Brahman caste having hunger for its chief thing (preeminent feature)". — For ullei see § 111.

4) Nom. *vartmā > vaṭṭā, which then goes over to the feminines (vaṭṭā looks exactly like mālā). Cp. ūṇimā, Erz. p. 63, l. 25; tambimā (fem.) =

At break of day they set out again; at noon they halted after the same fashion. In the same way the Ḍhakka ate; gave him nothing. Nevertheless [1]) Mūladeva thought on the third day: "We have almost entirely cut through the forest. Therefore he will surely give me something". Meanwhile he did not even then give him anything. They came out of the wood. The roads of the two became separated. Thereupon the doctor said: "Sir, this is your road; but this is mine. Therefore do you travel by that. Mūladeva said: "Listen doctor! I have arrived by reason of your supernatural power. So Mūladeva is my name. If it come to pass that you sometime need me somehow [2]), then come to Beṇṇāyaḍa. And what is your name?" The Ḍhakka said: "Saddhaḍa; according to the nickname given me by the people Nigghiṇasamma [3]) is my name". Thereupon the doctor started out for his village, and Mūladeva toward Beṇṇāyaḍa.

On the way he saw a settlement. He entered there for alms. He wandered through the whole village, but got sour gruel, nothing else. He went toward a pond. At this juncture he saw a great ascetic with body dried up by penance, and of great dignity, enter in order

*tāmriman, Gauḍavaha 1140, and end of § 401. — Vaṭṭiya, "bowl", may be derived from vartika (vartikā) "rounded vessel", although this meaning is not found in Skt. Cp. vaṭṭasamugga C fol. 312*a*.

1) Jāva also means "indessen" (i. e. "da" and "dennoch", however). Cp. ZDMG. Vol. 42, p. 501, l. 30; 502, l. 21. With nicchinnā aḍavī and chijjai (l. 16) cp. Fick, Sagarasage p. 9, l. 12 bhanjanto thalaselavaṇe, which does not mean "vernichtend", but "durchschneidend, durquerend", possibly "ein Strombett brechend".

2) So if we are guided by Jacobi. But both the natural meaning of sijjhai and the Brahman's subsequent action rather point to: "If at any time any design of mine succeed (if I prosper) then, etc."

3) About equivalent to "Priest Pitiless".

to break a fast of one month. And when Mūladeva had seen him the hairs of his body bristled with joy and he thought: "Ah, fortunate and happy am I into whose range of sight this great ascetic has come at this time. Therefore at all events [1]) I shall prosper. And also:

> "As a wish-yielding tree in the desert, as a rain of gold in the house of a poor man, as a king of elephants in the elephants' stable [2]), so is this great-souled saint here".

And furthermore:

> "Purified by insight [3]) and knowledge; attentive to the five great vows [4]); steadfast; endowed with patience, gentleness, and uprightness; excelling on account of emancipation; delighting in study, meditation, and self-mortification; having a clear mind; possessed of the five samiti virtues; guarded in the threefold way; having no property; free from the attachments of the householder ...." [5]).

This monk is an excellent receptacle. Therefore:

> "One's property put as grain into such a receptacle which is a good field, and irrigated with the water of a pure disposition [6]), brings forth endless fruit here and in the next world".

1) Separate avassa from bhaviyavvaṃ.

2) Or, "the Caṇḍāla's house"? — Concerning mahappā see § 277.

3) Or perhaps rather "faith", one of the three "jewels" (which are knowledge, faith, life [Wandel]).

4) The five great vows together with their clauses are laid down in Ayāraṃgasuttaṃ II, 15, I, 1 ff. (p. 131 ff. in Jacobi's edition, translated in SBE. Vol. 22).

5) Or, "to the householder", a thing also forbidden to the Jaina monk. — The original also has neither subject nor predicate. It is a quotation torn out from some book.

6) My rendering of lesa is rather inadequate. But technical terms are

"So how should there be room for hesitating [1]) here? I shall give him this sour gruel. For this is an illiberal village, and this great-souled one after making a call [2]) in a few houses will turn back. But I shall wander through it two or three times; then I shall get something again. Another, a second village is near; so I shall offer him all this [sour gruel]". Thereupon he made a low obeisance and handed the holy man the sour gruel. And the monk, who was aware of his excellent state of soul and who knew the extreme purity of the thing offered and of everything connected with it [3]), said: "Man of pious character, give me a little". And he held out his bowl. And he gave the sour gruel, growing in perfection [4]). And he said:

"Blessed indeed are the men who have sour gruel when a monk breaks his fast".

hard to translate. The lesa are treated in Uttarajj. XXXIV. This fanciful doctrine of the Jainas almost looks like a queer perversion of the three guṇas of the Sāṅkhya philosophy. Two times three is six, and also all the other amplifications would accord well with the spirit displayed by Jinism in the adaptation of material taken over. Cp. also my book Kshemendras Samayamātṛika, p. XXI, note.

1) Ālociyā, German "Bedenken".

2) Darisāva, an interesting noun from the causat. darisāvei, "to cause to see" (cp. English to see = to visit, call on", and Skt. melāpa(ka), evidently a Prākritism and as such used especially by Jaina writers).

3) Something offered to a Jaina monk must be pure in regard to davva (dravya, substance, the thing itself); khetta (kshetra, place, the monk may not go beyond a certain limit in his begging tour); kāla (time, he must beg at a certain time of the day), and bhāva (disposition. tendency, aim of the giver). Rules for the monk are laid down, for instance, in the Kalpasūtra and in the Āyāraṃgasuttaṃ, both translated by Jacobi in the 22d volume of the Sacred Books of the East.

4) Or, "excellence, preeminence". There is no necessity for supplying anything. Thirty-four atiçaya are ascribed to the Arhats. These cannot be intended here.

At this point a deity traveling through the air [1]), devoted to holy ascetics, and pleased with the devotion of Mūladeva said; "Son Mūladeva, you have done a beautiful thing. Therefore ask by means of the last half of this stanza what you would like; that I may bring it all about". Mūladeva said:

"The courtesan Devadattā, a thousand elephants, and a kingdom".

The deity said: "Son, live free from anxious thought. Surely by the might of the holy ascetic's feet you will in a short time obtain it [all]". Mūladeva said: "Reverend lady, that is so". Thereupon, having worshipped the holy sage, he returned; but the sage went into the public garden. Mūladeva got other alms. He ate, set out toward Beṇṇāyaḍa, and arrived there in due course.

He went to sleep outside in the travelers' shed. And in the last watch of the night he had a dream: "The full-orbed moon in all her pure lustre entered my belly". Another one of the ragged beggars also had the very same dream, and he told the beggars. Then one of them said: "You will get today a very big cake rich with ghee and sugar". Mūladeva thought: "They do not know the real import of the dream", and said nothing. The beggar went for alms and received a cake, just as indicated, from the mistress of a house. And he was delighted and reported it to the beggars. But Mūladeva went to a garden. There he won the good will of the garland-maker [2]) by assisting him in picking flowers. He gave [Mūladeva] flowers and fruits. These he took,

1) Lit., "through the interval of the heaven".

2) The gardener, florist.

made himself clean, went to a scholar in the science of dreams, and made him a low obeisance. And he asked [the teacher of dream lore] for information about his welfare and health [1]). [And he gave him the flowers etc.] The interpreter of dreams too addressed him with great respect and asked him what he wanted. And Mūladeva joined his hands [2]) and told him the story of his dream. And the professor said with joy: "I will tell you the fruit of the dream in an auspicious hour: today meanwhile be my guest". Mūladeva agreed. He bathed and feasted in sumptuous fashion. And after the meal the professor said to him: "Son, I have [3]) a most splendid daughter here; therefore do you marry her from regard to me". Mūladeva said: "Father, why do you make a man your son-in-law whose family and character you do not know?" The professor said: "Son, by one's conduct already one's family, though untold, is known". And it is said:

> "Conduct declares the family, speech declares the country, fluttering flurry declares love, appearance [4]) declares what one eats".

"Likewise: [5])

> "Who produces fragrance in the lotus flower, and sweetness in the sugar cane, and graceful sport in fine elephants, and well-bread demeanor in those who have been born in noble families?

1) That is, he asked him: "How do you do".

2) The Dhātupāṭha contains the root jud, jut, "to bind". With that, I think, our joḍei connects. But the form of the root as given by the Dhātupāṭha is the Prākrit of *yut = yu, "to unite, to join". Cp. ci: cit; (dyu): dyut; (vṛ): vṛit.

3) Lit., "I have got". But cp. Appendix.

4) Or, "the body". 5) Or, "Thus it is".

"Or rather:

"If there be excellent qualities, what of family then! The man of excellent qualities indeed has no concern with family. A stainless family is even a grievous stain for those who are destitute of good qualities".

By such and similar speeches he made him consent and marry [her] in an auspicious hour. And he told him the fruit of the dream: "Within seven days you will be king". And hearing this he became joyful in mind. And he stayed there in pleasant ease. And on the fifth day he went outside of the city and sat down in the shade of a Campaka tree.

Now the king in that city had died sonless. Then the five divine things [1]) were deputed. After roaming about in the middle of the city, they went out; they came to Mūladeva. He was seen in the shade that did not shift [2]). Having seen him the elephant trumpeted, the steed neighed, the golden pitcher sprinkled him, the chowries fanned him, and the parasol stood over him. Thereupon the people uttered cries of "Hail, Hail!" The elephant lifted him on its back; he was brought into the city and installed by the ministers of state and the vassals. And a deity in the expanse of the

1) "The five insignia of royalty" (Jacobi) is hardly correct. For with the Jainas too these are: Sword, parasol, crown, shoes, chowries. Aupapātikasūtra § 19, 54. But here (as in Hemacandra's story of king Nanda referred to already) we have: Elephant, steed, golden pitcher, chowries, parasol. Cp. note 3) p. 131 and add. F. A. Steel, Tales of the Punjab p. 131.

2) In regard to this phenomenon, which also has European parallels, compare Lalitavistara ed. Lefmann pp. 132, 134; Raghuvaṃça XII, 21; Tawney's Prabandhacintāmaṇi p. 161; Haberlandt, Der indische Geist p. 38; Divyāvadāna (ed. Cowell & Neil) p. 391; Alabaster, Wheel of the Law p. 118.

heavens said: "Hear! hear! this is a most mighty king, Vikramarāja by name, who is a perfect master of all arts and whose body is inhabited by a divinity [1]). Therefore I shall not forgive him who abides not in his commandments". Thereupon the whole train, the vassals, the counsellors, the family priests, and other men, became submissive [2]) to his rule. And thereafter he lived enjoying brilliant pleasures of the senses. He entered into intercourse with Viyāradhavala, the lord of Ujjeṇī; most intimate mutual friendship sprang up forthwith [3]).

Now, when Devadattā had seen such an insult to Mūladeva she was extremely disaffected toward Ayala. Thereupon she upbraided Ayala: "Sir, I am a prostitute, but I am not your legal wife [4]). Nevertheless you demean yourself that way when you stay in my house. Therefore do not trouble [5]) yourself about me anymore". Having spoken thus she went into the presence of the king. And she fell down at his feet and said to him: "Do me a favor in virtue of that boon [which you granted me formerly and which I forbore to ask then, reserving it for a future occasion]". The king said: "Speak; the

1) The *sang froid* shown by the Jainas in using celebrated names of Hindu history and current tales for their own purposes is simply wonderful. Their fancy shrinks back from nothing in the way of transforming the material they appropriate. So it is not at all surprising that the Salomon and Harun al Rashid of Indian storyland, King Vikrama, the thirty-two tales of whose throne also were favorites with the Jainas, is dealt with in the manner of our narrative. Cp. Prabandhacintāmaṇi (Tawney) p. 2 ff.

2) Vihea = vidheya.

3) Put the comma (or a period) before jāva.

4) Literally, "family-house wife", a woman of good family, married to a man and bound to be faithful to him; about the same as kulavadhū, kulāṅganā, "a respectable woman, a virtuous wife".

5) Khidyati > khijjai; from this present stem our gerundiv.

favor to you is done already. What else are you going to say?" Devadattā said: "Then, O lord, no other man save Mūladeva is to be forced on me [1]). This Ayala must be forbidden to come to my house". The king said: "Very well; as it pleases you. But, tell me, what now is this business?" Thereupon it was told by Māhavī. The king became incensed against Ayala. And he said: "What! this city has these two jewels; and these he ill-treats [2]) shamefully!" Thereupon Ayala was summoned, beaten and thus spoken to: "Sirrah, are you king here that you demean yourself in such a way? Therefore look about for protection now! I'll make you lose your life". Devadattā said: "Lord, why should you kill this Pariah? [3]) Therefore let him go". The king said: "Sirrah, in accordance with the words of this most illustrious lady you are now released; but expiation [of the crime] will come about only through his being brought here" [4]). Then he fell at his feet and went out of the king's court. He set about to search for him in all directions and still he found him not. Thereupon on account of

1) Lit., "mir anzubefehlen".

2) There is nothing wrong in khalīkarei (for which Jacobi would substitute khilīkarei). — Concerning the high esteem in which the courtesan was held in Ancient India, see the Introduction to my Daçakumāracaritam p. 46 sqq. and my Kshemendra's Samayamātrika pp. IX sqq.

3) Pratiskabdha = pratitstabdha. "Stabdha" means "stiff". So paḍikhadda = made a "stiff", killed? Following the Skt. meaning of pratiskabh we would have to translate: "What of checking (punishing) such a Caṇḍāla!" i. e. he is even beneath your interference with him. *Çunakapāca > suṇahapāya, "one who cooks (and eats) dogs, a Pariah".

4) Lit., "purification". Jacobi offers "volständige Verzeihung", which suits neither the context, nor the usual sense of the word very well. The king has in *no* way forgiven Ayala's misdeed. He is in the monarch's eyes a punishable criminal till he produces Mūladeva.

this very deficiency[1]) he loaded ships with goods and sailed for Persia.

Now Mūladeva sent a letter and presents to Devadattā and to this king. And he said to the king: "I cherish a great attachment to this Devadattā: so, if she likes, or you please, then do me a favor; send her!" Thereupon the king said to the royal doorkeepers: "Hear, what is this? Have such words been caused to be written by Vikramarāja? Is there any difference between me and him? His is even this whole kingdom; how much more Devadattā. Let her only desire it". Thereupon Devadattā was called. The affair was stated. "Therefore, if you please, go to him". She said: "Your most gracious command is the wish of my heart[2]) after I have been granted permission by you". Thereupon being honored with great riches, she was sent and went. And Mūladeva conducted her into the city with great pomp. And it became mutually one realm for them. Mūladeva lived together with her, enjoying the pleasures of the senses, engrossed with making and worshipping temples and images of the Jinas.

Now that Ayala having made much money in Persia and having loaded a ship with magnificent goods, came to Beṇṇāyaḍa; and he lodged outside [of the city]. He asked the people: "By what name is the king here called?" They told him: "By the name of Vikramarāja". Thereupon he filled a dish with coins, gold, and

1) *Uniman, nom. ūnimā becomes a feminine ūṇimā and means "the state of one who is deprived of something, who is deficient, inferior, weaker, incapable (perhaps also, sickened, depressed, dem etwas fehlt)".

2) Lit., "your great favor is conducive to —, productive of desire, becomes a desire with me who am permitted by you"

pearls[1]) and went to see the king. The king had a seat given to him. He sat down and was recognized [by Mūladeva]; but Ayala did not know him. The king asked: "Whence has the great merchant come?"[2]) He said: "From Persia". On being honored by the king Ayala said: "Lord, send an overseer[3]) to inspect my goods". Then the king said: "I come *myself*". Then the king went together with the appraiser and was shown the wares in the ships, consisting of conches, betel nuts, sandal wood, aloe, Bengal madder etc. And the king asked in the presence of the appraiser: "Hear great merchant, is it just so much?" He said: "Your Majesty, it is just so much". The king said: "Give the great merchant half, but weigh in my presence". The appraiser weighed the goods in the bale[4]). By means of the weight, of kicks, and of piercing with an instrument for this purpose most precious wares were discovered, that were put inside the madder etc. The king had the bales opened[5]), and when they were thoroughly examined, there was

1) Or, "with wrought gold, unwrought gold and pearls". See Hoernle's Uvāsagadasāo II, p. 12, note 22; Uttarajjh. p. 296 (comm. to IX, 46).

2) Read seṭṭhī with the MSS. and cp. p. 36, l. 2 of Erz.

3) With uvarima cp. Skt. paçcima, agrima; Pāli puratthima, heṭṭhima; Prākrit purumilla (Gaudavaha 1093), i. e. purima > puruma + illa, and see § 602.

4) Or, "in the bundle". This meaning is clear from the context. There is a root cul, "to raise"; so perhaps culya > colla "heap", etc. Or maybe the word means "bag, sack". If so, the derivation might be colya > colla, from cola, "cloth". For merchants hiding spoons of gold in sacks of madder, cp. Prabandhacintāmaṇi p. 105. Concerning pañakula see ib. p. 18. Perhaps the best rendering of pancaula would have been "officer of the finances".

As to colla, cp. also nicola, "case, bag", dealt with in the note to stanza 212 of Agaḍadatta, and Appendix.

5) The connection points to this meaning of ukkhellāviya. Connected with the root kil, "to throw, ut + kil to throw open"?

seen in one place gold, in another silver[1]), in another goods of great value consisting of gems, pearls, corals etc. And having seen that, he was indignant and gave command to his men: "Zounds! bind this manifest thief". And he was bound by them, while his heart went pitapat[2]). And having given him over to the guards, the king went into his palace.

And he was led by the chief of the guards into the king's presence. And when the king saw him firmly bound he said: "Release him! release him!" He was released by the others. The king asked him: "Do you know me"; He said: "Who should not know the great princes of men who are famed over the whole earth?" The king said: "Enough of speaking civilities! Tell me frankly, do you know me?" Ayala said: "Your majesty, I do not quite know you". Thereupon the king had Devadattā called; she came like a peerless Apsaras, wearing ornaments on all her limbs[3]). Ayala knew her. He was very much ashamed in his heart. And she said: "Hear! this is that Mūladeva to whom you said that time: "May you do me also a service some day when by the dispensation of fate I have got into misfortune". So this is the opportunity. And now the king, who is so tender to humble and afflicted people, has released you, although you have incurred danger of property and life". When he had heard this he was abashed in his mind, and saying: "It is great grace", he fell at the feet

1) Ruppa may also represent rukman (§ 277). If that should be meant here, it would be the same as hiranya, "wrought gold" (or, gold coin).

2) Cp. dhagaddhagiti, Pariçishṭaparvan XI, 156.

3) See the gorgeous description of the Apsarases in Aupapātikas. § 38.

of the king and of Devadattā. And he said: "So let the lord forgive me that disdainful oppression which I, Rāhulike, inflicted on your majesty at that time, you who cause all the people peaceful bliss, who shine in all the arts, and who are of stainless nature, thus resembling the full moon[1]). In his anger at the trouble inflicted on you the great king does not grant me entrance into Ujjeṇī". Mūladeva said: "I have already forgiven you to whom the queen has shown her favor". Thereupon he again fell at the feet of the two out of supreme respect. And Devadattā had him bathed and clad in most costly raiment; the king bestowed gifts on him[2]). He was sent to Ujjeṇī. At the request of king Mūladeva Viyāradhavala pardoned him.

Nigghiṇasamma too came to Beṇṇāyaḍa when he heard that Mūladeva was established in regal power. And he saw the king. And in homage to the "invisible" the king gave that very village[3]). Having made a low obeisance and declared: "It is a great kindness", he went to the village.

Now that beggar heard: "Mūladeva too has dreamed just such a dream as I. But by virtue of complete absorption in the idea he has become king". He thought:

1) The epithets have a double bearing. Therefore nisesakalāsohiya as referring to the moon means "shining with all her digits".

2) Or perhaps better, "remitted the duty" (erliess ihm die Abgabe). Dān has that meaning in the modern vernacular. In line 14 kareha seṭṭhissa addhadāṇam = fix half of the duty for the merchant (make him pay only half of the duty?).

3) He made Nigghiṇasamma lord of the village in which Nigghiṇasamma lived. — Adrishṭa, "the invisible", in Skt. means: "virtue or vice as the eventual cause of pleasure or pain". Jacobi says: "adiṭṭha = dharma", "das Gute".

"I shall go where there is milk and, having drunk that, I shall sleep, so that I may dream that dream again". Maybe he dreamed it: but there is no light to be got from man [1]).

1) This arch remark is a rare bit of choice humor. It may mean so much. Taken by itself the dictum: "Na manusāo vibhāsā", "there is no light to be obtained from man", embodies a grand and profound thought.

> Nor any light
> Shall any gazer see with mortal eyes,
> Or any searcher know by human mind;
> Veil after veil will lift, still there must be
> Veil upon veil behind.
>
> Sir Edwin Arnold's "Light of Asia".

Less probable, I think, is the rendering: "He may even (perhaps) dream it". With api cp. the German "auch" in such sentences.

Vibhāsā would be the same in Skt.

MAṆḌIYA.

MAṆḌIYA[1]).

In the city of Beṇṇāyaḍa a tailor, Maṇḍiya by name, was addicted to taking other men's property. And declaring among the people: "I have a bad disease [2]) he was always besmeared with moist salve in the region of the knee, tied a bandage around [3]), and thus lived on his tailor's art in the king's highway. And also when he walked, he walked some way or other with wearisome effort, his foot being supported by means of a staff. And at night he dug a hole in the walls of houses and took a multitude of things. — Near the city, in a part of the garden, there was an underground dwelling — there he deposited them. And there lived his sister, a maiden. In the middle of that underground dwelling there was a well. And every accomplice whom

1) The Sanskrit version is found in Uttarajjh. p. 190. Tuṇṇāya I have connected with tunnavāya. But Jacobi's "beggar" is probably right.

2) Read with the MSS. gaḍa = gada. If we accepted Jacobi's emendation we would have to translate: "I have a bad boil (tumor)". According to the dīpikā he even claimed that he had a number of them. It reads: pādayor me gaṇḍānīti vadan. Uttarajjh. p. 190, l. 7. There is just a bare possibility that gaḍa derives from gaḍ to run (used of liquids). That would amount to: "I have a bad running sore".

3) Lit., "cloth for a wound (a sore)". Read with AB: jāṇudese niccam eva addāvalevalitto. Jacobi's text would mean: "Declaring among the people by means of the region of his knee always besmeared with moist salve: "I have a bad tumor", and having a bandage tied about it, he lived, etc." Or, "Declaring among the people: "I have a bad boil" and being, by means of his knee always besmeared with moist salve, a man who has a bandage tied about". Both ideas would be a little strange.

that thief enticed by means of money and brought there as carrier of [stolen] goods, his sister bade sit down on a seat placed there previously near the pit; and taking hold of his feet under the pretext[1]) of washing them she hurled him into that well. Thereupon he perished. Thus the time went by while the tailor robbed the town. The thief-catchers could not catch him. Thereupon there arose much clamor in the city. And Mūladeva was king there, who had become such in the manner already mentioned. And the affair of the burglar was told him by the citizens as follows: "It is a long time that some burglar has been stealing here in the city. And nobody can catch him. Therefore employ some means". Then he appointed another chief of the city guards; he too could not catch the thief. Then Mūladeva himself went out during the night, having put on[2]) dark-colored habiliments[3]). While Mūladeva, not being known[4]), lay down and remained in a shed this thief Maṇḍiya came and said: "Who stays here?" Mūladeva said: "I, a beggar". He said: "Come I will make you a man". Mūladeva got up. A hole was bored [by the thief] into the house of a rich man. The thief brought out a multitude of valuable things and laid them on Mūladeva. They started for the outskirts of the city. Mūladeva went before, the thief behind with sword

1) Lit., "under color".

2) Prāvṛiṇāmi (nā-class for nu-class) > pāvuṇāmi > pāuṇāmi. See §§ 502—505 and E. Müller, The Pali Language p. 105.

3) Of course, the dark-colored dress of Hindu thieves and other people who prowl about at night is used for the same reason as the green suit of hunters (which is customary also in India). Raghuvaṃça IX, 51).

4) § 548.

drawn. They came to the underground dwelling. The thief began to bury these valuables. And he said to his sister: "Wash the feet of this guest". She bade him sit down on the seat put down near the brink of the well. She took hold of his foot under the pretence of washing it and thought: "I'll push him into the well". Since his feet were extremely delicate, she knew: "This is some man who formerly enjoyed kingly power; his limbs are weakly"[1]). Pity arose in her. Thereupon she made a sign to him at his feet: "Fly!" "Do not let yourself be killed". After that he fled. She made an outcry: "He has fled! he has fled!" Maṇḍiya drew his sword and followed[2]) on the road. Mūladeva, seeing that he was extremely near to him on the king's highway, hid behind a linga of Çiva on the square. The thief thought: "This is the man", cleft that linga of Çiva in twain with his sword, that was shaped like a heron's beak[3]), returned, and went into the underground dwelling. Having stayed there over night he went outside from there at the break of day. In the middle of the market

1) Vihaliya from vihalei = vihvalayati. See §§ 206, 332 and cp. āheṇa = āhvayana; paheṇa = prahvayana (Ayāraṃgasuttam II, 1, 4 § 1).

2) Olagga = avalagna, "hanging to, clinging to". He stuck to him on the road (er heftete sich an seine Fersen).

3) I translate according to Jacobi. Cp. Pariçishtaparvan VI, 204:

Cirasaṃgopitaṃ kaṅka —
mayīm ādāya kartrikām
pracchannām dhārayāmāsa
sa jighaṃsur Udāyinam.

In VI, 216 Hemacandra calls the same weapon kaṅkakartrikā, which is more intelligible. Also kaṅkamaya may perhaps mean "made like a heron (i. e. like a heron's beak)", but as we find also kaṅkalohamayakhaḍga (for instance, in Uttarajjh. p. 194, l. 4) the correct rendering would rather seem to be "made of kaṅka-iron". Still there is a possibility that this kind of iron owes its origin to the difficulty presented by kaṅkamaya.

place he worked at his tailor's trade. The king had him called by his men. He thought: "That man clearly was not killed, and surely it must be the king". He was brought by the men. The king rose in greeting, honored him, bade him sit down on a seat, addressed many pleasant words to him, and then said: "Give me your sister to wife". He gave her and she was married by the king. And the king gave him objects of enjoyment. When a few days had elapsed the king said to Maṇḍiya: "I need money". He gave him a heap of money. He was honored by the king. On another day he was asked again; and again he gave. And the king paid this thief exceeding honor and respect. After this fashion he made him give[1]) everything [that he had taken]. The king asked his sister. She declared: "That is all his wealth". Thereupon having caused all that wealth to be given [back to the rightful owners] in conformity with a list previously communicated, he had Maṇḍiya impaled.

1) An interesting causative with double-paya, i. e. *dapayati > davei; *dapāpayati > davāvei. — With this story compare Devendra N. Dass, Sketches of Hindoo Life (London 1887) pp. 151—53.

AGALADATTA.

AGALADATTA [1].

King Jiyasattu in Ujjeṇī had a charioteer, Amoharaha by name; his wife was Jasamatī. She had a son, Agaladatta by name. And when he was still in his childhood, his father passed away. And one day he questioned his mother who was continually weeping [2]. At his pressing request she declared as follows: "This charioteer Amohapahāri has stepped into the dignity that belonged to your father. Seeing such a painful thing before my very eyes and that you have not acquired the sciences, I am exceedingly grieved". He said: "Is there anyone who will teach me?" She said: "There is a friend of your father's in Kosambī, Daḍhappāhari by name". He went to Kosambī. He saw Daḍhappāhari, a teacher who was an expert in archery [3], with the sword, and in

1) See Uttarajjh. pp. 182—184 and cp. Jātaka Nr. 163. Both this prose version and the metrical form of the tale (Erz. pp. 68 sqq.) have been translated into Italian by Ambrogio Ballini (Agaḍadatta, Firenze 1903), My own translation was finished long before I received Ballini's booklet. But in the notes I added his interpretation of several passages.

2) Read royamāṇiṃ. The dīpikā also is in favor of this emendation. It tells us: So abhīkshṇaṃ rudatīṃ mātaraṃ dṛishṭvā pṛicchati: Mātar, vāraṃ vāraṃ kiṃ rodishi?

3) Īsattha is neither ishvastra (Leumann, Jacobi), nor ishuçāstra (Pischel §§ 117, 148), but = *ishvastrya. In Pāli we have issattho = ishvastra (one who has the arrow for his weapon, archer), which is = issāsa (also in mahissāso, "great archer", Theragāthā 1210). Issattho occurs in Milindap. pp. 250, 305. 418, 49. From that with the suffix ya we get issatthaṃ, "archery". Anguttara-Nik. Vol. III, p. 225.

traveling by chariot. By him he was perfected, as if he had been his own son, in archery, in throwing the disc against the enemy's disc, in the use of engine missiles, and in other accomplishments.

When he had mastered the sciences he went one day with the permission of his teacher to the court of the king in order to show his proficiency. And there he exhibited everything just as he had been taught, how to hold the sword and the shield, and other acquirements. The hearts of all the people were ravished. The king said: "This is nothing wonderful'" And he was not surprised at all. And he said: "What, what shall I give you? [1]). He answered respectfully: "Lord, if you do not give me your approbation, what is the use of another gift?"

At this very place and time the king was requested by his subjects in the city: "In the city of the beloved of the gods [2]) breaking into houses has not been heard of before. And now carrying away of valuable things and theft is being commited by some one. Therefore indeed may the beloved of the gods deign to guard the city". Thereupon the chief of the city guards was commanded by the king: "Do you bring it about that they are caught within seven days". Hearing this, Agaladatta reckoned: "This is a chance for me to go", and respectfully spoke to the king as follows: "Within seven days I shall bring them to your feet, O lord". And the king agreed to these words and gave him permission, saying: "Do so".

Thereupon he departed from the king's court with

1) Or perhaps, "How now? What shall I give you?"
2) Plur. majestatis. The king is meant. Cp. § 111.

glad and rejoicing heart. And he reflected as follows: "Bad men and thieves prowl about in dramshops and other such places, concealed by various dresses and signs [of other professions]. Therefore I shall explore these places myself and by means of spies". Having had them explored, he went out of the city, and when he had hastened out, he sat down and remained in a place under a mango tree of cool shade, clad in ragged and dirty garments, pondering on a means of catching the thief. And presently a religious mendicant who was muttering and mumbling something approached the shade of this very mango tree. He broke off young shoots and branches of the mango tree and sat down [on them]. And Agaladatta saw that he had firm calves and long legs[1]. And having seen him he suspected in his mind: "The signs betray the evildoer. Surely he is the thief". And the religious mendicant said to him: "Child, from where do you roam about and for what reason?" Thereupon he answered: "Reverend sir, I wandered out of Ujjeṇī as my property is wasted away". He said: "Son, I shall give you much precious wealth". Agaladatta said: "You have shown me a kindness". And thus the sun became invisible; the evening twilight passed away. He pulled out a sword from his three staves and girded up his loins. Having risen he said: "Let us go to the city". Thereupon Agaladatta followed him with suspicion, and thought: "This is that thief." They entered the city.

1) Uvvaddha is rather = udbaddha. Udvṛiddha would in the natural course of events develop to uvvaḍḍha. Cp. § 291. But it is not impossible that Skt. udbaddha owes its origin to a wrong translation from Prākrit. Some derivatives of vṛidh have the dental in Prākrit. Udbadha, "tied up, compressed, compact", however, is not unnatural.

And there was the house of some one which was worth looking at with wide open eyes and indicative of a wealth of complete excellence [1]). And there the religious mendicant made a breach in the form of a sirivaccha [2]) and went in. He brought out baskets filled with many wares. And having stationed him there he left. Agaladatta thought: "I shall sift the thing to the bottom [3]). And forthwith the religious mendicant came from the temple of a Yaksha, bringing poor men of his own [4]). And these he bade take the baskets and all hurry out of the city.

And the religious mendicant said: "Son, here in the dilapidated park, let us indulge in the recreation of sleep for a short hour, till the night passes. Thereupon we will go". Thereupon Agaladatta said: "Father, let us do so". Then these men put the baskets down and they fell fast asleep. And that religious mendicant and Agaladatta, having spread their beds, lay there feigning sleep. And Agaladatta softly got up, slipped away, and

1) Taking puṇṇa = pūrṇa. Or, "indicative of the splendor of extraordinary religious merit" (i. e., showing that this man had in a previous existence performed splendid good works of an extraordinary kind). Or, "exhibiting a splendor that was the natural result of superior pious deeds done in a former existence".

2) The picture of one is to be seen in Schlagintweit's Indien in Wort und Bild II, p. 105. Burglars seem to have made holes of this auspicious shape often, and according to Skt. lexicographers çrīvatsa designates also a hole of particular form made through a wall by a housebreaker. Naturally thieves and robbers cherish all kinds of superstitions in India, the Eldorado of superstitions. Like other criminals, also among us, they are frequently of a religious turn of mind. Cp. Crooke, Popular Religion and Folk Lore of Northern India p. 342; Pariçishṭaparvan II, 173 (thieves carry twig of crow's nest, "which opens locks and holds houses spellbound"; they also use particular spells etc. for these purposes).

3) Lit., "follow the thing to the end" (see what comes of it).

4) Svakīya + illa + ka > saīa + ellaya > saiellaya. Cp. §§ 595, 119, 79 sqq.

stood concealed by a tree[1]). When the religious mendicant knew that these men had fallen fast asleep he killed them, slaying them with calm assurance. And not seeing Agaladatta on his bed of leaves, he began to search for him. And Agaladatta, whose body was hidden by the branches, smote him with his sword in the region of the shoulders while he searched for him and came toward him; and he fell sorely wounded. And when consciousness had returned he said to Agaladatta: "Child, take this sword; go to the place back of the cemetery. Having gone there make a sound at the side of the wall of Santijjā's temple[2]). There my sister lives in an underground dwelling; show her the sword. And she will become your wife, and you will be lord of all the riches there. I, for my part, am sorely wounded and my life is passed". And Agaladatta went, taking the sword with him. And he saw her in that temple like[3]) the goddess dwelling in the temple[4]). And

1) Or, "by trees".

2) Santijjāghara can hardly have the meaning attributed to it by Jacobi. The long ā would remain unexplainable, and I do not like to change to santijjaghara. Monier-Williams' dictionary contains the name of a goddess Çāntivā, which could become Santiya > Santiyya > Santijjā. Or the word may have been Santiyā from the beginning. It would seem to denote some genius of peace, bliss, prosperity. Cp. çānti and Çānti. Or is it a deity for averting evil omens?

3) Lit., "saw her [looming] from that temple to behold like" etc. (anzuschauen wie).

4) She looked as if she had been that goddess; so beautiful was she. This seems to be the most natural way of taking the passage. But maybe we have to translate: "beautiful to behold like a Bhavaṇavāsi goddess" (as suggested by Jacobi). The Bhavavāsin are: Asura-, Nāga-, Suparṇa-, Vidyut-, Agni-, Dvīpa-, Udadhi-, Vāta-, and Stanitakumāra, or: Asura Genii, Serpent Genii, Garuḍa Genii, Genii of the Lightning, Genii of the Fire, Genii of the Islands, Genii of the Ocean, Genii of the Wind, and Genii of Thunder.

she said: "From where are you?" Agaladatta showed the sword. And her face and her heart were dejected; but she hid her grief and conducted him with zealous hurry into the temple of Santijjā. She offered him a seat; Agaladatta sat down. Suspicious, he watched her doings. And she prepared the couch with extreme care. And she said: "Take a rest here". Thereupon he did not yield to the lassitude of sleep; but when her thoughts were distracted [1]) [by something else] he went to another place and stood there concealed. And above the couch a stone had previously been made ready; she caused it to fall, and the bed was smashed. And she said with glad and gleeful heart: "Ah, I have killed the slayer of my brother!" And Agaladatta rushed forth from there, seized her by the hair, and said: "Ah, daughter of a slave wench, who could kill me?" Thereupon she fell at his feet, saying: "I have come for protection". He comforted her with the words. "Do not fear" [2]). And he took her and went to the king's court. He was honored by the king and by the subjects in the city, and enjoyable things fell to his lot.

Thus good fortune falls to the lot of others, too, who are earnest.

1) Vikhittacittāe is loc. sg. fem. (= vikshiptacittāyām).
2) §§ 501, 213, 263. Vīhei = bīhei.

AGAḌADATTA.

AGAḌADATTA [1].

1. There is in the world a most famous city, Sankhapura by name, abounding in excellences. And in that city there lived a king who caused his people joy; Sundara was his name.

2. He had a peerless wife, Sulasā by name, the first lady of his harem, equal to him in descent and beauty, creating delights of the eye for all the people.

3. From her womb there was born a son, Agaḍadatta by name. Growing day by day he reached the most beautiful bloom of youth [2]. And of what kind was he?

4. Void of virtue, thrift, and pity, not impressed [3] with the words of his superiors, a speaker of untruth, eager for amorous dalliance with the wives of others, without scruple, intoxicated with pride.

5. Liquor he drank, in gambling he delighted, meat and honey he ate [4]; surrounded by bands of actors and swarms of strumpets he strolled about in the middle of the city.

1) A Skt. version is found in the Uttarajjh., pp. 184—189. A metrical translation I have given in my book Kāvyasaṃgraha. Metrische Übersetzungen aus indischen und andern Sprachen. (Leipzig 1903).

2) Or, "growing most beautifully he reached the age of puberty".

3) Lit., "left by". But C reads guruviṇaya "devoid of modesty to his gurus", which is better.

4) A most impressive discourse stating why liquor should not be drunk, nor meat, honey, etc. eaten, we have in Hemacandra's Yogaçāstra III, 8 sqq. (ZDMG. 28, pp. 201 sqq.). Cp. Amitagati's Subhā-shitasaṃdoha XX—XXII (ZDMG. 61 p. 112 ff.).

6. One day the best people of the city announced this affair to the king: "Sovereign of men, unbecoming things have been done by the prince in the city".

7. When the king had heard the words of the towns-people, his eyes waxed red with violent wrath, his head grew terrible with a very marked contraction of the brows [1]), and thus he began to speak:

8. "Hark ye! tell the prince: "Quickly abandon my realm and go elsewhere, and do not say a word that you are not told.""

9. When the prince learned of the matter he left his own pleasant city, and with his sword for his only companion he set forth, his anger being increased by mighty pride.

10. Traversing mountains, rivers, forests, cities, stations of cowherds, and a multitude of villages [2]), far away from his own city, he came to the city of Benares.

11. Companionless he rambled about in the middle of the city, through three-cornered places, squares etc., filled with anger in his heart, like the elephant that has been lost from the herd.

12. And while the king's son thereupon wandered about in the streets of the city he saw a man of knowledge, who was accompanied by many young men.

And what was he like?

1) The Skt. lexicographers give "terrible" as a meaning of bhāsura. That would fit well here. ZDMG. 34, pp. 274, l. 2 contains a similar phrase: bhiuḍibhāsuraṃ vayaṇam kāūṇa, having made his face terrible with a frown". The usual meaning "shining" (clearly marked) would do too in our stanza.

2) Or perhaps better: "and a multitude of cities, stations of cowherds, and villages".

13-14. Clever in the sciences, in arms, and in the arts [1]), wise, knowing the feelings of the heart, very profound, devoted to the service of others, full of compassion, endowed with excellences of form, Pavaṇacaṇḍa by name; but fierce as the wind [2]) was he for his opponents in disputation, not for his pupils. The sciences of chariot, horse, and elephant he taught there the sons of kings [3]).

15. Into his presence went Agaḍadatta, made a low obeisance to his feet, and sat down. "From whence come you, fair sir?" Pavaṇacaṇḍa then accosted him.

16. Having gone aside [with him], the prince told Pavaṇacaṇḍa his story, how he had departed from Sankhapura.

17. Thereupon Caṇḍa [4]) said to him: "Stay here, learning the arts; but do not divulge your secret to any one, O slender youth".

18. The teacher rose, arrived at his own house together with the king's son, and said to his wife [5]): "This is my brother's son".

19. When he had caused the excellent prince to be bathed, and had given him precious garments and ornaments, Pavaṇacaṇḍa said these words to him at the close of the meal: [6])

20. "House, money, train of servants, carriages, and

1) Or, "in the matter of the sciences?" Or, "missile, sword, and arts?"

2) This is the meaning of the name of Pavaṇacaṇḍa.

3) Or, "he taught the son's of the king there".

4) A kind of "Koseform" for the long form Pavaṇacaṇḍa. Either the first or the second part of a compound proper noun was used that way. Cp. Jātaka N°. 257.

5) Mahilā, from mah, "to be glad, to frolic". Cp. vilāsinī.

6) In regard to iṇaṃ see § 431.

horses etc. — everything that belongs to me[1]) is at your disposal. Enjoy yourself as your heart desires, O prince".

21. Thus he remained in this man's house, delighted in mind, abandoning his cruel intentions, studying all the arts.

22. Having his heart pervaded with deep humility toward his teacher, a joy to the souls of all the people, he grasped the seventy-two arts in a short time.

23. In this wise this excellent prince, who had acquired the arts, tarried in the garden of the house every day, engaged in strenuous application, utterly absorbed in that matter.

24. Near the garden there was a chief merchant's house, charming with its windows, high, extremely extensive.

25. There abode the merchant's lovely daughter, Mayaṇamanjarī by name. Ascending the top of the house she daily saw the prince.

26. Now she, falling in love with him, looked at him incessantly and threw flowers, fruits, leaves, and little clods[2]), musing on something[3]).

27. Although the maid indeed had slipped into his heart, the prince regarded her not, in his passion for the arts, from fear of his superiors[4]), and on account of his eagerness for the acquisition of learning.

28. One day, intent on the acquisition of the arts, he

1) Santa (= Skt. sant) + ika > santika > santiya.

2) § 304.

3) Or, "thinking a little, somewhat meditavely".

4) But probably plur. majest. (honoris causa); and so translate: "from fear of his teacher".

was hit with a bunch of açoka blossoms by the girl, whose heart was distressed by the violent onslaught of Love [1]).

29. And on this day the prince looked closely at the maid, who hid her slender body amid the young branches of the açoka and was bewildered with fluttering flurry. And he thought:

30. "See! [2]) is this a woman of the gods? or may she be a Nāga girl? or is this Kamalā? or is it Sarasvatī in visible form?

31. But I'll rather ask her for what purpose she stays there". Having reflected thus in his heart, the prince said to her aloud:

32. "Who are you, matchless maiden? why do you show yourself only a little? why do you perturb me who am intent on the acquisition of learning, O slender one?"

33. Having heard the words of the prince, she said, her eyes opening wide, her face laughing, and a radiating brightness gleaming from her teeth: [3])

34. "I am the daughter of Bandhudatta, the principal merchant of the city, Mayaṇamanjarī by name, and married right here in the city" [4]).

1) Gurupasara of the MSS. (also of C) [prasara "free course"] should be retained.

2) According to Jacobi's vocabulary uaha is = uyāhu (cp. Pāli udāhu), "or". I cannot see how that is possible. Why not uaha 2d plur. imperat., which is so frequently found in Prākrit? Cp. Pischel § 471.

3) Lit. "having a row of rays of the teeth that manifests itself". Payaḍanta cannot be passive, but represents prakaṭanta, Skt. prakaṭat. Rāvaṇavaha, 8, 90 offers the same form, and 10, 44 paaḍanti. Goldschmidt wrongly derives from prakaṭayati. Prakaṭayanti may become paaḍaanti > paaḍanti. But the sense in the passages quoted is not that of the causative.

4) She has been married at an early age, in keeping with the Hindu custom, and remains in her father's house until she has grown up and matrimony is consummated.

35. "Since that day when I saw you[1]), beautiful one, who are like the god with the flowery bow, the tree of sorrow has grown up in my heart.

"For:

36. "Even sleep has fled from my eyes, the fever in my body has only increased, even food is distasteful to me, there is a violent pain in my head.

37. "So long only one is happy as nobody becomes dear to him. He who is attached to a dear one has delivered himself over to sorrow.

38. "A wretched being, impelled by certain deeds done in a former life, and desirous of happiness, falls in love with a person hard to obtain.

39. "Therefore if you do not engage with me in loving intercourse, which ravishes the hearts of young women, there will be murder on your soul[2]); for evidently I cannot live"[3]).

40. Having heard the words of this damsel, he reflected in his heart: "Clearly she will die, as her body is burning with the great fire of love.

41. "In the çastras Mahābhārata and Rāmāyaṇa we are told this distinctly that there are clearly ten amorous states for people in love.

1) Lit., "Since which day thou hast been seen, since that day etc."

2) Lit., "there will be an own murder for you". Read hohī with the MSS. Vajjhā is not uncommon in Prākrit [see, for instance, ZDMG. 34, p. 259, st. 5 of the Kālakācārya-kathānakam; Avaçyaka-Erzählungen p. 43, below the text the sixt line; Setubandha I, 16, where the scholiast is wrong].

3) The student of Ancient Hindu life knows that in love-affairs the woman, and not the man, is the active and aggressive party. She makes the first advances and she in the end goes to the lover's house, if in any way possible, in order to enjoy with him the consummation of amorous bliss. Cp. Th. Krabbes, Die Frau im altfranzös. Karls-Epos p. 20 ff.

42. "The first produces anxious thought; in the second one yearns for the bliss of union; in the third long-drawn, hot sighs arise.

43. "The fourth produces fever; in the fifth state the body burns: in the sixth stage food is disagreeable to the person in love.

44. "In the seventh there is fainting; in the eighth state madness sets in; danger of life there is for one who has reached the ninth state.

45. "The lover who enters the tenth state is inevitably deprived of life [1]). So in separation from me this girl will be exposed even to danger of life" [2]).

46. When the royal prince, who was well versed in the emotions, had meditated in his heart, he addressed that young maiden in a love-abounding manner, with sweet words:

47. "Beautiful one, know that I am the first son — Agaḍadatta by name — of king Sundara, whose actions are beautiful and whose fame is far-spread.

48. Having come here to a teacher of the arts in order to acquire the arts; I shall take you with me on the day when I go and return home [3]).

49. Speaking thus in many a manner, with the greatest difficulty he made the deer-eyed girl, whose body was thorned with the multitude of love's darts, compose herself.

1) Concerning the ten stages of "love in separation" see R. Schmidt, Beiträge zur indischen Erotik (Leipzig 1902) pp. 124 ff. Death on account of "love in separation" is also a medieval conception. Wolfram's Parzifal XIII, 359—867; and esp. 489 ff.; Hartmann's Iwein 1546—1556.

2) Saṃsayaṃ kāhī lit means: "she will bring about danger (or doubt) of life".

3) Lit., "On which day I shall return home on *that* I shall go taking [you] with me". Tae = *take, i. e. loc. from pronominal stem ta + ka. C's reading pavasissaṃ "when I depart" is more natural.

50. That son of a king whose heart was enamored of her excellences and beauty, thereupon when he had arrived in his house meditated a means for their union.

51. On the next day that royal scion came along the street on his road[1]), mounted on a steed. Then there arose a hubbub in the city.

And also:

52. Has the ocean broken out?[2]) or is a terrible fire blazing? or has the enemy's army arrived? or has a lightning-bolt fallen?

53-54. At this point the prince suddenly with an astonished mind saw a mad elephant in rut who had felled the strong post to which he had been tied, who had been left by his keeper, and who was killing all who came within reach of his trunk, and who moved hither, enraged without cause, like the god of death.

55. With the rope that bound his foot torn in pieces, smashing houses, marked-stalls, and temples, infuriated in a moment, that elephant came before the prince.

56. When the people of the city saw the prince who possessed such a beautiful form, they cried with a loud voice: "Run away! run away from the path of the elephant!"

57. But the prince left his own steed and walking along with most dexterous gait he called the prince of elephants, who was like Indra's prince of elephants.

58. When the elephant, from whom there flowed[3]) a stream of ichor juice, heard the voice of the prince he

1) Or less probably, "on the path of the street".
2) Or, as Jacobi would have it, "become perturbed".
3) § 325.

quickly rushed forward, infuriated against the prince, like the god of death.

59. And the prince with joyful soul rolled up [1]) his upper garment and threw it down before the trunk of the on-rushing elephant.

60. Panting [2]) with rage the elephant gave it many a thrust [3]). But the prince hit the animal on the region of the back with hard blows of the fist.

61. Thereupon, panting with fury, it rushed and ran and shook and stumbled and tried to strike with its tusks and whirled about in a circle.

62. After he had sported with that fine elephant for an exceedingly long time and had rendered it submissive to his will, he forthwith mounted its back.

63. Now the most excellent prince of men, together with the ladies of his harem, looked on this sport with the elephant, which ravished the hearts of all the people.

64-65. Seeing the prince on the back of the elephant like the lord of the gods, that king asked the company of his servants: "Who is this boy, this treasure of excellences, in splendor the sun and likewise in lovely gentleness the lord of the night [4]), accomplished in all

1) § 107. Cp. Pāli saṃvelli in expressions like the following daḷhaṃ katvā saṃvelliṃ = kacchaṃ bandhitvā, "having rolled up his garment, having taken up the end of the garment and tucked it into the girdle", Jātaka V, p. 306, stanza 56; saṃvelliyaṃ nivāseti, "to wear the under-garment rolled up". Vinaya Vol. II, p. 137. Buddhaghosha explains the latter passage: mallakammakārādayo viya kacchaṃ bandhitvā nivāseti. Skt. vellita also means "bent, curved".

2) Dhamadhamenta presents dhamati with reduplication of the whole present stem.

3) Chobha = kshobha (just as chubhai, chuhai, chūḍha from kshubh).

4) Or, as we would say, "the queen of the night". But the moon is masculine in the Hindu languages.

the arts and sciences, eloquent, heroic, and handsome?"

66. Thereupon one of them said: "In the house of the teacher of the arts, O lord of men, there[1]) I have seen him engaged in strenuous application to the arts".

67. Then the delighted ruler of men asked that teacher of the arts: "Who is this excellent man, who is extremely clever in the excellent science of elephants?"[2]).

68. When the teacher of the arts had asked for safety he told the story of the prince with its details to the ruler of men, who was attended by many people.

69. Having heard this, the king, who experienced great satisfaction in his heart, despatched his door-keeper: "Bring the prince into my presence".

70. And sitting[3]) on the elephant's back he was then accosted by the door-keeper: "The lord of men summons you; come to the king's court, O prince".

71. In accordance with the king's behest the prince thereupon fastened the elephant to the post and came into the king's presence with a heart full of misgivings.

72. Before he had made a low obeisance by placing his knees, hands, and head on the ground in deep humility, he was embraced by the king.

73. Extremely honored with betel, a seat, respect, presents and honor, and in other ways[4]), the prince sat down with serene soul at the side of the king.

1) § 293.
2) Or, "in the science to master excellent elephants".
3) Pariṭṭhiyao = *parishṭhitakaḥ.
4) Or, "most extraordinarily honored with the honor of the tributes of respect consisting in betel and a seat and with other [marks of distinction]".

Thereupon the king thought: "This is one of the noblest of men. For:

74. "Modesty is the root of manliness; the root of success determination; virtue is the root of blessings; pride the root of ruin.

"And another saying:

75. "Who paints the peacock so bright? who imparts [1]) their gait to the royal swans? who fragrance to the lotus flowers and modesty to those who are born in noble families?

"And also:

76. "The ears of rice bend with their weight, on account of their water the clouds, the tops of the trees with their burdens of fruit, and by reason of their modesty noble men; but not from fear of anybody".

77-78. Thereupon the prince was asked for intelligence of his welfare [2]) by the king, who was delighted with

1) Lit., "produces". The haṃsagati (gait of the swan") is typical of gracefulness and the Hindus are fond of comparing the way in which beautiful women move or walk to the movement of the swan. Probably they think after all, more of the bird's majestic gliding on the water and not of its wabbling way of walking, although this is the prevailing interpretation. Gati may mean both. Still I am not perfectly sure that the translation I gave in my Kāvyasaṃgraha p. 82 ("das stolze Zieh'n") is the only legitimate one. Parallels from European writers correspond to the "stolze Ziehn". So, for instance, Pushkin, Poltawa, 1st Canto:

Ея движенья
То лебедя пустынныхъ водъ
Напоминаютъ плавный ходъ.

But the modern Finnish poet Eino Leino would seem to voice a slightly different notion. In his Tarina suuresta tammesta (Borgå, Werner Söderström, p. 31) we read:

Neiet joutsenena souten joutui.

"Swanlike rocking thither came the maidens". And in Finnish popular poetry the maiden walks like a duck, e. g. Kanteletar[3] II, 233.

2) "Asked how he fared, how he was doing". Pauttio, the plural, implies all the different details.

his modesty, and also questioned in detail with regard to his acquirement of the sciences; and when he from shame did not reveal the acquisition of his own accomplishments, then the teacher said: "Lord, he is proficient in everything".

But great king:

79. "Those who are of noble character are ashamed when their own great splendor is being extolled; but the others are beside themselves [1]) even if they are falsely praised".

80. And while thus that king's mind was enraptured [2]) with the behaviour of the prince, there came all the people of the city to the king.

81. Fine jewels and garments, fragrant flowers, together with fruits were put down before the king by the city community, that had incurred disgrace [3]).

82. This present [4]) of the townspeople was handed over by the king to the prince. Then falling at the king's feet they began to make their petition.

It was as follows:

83. "Your majesty, this city of yours, that boasts an abundance of riches surpassing the wealth of Kuvera's town, has become a thief's house within a few days.

1) Lit., "do not find room in their own bodies" (from vanity).

2) Khitta, literally "thrown", means "distracted, transported" (with joy etc.), rather than "astonished" (Jacobi). Cp. vikhitta in Erz. p. 68, l. 17.

3) The disgrace of being robbed by a thief is meant.

4) Kosalla might perfectly well be = kauçalya, "prosperity, cleverness", considering the necessity and good effect of a present in the Orient. But probably the word represents kauçalya in the sense of "going along with the kuçalam" (or kuçalī), the respectful greeting. Or perhaps, kosa (= koça, sheath, covering. envelope) + alla (§ 595 in fine), i. e., something covered up, wrapped up. Cp. Pāli paṇṇākāra in Childers.

84. "The city, O chief of men, is being robbed by some wicked burglar, who is clever in digging holes [into houses]. Protect us now. What [need] of many words?"

85. With harsh words the king said to the chief of the guards of the excellent town: "Heigh, sirrah! even while you look on, the whole town is being robbed!"

86. Then he pleaded: "Your majesty, it is many days that we have watched for the thief. Nevertheless he has not yet been seen anywhere".

87. At this juncture the king was requested by prince Agaḍadatta: "Sovereign, give me orders; I shall find the robber of the city quickly.

88. "If within seven days I do not find the thief of the city, I shall burn my own body in the flames [1]) of flaming fire".

89. When the ruler of men had heard these words of the prince together with his promise, he gave him permission and said: "May your desire be fulfilled".

90. Then having taken that vow and having made a low obeisance to the king he wandered about in the city without anxiety, watching the haunts of the thieves.

That is to say: [2])

91-92. In the houses of prostitutes, in taprooms, in gambling places, and in the stalls of the bakers; in the sheds of the parks where one can get water to drink, in the huts of ascetics, in empty temples, on the

1) Lit., "flame-rows".

2) Avi ya exactly corresponds to the German idiom "und zwar", both here and between stanzas 51 and 52 (where I have translated rather awkwardly "and also").

squares, in the market quadrangles[1]) in the bazaars of the market, the prince strolled about all alone, watching the movements of the thieves.

93. Then, when the sixth day had passed and the thief had not been seen, on the seventh day the prince was exceedingly seized with anxious thoughts.

94. "Shall I wander to a foreign country? or shall I go to my father, taking that deer-eyed damsel with me? Or shall I betake myself to the wildwood?

95. "But it is not becoming for men who have sprung from a taintless family that something they have promised with their tongues should turn out otherwise. For:

96. "Let their heads be cut off, let there be bondage for them, let prosperity depart altogether, let happen what will happen, if excellent men keep what they have promised[2]).

97. "Not indeed the wearing of dead men's bones as a badge is the "great vow"; to keep what one has promised, that is the great vow of strong-minded men"[3]).

98. Thus fostering many doubting thoughts in his own mind, this prince got outside of the city at the time of the afternoon.

99-100. Under[4]) a mango tree that was dense with

1) Formed by the booths on all four sides. 2) Cp. Kathākoça p. 179.

3) Naraṭṭhi = nara + asthi. Muddā = mudrā is used the same way in Skt. The "man's-bone-badge", we know, is the great pride of the Pācupata ascetics, whom our tale exhibits in a very unfavorable light. The religious vows they observe they call the "great vows", and hence they are termed mahāvratika or mahāvratin, "people of the great vow". Neyaṃ = Skt. na + etad.

4) Lit., "in that which is below"; loc. sg. of neuter adj. heṭṭha + ka. See § 107.

a multitude of fine shoots, and cast a cool shade and abounded in towering, mighty boughs, he was sitting, his body exhausted[1]) with the burden of anxious thoughts, and was looking about in all directions like a Vidyādhara who is deprived of his magic.

101-102. At this juncture suddenly a wandering ascetic arrived whose costume consisted of a red garment[2]) and who wore a sheaf of hair on his bald head by way of a crown-tuft. Provided with three staves, a water-pot, and a chowrie, holding also a rosary[3]) and mur-

1) Suḍhiya (which occurs as vario lectio a number of times also in Hāla; see Index sub suḍia) has by Goldschmidt been wrongly derived from a supposed root suṭh. Pāli sodheti points to the Prākṛit root suḍh. This Pāli verb occurs in Theragāthā 149, and the comm. translates it by bādheti. heṭhayati. Does it represent a samprasāraṇa form *sudh = svadh, from which we would have to derive Skt. svadhiti? Goldschmidt assumes a root sudh in his Setubandha. But this is a second mistake. The root of the forms given by him as coming from that hypothetical sudh is in reality the same as Skt. çumbh, çubh, from which we have so many forms in Pāli; for instance, āsumbhati, "to hurl, to throw" Jāt. III, 435, l. 21 (varia lectio khipi); nisumbhati, "to trample under foot, to dash to the ground, to kill, Therīgāthā 302 (Skt. niçumbhati); parisumbhati, "to strike" (= paharati), Jāt. III, 347, stanza 49; VI, 376, l. 18; saṃsumbhati, "to roll" (vaṭṭeti) Jāt. VI, 88, stanza 355; sumbhati, "to strike" (= paharati, poṭheti), Jāt. III, p. 185, st. 51; VI, p. 549, st. 2161.

2) Lit., "ruddle garment". The red robe of the Brahman ascetics is often spoken of in the Jaina books. Aupapātikas. § 86; Bhagavatī p. 255; and on account of their dress they are nicknamed "ruddles" (geruya) and termed rattapaḍa, "they of the red cloth". Leumann in ZDMG. 48, pp. 65, 56.

3) Gaṇayatrī > gaṇettī + ka, "Zählerin". Muṇḍiyasirakuccasaccūla literally means: "crowntufted by means of a bunch on his shaven head". Cūḍā denotes a single lock of hair left on the crown of the shaven head, and muṇḍiya is extremely common, also in Jaina books, with reference to the bald head of those who have renounced the world. The tuft of hair on the shaven head tallies exactly with the descriptions of the Brahman monk that are so frequently encountered in Hindu literature. Kūrca > kucca denotes a bundle, especially a bundle of grass or straw. Evidently the ascetic had an immense shock of hair on his crown; therefore I translate by "sheaf". Kucca could even be taken as "a bunch of

muring and mumbling something or other, he came in front of the prince.

103. His staff-like arms resembled the trunk of an elephant, spacious was his chest, shaggy his hair; he was endowed with the fresh bloom of youth, fierce, red-eyed, and long-legged.

104. Now having gazed on him steadfastly, the prince, full of suspicion, thought in his heart: "On account of such an appearance this must clearly be the thief"[1]).

105. At this point he said to the prince with pleasant words: "From where are you, excellent man, and for what reason do you stay here?"

106. Having found out his real condition, the prince, who had a clever intellect[2]), declared: "Overcome by poverty I wander about in the city with an empty heart".

107. "Do not sorrow, my son. Today I will do away with your poverty. I will give you the riches you desire". So said the wandering ascetic.

108. The prince prated: "By the grace of your feet my poverty will vanish and will the matter desired by me be accomplished".

109. While they talked thus the lord of day, leaving

sacred kuça grass which the man wore on his head. Cp. Kshemendra's Kalāvilāsa I, 67 ff. But the epithet pharusakesa in the next stanza militates against this view. — The compound could also be taken as a dvandva — "whose head and beard were shaven (shorn) and who wore a crowntuft". But I doubt that muṇḍito could be used of the beard, although the dīpikā supports this view. It reads muṇḍitaçiraḥkūrcas. Jacobi seems to be of the commentator's opinion.

1) Aha of course, is = Skt. atha.

2) Lit., "clever as to his intellect" (or perhaps, "in his judgment", or "in his designs").

the range of the eyes, disappeared as a good man from fear of a sin.

110-111. When the glow of the evening twilight had gone and the mass of night's darkness became manifest, the ascetic drew a sword of frightful aspect out of the scabbard, started with quick steps, and said to the prince: "Follow me[1]), in order that I may accomplish every purpose you have in view. What [need] of many words".

112. And straightway the two came quickly into the middle[2]) of the city and after roaming about a little sat down in a certain place.

113. And forthwith the wandering ascetics scratched [the outlines of] a breach on a rich merchant's towering palace, on a part of the wall that was easily broken through.

114. When a breach in the wall had been made he dug out with a very sharp tool an extremely well concealed hole, which resembled a sirivaccha and which made it easy to get in and out.

115. Having looked in attentively for a long time, the rogue entered [the house] with gentle steps and dragged out right there most precious goods, many baskets full.

116. Stationing the prince there he fetched poor men from a temple[3]) and made them take these [baskets]; and out of the city they went forthwith.

1) Lit, "come to my back".

2) Majjhayāra most probably is = madhyakāra.

3) Wayfarers and beggars frequently had to sleep in temples. Cp. Kuṭṭanīmatam 223 and my note to 221 in my translation of Dāmodaragupta's work. — Tāo in the following is most probably fem. plur., less likely abl. sg. (connecting with nayarāo).

Then the prince reflected:

117. "Shall I draw my sword and slay the miscreant here by a trick. But to slay by trick becomes not us who have been born in noble families.

118. "Going to his dwelling I shall see how much property he has stolen, for the sake of which he continually robs this host of townspeople".

119. Thus these two, having taken their plunder and departed from the peerless town, arrived in the park of the city, fatigued by their heavy burdens.

120. The religious mendicant said to the prince, in order to kill him by a trick: "Noble man, the night is long; [1]) let us rest here in the park".

121. The prince agreeing, they sat down there in the park, [saying]: "Yes, let us enjoy a nap", but both of them suspicious in their hearts.

122. In a moment they both feigned sleep, one to the right, the other to the left at the foot of a tree [2]), each intent on killing the other.

123. The men who had served as carriers [3]) all went to sleep with confident minds, but the prince rose from his bed [of leaves and twigs] and softly slipped away.

124. Taking his sword in his hand he stood at the foot of another great tree vigilently watching that man's doings.

125-126. Seeing that they slept the thief killed these

1) Or "the gloom of the night is intense". — Chalaghātamaraṇa lit., killing by a tricky stroke".

2) Lit., both had fallen asleep in a false sleep to the right and to the left of a tree's root.

3) Vāhitra + ika > vāhitrika > vāhittiya ("ein Mann der Trage"). — For uṭṭhettā cp. Erz. p. 42 l. 3 (uṭṭhehi); p. 69, l. 28 (uṭṭheuṃ), and § 582.

men, and while he looked there for the prince, not seeing him on his bed, the prince called the miscreant, drew his sword, and struck him about[1]) the shanks, free from fear and endowed with terrible strength.

127. By one stroke his two shanks dropped down; like a tree cut by the disc he was felled precipitately to the ground.

128. Unable to walk and having only a remnant of life left[2]), he said to him: "I was that far-famed thief, Bhuyaṃgana by name.

129. "So, too, there is here in the cemetry a dwelling in the interior of the earth. There lives my sister, a young girl, Vīramaī by name.

130. "Go to the foot of the fig tree and call her, that she may quickly open the door of the underground dwelling.

131. "Having married her, fair sir, take the *whole* heap of riches. Live there in ease and pleasure, or go to a settlement [of men].

132. While he was talking thus, the prince spoke words of comfort to him for a moment. He then took the thief's sword and came to the grounds of the dead.

133. Having gone there he made a sound at the foot of the fig tree for that young damsel; and she came and opened the door of the house.

134. Looking intently on the beautiful form of the girl for a long time, he was astonished immediately and he thought in his own heart: "She is the very essence of love".

1) Lit., "in the vicinity of" (German, Beingegend).

2) I. e., "on the point of dying". Less likely would be the rendering: "having only life left" (not strength etc.).

135. And he was questioned by her: "Fair sir, from where and for what purpose have you come?" He told her what had happened. When she had heard it she was anguished in her heart[1]).

136. Speaking sweet words she conducted the prince into the underworld palace. With great respect she offered him a splendid seat there.

137. In *loving* wise she said to him: "I and this flood of vast riches, everything is at your disposal. Fair sir, amuse yourself as you like".

138. Showing him the sleeping apartment she said: "Rest here on the couch; I, on the other hand, will go and fetch ointment for you".

139. Speaking thus she immediately went out of the sleeping chamber. But the prince then thought in his heart of the science of prudent policy.

140. "Trickery, untruth, greed, silliness, rashness, impurity, and cruelty[2]) likewise are the inborn faults of women.

1) Dūmei is a denom. from *dūman, du just as ṇūmei, ṇūmai from *nūman (Prākrit ṇūma). See Weber, Hāla 91. In Skt. we have doman; but dūman is very natural, as the most common forms of the verb are dūyate etc. Cp. § 540. Pahamma = vivara, çvabhra I range under the same head, setting it down = *prakhanman. Setubandha IX, 43.

2) Nissaṃsayā does not mean "Niederträchtigkeit" (Jacobi), but "cruelty" (the usual signification of nṛiçaṃsatā). In Uttarajjh. XXXIV, 22 we find nissaṃso, which the commentator correctly explains in the following manner: yo nṛiçaṃso bhavati nistrimçah jīvaṃ hiṃsan yo manāg api çaṅkāṃ na karoti sa nṛiçaṃsa ityucyate. Our stanza recurs in Uhle's Vetālapaṃcaviṃçati p. 14, ll. 28—28 (cp. Böhtlingk, Ind. Sprüche [2] 328):

Anṛitam, sāhasaṃ, māyā,
mūrkhatvam, atilobhatā,
açaucaṃ, nirdayatvaṃ ca
strīṇāṃ doshāḥ svabhāvajāḥ.

Nissaṃsayā is here translated by nirdayatva, "pitilessness".

"And another saying:

141-142. "Women are not won over by ardent love, not by learning and not by excellent qualities, not by modesty and not by pride, and not by a hundred thousand caresses, and neither by harsh nor by tender words, not by power, not by bloom of youth. Hard to win over is the heart of women. Ponder this carefully [1]).

1) The reading of the MSS. should not be tampered with. So I reject Jacobi's corrections. Upon the whole, I acknowledge neither metrical considerations, nor the rules of the grammarians as a warrant for altering readings of such excellent MSS. as those used by Jacobi. He has been unfortunate a number of times in changing the readings of the MSS. of our tales. The same is true of Fick in his edition of the Jinistic Sagara myth. From the very nature of their works the grammarians cannot be supposed to give every possible form. And if Pāli stanzas often are metrically faulty (and everybody knows that they are), why should Apabhraṃça verses always be correct?

For gheppahiṃ (gheppahĩ) see §§ 453, 456 and the paragraphs in the index sub gheppai. Susiṇeha (i. e. su + sneha) may well form an instrumental susiṇehiṃ. The two vowels i and e (and u and o) apparently were not clearly and distinctly separated in their Klangfarbe. The same is to be said of these vowels in English. So siṇehiṃ = siṇeheṃ is not to be suspected; and even Pischel the Pitiless sanctions it, for in his Materialien zur Kenntnis des Apabhraṃça, N°. 358 he admits nicchaĩ (nicchaiṃ) = niççayena. Cāduya = cāṭuka; khara = kshara. Vihavi = vihaviṃ, vihaveṃ, vihavẽ seems permissible too. The anunāsika and the anusvāra are in Prākrit added and dropped with the greatest facility. Durgṛihya > duggihya > dugiyha > dugijjha > dugejjha. Mahilahiṃ may be taken as loc. sg., "the heart in woman". But in the masculine a-stems we have Apabhraṃça *putrāsām > puttāhā̃ > puttahā̃, and in AMg. the genitive pl. fem. tāsim. So perhaps a genitive plur. fem. *mahilāsām > mahilāsiṃ > mahilāhiṃ > mahilahiṃ would not be an impossibility. I think that similar genitives plur. are also found in AMg. When we encounter bhūehiṃ sataṃ in Āyāraṃgasuttaṃ I, 3, 1 § 2, stanza 1, the only natural explanation appears to be: *bhūtesham > bhūesiṃ > bhuehiṃ. We expect the genitive plur. in our stanza. — Cintahiṃ I take = cintahi (2d sg. imperat.). Cintahi = cintehi represents an ordinary phenomenon in Apabhraṃça (Cp. stanza 307 in our poem). If we do not want to depart from the rules of the grammarians cintahiṃ (cintahĩ) would either be 3d pl. indicative, or 3d pl. imperat. There is no sense in the former here; the latter would require the translation:

"Therefore:

143. "The man deluded by love, who is filled with affection for the bevy of young women falls into a sea of trouble that is hard to cross, — there is no doubt of that".

"They (i. e. people) should ponder on it carefully". The 3d singular in the sense of the German "man" is very common in Skt.; the plural is also used. But with the imperative the second sg. is the rule. [C has the imperative 2d pl. cintaha āyariṇa, = cintahu]. — Vijjaiṃ and lajjaiṃ do not seem so monstrous to me. The change of the final e to i would be natural enough and is of frequent occurrence in Māhārāshṭrī. For a genitive which ends in i cp. the second stanza in Pischel's Materialien zur Kenntnis des Apabhramça. About the addition of the anusvāra I have spoken already. Concerning Māhārāshṭrī forms terminating with āiṃ cp. ZDMG. 33, p. 450. An interesting case is the following stanza of the Vikramorvaçīyam:

Jalahara saṃhara ehu! Kopaï ādhattao
aviraladhārāsāradisāmuhākantao
e maï puhavi bhamante. Jai pia pekhīhimi
tavve jaṃ ju karīhisi taṃ tu sahīhimi.

I translate: "Wolke, lass das! Das Angesicht der Weltgegenden mit dichten Gussregenschauern überziehend, ist sie in Zorn verfallen. (zum Zorn entschlossen, bereit) wider mich, o weh (or, following Pischel's ē, wider mich hier), der ich die Erde durchschweife. Wenn ich die Geliebte sehe, so werde ich ertragen was immer du mir auch thun magst". The MSS. have the readings kopai, kopaiṃ, kopaï, and all these variants seem to be substantially correct and to stand for Skt. kopake = kope. The sudden change from the second person to the third in the address to the cloud is very good as portraying the king's wandering mind. The king is a poor wanderer now; so the cloud can afford to treat him shamefully. It will be seen at a glance that my interpretation is based solely on the text which we have in the MSS. Pischel has to make changes in order to arrive at his rendering. Even if we accepted one of his emendations (one that he himself does not consider necessary), viz. āḍhantao for āḍhattao, we ought to translate: "Wer *billigt*, dass du" etc. (cp. the king's words between stanzas 3 and 4 of the 5th act. in Pandits second edition p. 114). "I, the king, do not allow it". Āḍhai as a synonym of parijāṇai, "to acknowledge", occurs often in the Jaina books. The most literal rendering is German "annehmen". Jai may also mean "ob". That would give the rendering: "der ich die Erde durchirre, ob ich nicht meine Geliebte wiedersehe. Dann etc.

144. And having meditated thus, that prince left the couch and crouched down in another place, putting an effigy of himself[1]) there [on the couch].

145. And the stone that was placed above the couch by means of a mechanical contrivance suddenly was let loose by her and dropped upon the bed.

146. Thinking that he had been crushed the wicked woman said with joyful heart "Slayer of my brother, do you now feel it in your heart?"

147. Having heard these words the prince rushed forth and upon her[2]); seizing her by her mass of hair he said words such as these to her:

148. "Ah, wicked woman, who could kill me by the power of his intellect? How should he who watches over another's house sleep in his own?"[3])

1) Paḍirūva, "Gegenbild", some effigy which resembled him (or, resembled a man). In a thief's lair you may expect to find such things, since they were used by the fraternity. Cp. Jātaka N°. 61 and especially Temple, Legends of the Panjāb I, p. 20. — Lukka is perhaps = *mlukna, from mluc, "to settle (crouch down)".

2) Āhutta I take to be = *ābhukta (bhuj, bhujáti), "bent, turned toward". — Pahāsai = pabhāsai (so C) in 146.

3) That is, how should he who watches in the interest of others neglect his own welfare! See my note on p. 220 of Kāvyasaṃgraha. Pavolini's and Ballini's explanation of this crux is a failure. I have followed Jacobi's emendation in my rendering. But also here the MSS. are in all probability correct, Chaṭṭhī is equivalent to Skt. shashṭhī. Shashṭhī is the technical term for the sixth night (or day) after the birth of a child. It is the most important night in a mortal's life according to the Hindu view. For then the Creator enters the mother's chamber and writes the child's destiny on its forehead. See Monier-Williams, Sub shashṭhī; Crooke, Popular Religion and Folklore of Northern India, p. 165; Bose, The Hindus as they are, p. 25. In that night female friends of the mother came to keep with her the shashṭhīprajāgara, "the Wake of the Sixth Night", as we read, for instance, in Kshemendra's Samayamāṭrikā VIII, 119. In the writings of the Jainas the Wake of the Sixth Night is mentioned frequently as being of the greatest importance. So Aupapātikasūtra § 107; Āyāraṃgasuttaṃ II, 12, 1 (p. 117); Nirayāvaliās.

149. And taking that young girl along, the prince went out of that dwelling in the earth; though previously in love, [now] entirely cured of love by her extremely cruel doings.

150. And going to the king he related what had happened in the night. "I have killed the thief with my sword and brought his sister here".

151. That very same underworld house he showed to the prince of men on the next day; the ruler of men made over that wealth left behind to the people of the town.

152-153. The delighted lord of men gave the prince his own daughter in marriage, whose name was Kamalasenā and who was like Kamalā, beloved of all the people; gave him a thousand excellent villages, a hundred kings of elephants, vast treasures, a lakh of soldiers on foot, and ten thousand steeds.

154. He who thus had won renown and was a full moon to the hearts and eyes of the people, deemed everything only a lie, since he was separated from the young maiden, whom he had not seen for a long time.

§ 43; Kalpasūtra I, 104. The meaning therefore would be: "How could one who watches during the sixth night of another sleep in her own". A woman goes to watch with her friends or neighbors on such an occasion. So how *could* she sleep when she herself and her own dear babe are concerned! I consider the line to be a proverb. Its general application is perfectly clear and would fit admirably into our context.

Shashṭhikā is a kind of rice. Perhaps shashthī was used in the same sense. Words ending with ī and ikā alternate frequently. Rice had to be carefully watched, especially on account of the parrots. Cp. my books Kshemendras Samayamatṛikā, p. 23, note 3 and Dāmodaraguptas Kuṭṭanīmatam, p. 146. So it does not seem impossible that the line meant: "How should he who watches other people's rice neglect his own!"

For:

155. So long there is modesty, so long pride and so long there is understanding to think of the other world, as the arrows of Love, that take away discrimination and life, do not prevail.

156. While the prince subject to love, thus dwelt in his own palace there came a beautiful woman[1]) to him.

157. When she had seated herself on the seat offered her, the prince said to her: "In what affair have you come here beautiful lady? Tell me your purpose".

158. She said: "Listen, prince, being of an attentive mind. I have been despatched to you by Mayaṇamanjarī.

159. "Fair sir, she who is tormented by the intense fire of separation sends you these words as a message: "Before my life departs sprinkle it with the water of union".

160-161. "And when she had heard of the other things: how you sported with the elephant, how you slew the thief, how you eluded the wicked woman, how the people with the king at their head showed you their approbation, she was extremely astonished in her heart. Even her life she sustains with great difficulty, longing to see you".

162. Having heard her words and given her the betel that was in his hands, he said to the woman in words whose essence was tender love:

1) Vilạyā = *vilakā, from vil, velati, vellati, vacillare, lascivare (cp. vilāsinī and mahilā)? In Pāli we find vilākā, "slender-waisted". (Jātaka V, p. 156, st. 108; V, p. 506, st. 476) and vilākamajjhā (IV, p. 19, st. 30). The root is lag (cp. Pāli lakana, "anchor" and laketi Majjh.-Nik. I, p. 127; Anguttara-Nik. III, pp. 230, 233). So the etymology vilagā, "the slender-waisted one" is perhaps better. Cp Skt. vilagnamadhyā.

163. "Clever lady, go and tell her: "Do not give way to your longing for some days. As soon as I get an opportunity I will set it all right"".

164. The next day men mounted on camels came unexpectedly, and when they entered the palace with a joyful soul they were beheld by the prince.

165. He embraced them joyfully and affectionately asked for tidings of his mother's and father's health, shedding a great flood of tears.

166. Then they said this: "Your mother and father are well, prince. Nevertheless, forsooth, they are continually afflicted with the great magic-wrought malady of separation from you [1]).

167. "If you do not go within a few days and see them, then, O prince, you will most assuredly go to people deprived of life" [2]).

168. Having heard this and bade his own host prepare themselves, he came into the presence of the king and spoke words of the following sort:

169. "Mounted on tall [3]) camels two men have come from my fathers side, in order to fetch me, O lord. Say what is befitting".

170. Thereupon the ruler of men said: "Go accordingly to your parents, O prince. Having gone there accompanied by your own retinue, come back again".

171. Giving him ornaments and honoring him with

1) Why Jacobi tahes gaha = Rāhu I fail to apprehend. The messenger seems to say: "They have good health, for that matter; but an unearthly disease torments them — separation from you".

2) Lit., "go (travel) for people deprived of life". Hardly gen. absol.

3) Ussuya = ucchuya (C) = Skt. ucchrita high. I do not believe in ussuya = utsuka swift.

sweet words, the ruler of men sent off the prince together with his own daughter.

172. Having formed his company for the journey [1]) and bidden the host begin their march [2]), the prince himself remained in the middle of the city with one chariot.

173. In the first watch of the night the prince despatched one of his own men to the messenger Saṃgamī, in order to give her intelligence.

174—175. He went and said to her: "Our army has set out on the road; the king's son tarries all alone on your account. Therefore, fair lady, go and quickly bring Mayaṇamanjarī hither, in order that the thing you desire to be done may be accomplished today".

176. On hearing his words Saṃgamī went in haste and hurry and told her mistress what had been said by that man of the prince.

177. When she had heard it an intense thrill of rapture rose impetuously in her all at once, and together with her good friend [Saṃgamī] she departed [3]) instantly from her own house.

178. Mounted on a litter [4]) Mayaṇamanjarī arrived in the presence of the prince. "Quickly mount [my chariot] slender maiden", thus said the king's son to her.

179. Then he urged on the horses, taking hold of the

1) Saṃjattī = saṃyātrī is hardly "Marschordnung" (Jacobi), but rather "Versammlung, Reisegesellschaft, Reisegeleite".

2) Lit., "made them give setting out, — march", cp. dadāti jhampam, "he gives a jump", e. e. he jumps. Payāṇaṃ dei, etc., very common in Pkt.

3) *Saṃcalyati > saṃcallai; from the present stem our participle.

4) Jacobi "wagon, carriage". In that case we have to translate: "She came to the prince. She mounted his chariot, being thus addressed by etc.'

reins with the left hand[1]); and driving out of the city[2]) he came among his own encamped army.

180. Speedily, as soon as he had arrived, he had the drum-signal for the march given, and the whole army started, forming a magnificent escort for the journey.

181. Traversing[3]) the country of the protector of the earth in uninterrupted marches, they came to a great wildwood full of beasts of prey and trees, and terrible.

182. While he traveled along on the path, which was tangled with most vexatious great trees, the rainy season, dear[4]) to all people, arrived.

183. And when the prince was journeying along in

1) Probably the prince's other hand and arm were occupied in a manner mentioned in several Runos of the Kalevala (in caressing his love).

2) "Driving out in the city (through the city)" is possible and found in such connection elsewhere. But perhaps we should read nayarīo.

3) Concerning the Apabhraṃça gerunds ending with vi and viṇu see § 588. Such a gerund formed with viṇu we also have in the confessedly difficult stanza:

> Lae, pekkha, viṇu hiaẽ bhāvami,
> jai vihijoẽ puṇu tahĩ pāvami.
> Tā raṇṇeviṇu karami nibbhantī.
> Puṇu ṇai mellai dāha kalantī.

Vikramorvaçīyam p. 131 in Shankar Paṇḍit's second edition; in Parab and Telang's IV, 67; Pischel, Materialien p. 63, N°. XXXIV. I translate: "O Liane, sieh, ohne mein Herz irre ich umher, ob ich nicht durch Schicksalsfügung wieder zu ihm gelange. Nachdem ich (mit meiner Liebsten) der Freude genossen, gebe ich mich daher dem Irrsal hin. Nimmer lässt es, das Glut bereitende, mich wieder". Dāha kalantī is Shankar Paṇḍit's reading. Telang's edition also notices dāha kaantī, which yields the same sense; for I take kaantī as a denom. from the p.p.p. kaa (= kṛita). It would correspond exactly with kaḍḍhai and other similar derivatives. Raṇṇeviṇu is from the present stem raṇṇai (Skt. raṇyati). Remember that BCLPT read raṇṇe. There is considerable evidence for mellau in the last pāda. The sense would remain essentially the same: "nimmer lasse ich es .... wieder" — Nibbhantī = *nibhrānti.

4) Dayā + ra > dayara (= dayita). It would be possible to translate: "on the path which was rough and full of big trees".

the midst of the forest at this soul-enchanting time, a chief of the Bhillas suddenly fell upon his army.

184. By his host, which was maddened with its own strength, the prince's army was scattered instantly to the four quarters of the compass, as a mass of clouds by the wind.

185. With his one chariot and accompanied by his sweetheart, the son of the king took his stand in the midst of the forest like a lion in the midst of a herd of elephants.

186. Thereupon that whole host of Bhillas, attacked with a succession of arrows, was discomfited and fled[1]) in different directions as a herd of [common] elephants before the scent-elephant[2]).

187. But when the chief of the Bhillas saw his own body of warriors flying he precipituously advanced against the prince, upbraiding [them] fiercely.

188. Incessantly these two discharged showers of arrows upon each other, but neither one was vanquished, on account of their skill in the science of the bow.

Thereupon the prince reflected:

189. "By intelligence, fraud, trick, likewise by the employment of spell and witchcraft the adversary is

1) Notice that we have both passive participles: *palāta > palāya and *palāna > palāṇa.

2) Concerning the gandhagaja see note 2) on page 57 of my book Kāvyasamgraha. Metrische Übersetzungen aus indischen und andern Sprachen (Leipzig). Prof. Lanman's view is favored by passages like the following: "As an elephant in rut scatters the other elephants by his mere odor". Stein's Rājataranginī I, 300 (cp. IV, 354). The fluid that exudes from a rutting elephant's temples is said to smell like the fragrance of the blossom of the mango tree. Kirātārjun. V, 26; Çiçupālav. XVII, 67.

slain against whom one cannot prevail by right conduct.

190. "So this chief of the Bhillas has acquired magnificent skill in the many various uses of the bow[1]). And he cannot be slain. Therefore I shall devise a stratagem".

191. And after such reflection the prince said to his wife there: "Make love [to the Bhilla], my dear. Sit down in the fore part of the chariot".

192. When she had sat down there, and when he saw the peerless perfection of her beauty, he fixed his gaze on her, smitten with the darts of Love.

193. So with an arrow resembling the petal of a dark blue lotus-flower and tipped with an awl he was suddenly wounded in the chest by the son of the king.

194. Hit in a mortal spot, the prince of the Bhillas dropped to the earth: opening his eyes only a little he said such words as the following:

And here they are: [2])

195. "I have not been slain by your arrow: I have been slain by the dart of the god with the flowery weapon. But what is there wonderful about this? Who indeed has not been outwitted[3]) by Love?"

196. Speaking thus the lord of the Bhillas suddenly

1) Lit., "in the hosts (sātha) of "knacks" of the bow" (guṇa exactly as German "Vorteil", in using an implement, in doing a certain thing). Or, "in the hosts of peculiarities of the bow" (ways in which it may be or is to be used). Sattha = çastra is possible, but less probable.

For māhappa = māhātmya see § 277.

2) Avi ya again = German "und zwar".

3) Both here and in Erz. 60, l. 12 the common meaning of chal, "to deceive" is perfectly satisfactory. I do not know if Prākrit chal may stand for "besiegen" (Jacobi), although the difference is small in our case. Vicchalai in st. 188 may also mean "to outwit".

died. At this point the prince looked about for his own retinue.

197. Since he [saw] neither chariots, nor steeds, nor servants, nor trusty warrior heroes the prince proceeded with his one chariot toward his own city.

198. After traversing this wildwood with the greatest difficulty, but free from fear, the prince came to a station of cowherds, which was charming with the herd of kine [1]).

199-200. In the meantime two men saw the prince from the station of cowherds [2]), came up to him, and said in sweet words: "Where are you from, chief of men, and where do you go? Tell us". "We go to Sankhapura" said the royal scion to them.

201. Thereupon they spoke again: "Noble man, we too will go to Sankhapura as your company on the journey, if you do us the great favor" [3]).

1) C has govī "with the bevy of herdswomen", which seems better.

2) Gukulāo can also be taken with pattā ("came from the station.... to the prince)". So Ballini. — Jāva inst. 197 probably better, "however".

3) The instrumental satthena "as your company" is interesting. My theory is this, The instrumental should rather be called sociative. That has been pointed out already. Vṛikeṇa, for instance, first means" with a wolf." By a natural step the idea of association, of accompaniment, passes into that of modality. So we get vṛikeṇa "as a wolf". This we have in our satthena. I give a few other examples. Agninā "as Agni", Bṛihadaraṇyakopanishad I, 4, 15; Sakko brāhmaṇavaṇṇinā.... upāgañchi, "Çakra approached as one who appears like a Brahman", Cariyāpiṭaka I, 10; cp. II, 2, 5; Therīgathā 130; Kosalarājā kumbhakāranivesane aññāta-kavasena paribbājakacchannena paṭivasati, "the king of Kosala lives in a potter's house as one who wears unknown costume" (i. e. incognito), "as one who is disguised as a religious mendicant", Mahāvagga X, 2, 3; supinantena nāgamā, "he did not go as one sleeping", Suttanipāta 293. See also Katthāvatthu p. 617. The next step is to use this sociative in comparisons. i. e. vṛikeṇa "like a wolf". This we find in Russian, where it is an ordinary thing. I cannot remember having seen in Hindu writings a perfectly clear case of such an instrumental. Still some examples

202. When he had agreed with the words: "So be it", and when he had hitched [1]) the horses to the chariot, the men who formed his escort said the following words:

203-204. On this road there is an extremely great forest and in its midst live the fierce robber Dujjohaṇa and the most dangerous elephant champion, maddened with rut and uttering a rumbling roar, and the snake that has poison in its look [2]), and likewise the dreadful tiger.

come very near this usage and it does not seem alien to the spirit of the Indian languages. In the Veda we have the well-known na = iva. An acceptable explanation has not come to my notice. I think, the solution may be this. Vrikā is the old form of the sociative, which is still found in the Veda, in the Prākrits, and in Pāli. Soon a certain na, which I take to be a sociative adverb or particle, was added in order to strengthen the force of the case form (just as the so-called prepositions were originally adverbs used in the same way with case forms and usually put after them). It was added with the insertion of that copulative i which appears so frequently in the noun, the pronoun, and the verb. Thus we get vṛikeṇa. Now, although the use of the sociative vṛikā or vṛikeṇa as a mode of expressing comparison or likeness does not seem to have survived, the sociative na as a separate word is employed to bring out that idea, and as such it drops its other sociative connotations. It "specializes". But whereever it is added as a kind of postposition it preserves its wider signification. So in the instrum., so in the second plur. of the verb. For I assume this na in forms like vadathana, "you speak together", itana, "go ye together". If my theory be correct the evolution is worthy of notice. The ideas set forth in Persson's very full and learned article in Indogermanische Forschungen II, p. 344 sqq. can be harmonized with my hypothesis.

Jai supasāo tumam hosi, lit., "if thou art good-kindness-having".

For the following stanza cp. note on stanza 256.

1) Apparently better, "urged on the horses in his chariot". Cp. note on st. 256.

2) A snake whose glance kills is meant. This kind of snake is often introduced to us in Prākrit and in Jaina works. Fick, Sagara-Sage p. 4, l. 8; Uvāsagadasāo § 107; Pariçishṭaparvau VIII, 112 (cp. Introduction p. 53); Rāvaṇavaha IV, 50, 63. See W. Hertz in Abhandlungen der bayrischen Akademie, philos.-philol. Klasse, Vol. XX, p. 107. These reptiles of the deadly eye dwell alone, shunning the company of others; for the beautiful stanza of the Lalitavistara (ed. Lefmann p. 314) declares:

205. There are also other hosts of wild animals, cruel, flesh-devouring, and terrible to behold. Only after knowing this in your heart go you by this road".

206. Thereupon the prince said: "Harbor no fear, start on the path. When we have arrived safely at Sankhapura I shall be liberal [1]). What [need] of many words".

207. Upon hearing this the others, the numerous men who formed the company on the journey, proceeded with the prince, leaving the torrent of fear [2]).

208-209. At this point a Pāçupata ascetic arrived there. His body was adorned with the diadem of long matted hair, his limbs were strewn with ashes; in his fist he held the trident; he was encircled with evil-averting amulets [3]); his fingers were busy with his

Na siṃhavṛindaṃ bhuvi dṛishṭapūrvam,
dṛishṭīvishāṇām api nāsti vṛindam:
tejasvināṃ satyaparākramāṇam
purushavarshabhāṇām api nāsti vṛindam.

We also find the "deadly Upas tree" in India, not to speak at all of the kimpāka. It is called vishadruma (vishataru etc.) and occurs a number of times in Sanskrit literature (also in Rāvaṇavaha III, 13; IX, 44). It grows on mountains and is so destructive that it withers the blossoms of other trees. For Rāvaṇavaha VII, 67 informs us: "where the flowers of the trees fade and become discolored, being touched (lit., struck) by the wind of the poison-leaved (tree)". The poison trees on the mountain are set in violent motion by the monkeys. The Skt. text of this line, which neither the commentators nor Goldschmidt have understood, should run as follows: Vishaparṇavātavyāhatamlāyamāna-visvavarṇa- (sive: visavarṇa-) pādapakusumam.

1) It seems that we have to read either sampatto or sampatte. Still I am not sure that sampattā could not be correct and that the three words might not form a kind of nominative absolute clause. Possibly jai (yadi) is to be supplied. It is wanting in the conditional sentense also in Buddhavaṃsa II, 124. Cp. Speyer, Sanskrit Syntax, § 487 and Erz. 84, 5.

2) This is rather "outlandish dialect". Fear is conceived as a rushing flood of water which carries people along or which drowns them.

3) It is perfectly clear that the ascetic was all alone. So Jacobi's "Begleitung" for paḍivāraya is impossible. I take paḍi in its natural

hermit's token; a splendid and most praiseworthy man was he.

210. And he said to the prince: "I also shall journey along to Sankhapura with your fine traveling company, my son, in order to visit the places of pilgrimage.

211. "And another thing: A few denarii are in my possession, which have been given to me by pious men for the purpose of offering oblations and worship to the gods.

212. "Take these, far-famed one, in order that I may travel on without fear". Having said a great deal of this sort he handed him the wrapper with the money [1]).

213. Then, greatly delighted, he gave the son of the king his blessing and started with the men of the convoy, clad in his costume as an artifice [2]).

214. The prince, knowing his real character, reflected in his inmost heart: "Traveling together with this man will not be good in the end".

215. Having meditated thus in his heart the prince drove his horses on. The chariot, rolling along on the road, came into a region of impenetrable forest.

216. The Pāçupata ascetic said these words to the men of the escort: "Today I must by all means do you the honors of hospitality.

sense and vāra from vṛi, "to cover, to ward off". Pariyariya may either be paricarita, or here perhaps more probably, *parivarita.

Yogis carrying the trident, the weapon of Çiva, are mentioned elsewhere too. Kuṭṭanīmatam 12; Prabandhacintāmaṇi, p. 178.

1) Skt. nicula means an upper garment, and the Ancient Hindus used to tie up their money in their outer garments. But niculaka, nicola, and nicolaka also denote a "case" (Futteral, PW²). So Jacobi's "bag" may be correct. I tried to use a term that would bear both the interpretations which are possible.

2) Lit., "deceit-made-costume-wearing".

217. "There is here in the midst of the wildwood a station of cowherds which boasts a heap of copious riches. There I have spent the rainy season[1]) engaged in self-mortifications.

218. "In that [station of cowherds] I have won over all the cowherds by my virtues. They will today give us to eat. Therefore you are my guests".

219. After this invitation the Pāçupata ascetic went away, and returned with immense pails which he had filled with rice boiled in milk[2]), ghee, and sour milk.

220. And when he had come he said to the prince in sweet words: "Son, afford me now the joy that my heart desires".

221. Thereupon the prince said: "I have a violent pain in my head, and it is ascetic's food; this meat is not meet for us"[3]).

1) § 167. For āvanta see § 165.

2) Or perhaps, it would be better, to render pāyasa by "milk" (not by "rice boiled in milk").

3) The Prākrit may be translated in the following ways: 1) A violent pain in my head set in (taking vaṭṭai with the preceeding words. The position of ca is in favor of this interpretation, at least prima facie; and in Pāli, too, we have vedanā vattati). And it is ascetic's food; this fare is not proper for us. 2) A violent pain rages in my head. And another thing, it is ascetic's food. This (food) is not proper for us. 3) There is a violent pain in my head. And the food is for ascetics (vaṭṭai with annam). This food is not proper for us. [This rendering seems to the best]. 4)..... head. And the food is ascetic's food. It is not proper for us. 5) .... head. And other food is for ascetics. This is not befitting. By different combination even a few more translations arise. The first four in sense all come to the same thing. The last translation offered would seem to make the prince speak like a good Jaina. According to Uttarajjh. XVII, 15 Jaina ascetics may not eat "milk, curds", and other things produced from milk". But this prohibition is not in harmony with other passages. In Prabandhacintāmaṇi, p. 115 an enemy of Hemacandra taunts the Jaina ascetics with the following words:

222. And the prince told all the men of his traveling company by a sign of the eye: "This food brought by him is not to be eaten".

223. Not heeding the prince, they ate these viands, that were mixed with poison; and as soon as they had eaten them they all suddenly became unconscious [1]).

224. When the Pāçupata ascetic knew that they had all betaken themselves to the house of Death, he rushed forth, discharging a shower of arrows in order to kill the prince.

225. The prince, filled with wrath, dodged the shower of arrows by rapid motions and hit him in a vital spot with an arrow that had a crescent-shaped head.

226. Now he fell to the earth and having only a remnant of life left, he said this: "Son, I am that invincible thief, Dujjohaṇa by name.

227. "Illustrious sir, you of fearless heart have pleased my heart. I have only a short time to live yet on account of the wound inflicted by your arrow [2]).

228. "Listen to my words. On the left side of this mountain, between two rivers, there is a delightful temple.

As for men who live on food blended with ghī, and accompanied with milk and curds,

How can they restrain their senses? Only consider the hypocrisy of it".

His accusation was founded on truth. So if translation n°. 5) given in this note be correct the prince may after all view the matter from the Brahman ascetic's point of view; and that would be so much more in keeping with the requirements of literary art. To all appearance too, Agadadatta is converted to the Jaina faith only at the end of the tale. If the first four interpretations are correct, they contain a bit of concealed irony.

1) Cp. Crooke, Things Indian (London 1906) p. 378.

2) Cp. Pariçishtaparvan I, 174 sqq.

229. "In the place back of that a thin flat stone is detected if great pains are taken[1]). Throw that over to the left[2]) and enter the underground house there.

230. "In the middle part of that there is my wife, endowed with matchless beauty and virtues[3]), in the fresh bloom of youth, modest, and artless, Jayasirī by name.

231. "Exceedingly great wealth is found in the interior of this house. So make that all your own, noble man.

232. "But as for me, the end is nigh. Grant me the billets [of the funeral pile] when my life has departed". While yet speaking thus he suddenly expired.

233. Collecting a great number of pieces of wood the prince granted him the fire. He mounted his most excellent chariot and went first to the place he had been told.

234. Between the two rivers, at the temple, he saw the stone, opened the door, and made a noise as he had been enjoined.

235. Thereupon that lovely young woman came instantly to the spot where the door was and said with a voice as sweet as that of the kokila: "Come into the interior of the house".

1) We could take cajjiya = *tyajyita (from the passive stem tyajyate). The variants of the MSS. sajjiya [also C] and vajjiya (= varjita) point to this. All three words mean "abandoned, let go", German, gelassen, *eingelassen*". So we would get the rendering: "a thin flat stone has been sunk in with great care". I think cajjai, "to see" is from the same root that gives us Skt. caksh. Some of the cognate languages show that the sonant of Prākrit is etymologically correct. Cp. § 326.

2) Vāme is not clear. The literal translation could also run like this: "Throw that over on the left" (standing or taking hold of it on the left side). That would amount to: "Throw it over to the right". I do not think that vāme can be taken with the words following it.

3) Or, "endowed with the excellences of peerless beauty" (or, "endowed with matchless excellences of beauty").

236. While the prince, seeing her beauty, gazed on her with rapture Mayaṇamanjarī struck him suddenly with a push of her hand.

And she said:

237. "Relatives, dear companions [1]), and friends, city and home I have left for your sake, shameless man, and you are attached to another woman".

238. Having heard her words the prince quit that wood [2]) immediately and mounting his peerless chariot he then proceeded ahead.

239. While with ease and pleasure he traversed the frightful forest thicket for some distance, he suddenly saw a flying band of Çabaras.

240. Now when the prince had seen the terror-stricken bands of the woodlanders, he thought in his own mind: "Here must be the elephant in rut".

241-242. While he looked toward that direction, full of suspicion in his heart, he saw a peerless elephant, white as the moon, as the conch, as the waterlily, dripping with a stream of ichor [3]), breaking the fine

1) Or, "father". So Jacobi. That would naturally be represented by piu (pii) in composition. But piyā is used too.

2) The wood surrounding the temple. Ballini's version: "rimarginata quella ferita [d'amore]" looks very captivating. "He shunned (got rid) of that wound [inflicted by Love] quickly" would do very well. In Pali we have a word vana, which I derive from the root van "to desire" etc., and which means "desire, lust". See Childers and Theragāthā 691; Vimānavatthu 50, 14. "He renounced (abandoned) this [amorous] desire" would be more natural than Ballini's rendering.

3) According to Hindu poets, who revel in exaggeration, the little bit of ichor which trickles from the rutting elephant's head is a torrent, and Māgha tells us that the elephants of Hari's army created new and mighty rivers by the ichor streaming from their temples. Çiçupālavadha XII, 60. We are even told that the rutting elephant drips ichor in sevenfold manner. Uvāsagadasāo Vol. II, p. 73, note 195.

great-trunked trees. Mayaṇamanjarī was instantly shuddering in her inmost heart.

243. Thereupon the prince said: "Sweet innocent, do not fear the young elephant [1]) of the wildwood. Bliss and unhappiness are for the great, but not for other men" [2]).

244. After having thus addressed his sweetheart he swiftly stepped down from the peerless chariot, and advancing he suddenly flung his upper garment before the elephant.

245. And when, in the same moment, that elephant gave a thrust into the outer garment the very dexterous prince of a sudden mounted on his back.

246. In the space of only one moment that mad elephant champion, the God of Death for many woodlanders, was rendered submissive by the prince, just as a snake by the employment of gem and spell.

247. Before his own beloved he descended from the

1) Jacobi takes kalaha also here as equivalent to Skt. kalaha. In that case we would have to translate: "Do not be afraid of the fight in the woods". But the prince knows that the elephant has no chance of a fight with him. It is better to connect kalaha with kalabha, "an elephant 30 years old". This kalaha occurs in Prasannarāghava II, 56, p. 44 (in the edition of Sh. M. Paranjpe and N. S. Panse, Poona 1894). An elephant reaches his greatest strength and vigor when he gets to be 40 years old. Çiçupālavadha XII, 60 and Mallinātha's scholion. Elsewhere it is the elephant of sixty years that is considered mightiest. Uttarajjh. XI, 18.

2) Those of the common herd live on like animals; no great events, happy or unhappy, stir their sluggish existence, and, above all, they lack the intensity of feeling that is necessary for rising to the highest heights of joy and descending to the deepest depths of sorrow. Furthermore,

Amai tutti color cui la sventura
Cinsse il capo di funebri ghirlande.
Perchè non ha diritto alla sciagura
Chi non è grande.

peerless elephant's back; and, mounted again on the chariot, he proceeded in the direction of his own city.

248. When the prince, accompanied by his beloved, had traversed some distance he saw the tiger sitting on the wayside.

249. Its shaggy mane bristled[1]) and with its long tail it lashed the ground. On seeing it the prince laughed and ran toward it.

250. Just as the tiger, which had prepared a terrible leap, gave a blow with its paw, the prince thrust his hand, which he had wrapped up[2]) in his garment, into its mouth.

251. But with his right hand he plunged the sword into its back. Smitten with a deep wound it fell plump upon the round earth.

252. And while the prince after conquering the tiger, was traversing a little part of the dense wood he saw the snake lying on the road.

How did it look?

253. Black as a swarm of bees and as collyrium, having a body that shone with the flood of rays from the precious stones in its hood, double-tongued, red-eyed,

1) Skt. uddhushita and uddhūshita are simply wrong translations of Prākrit uddhusita = uddhṛishita (hṛish). The second u is due to assimilation of vowels. An interesting case of such assimilation is harima, "shameful" (Uttarajjh. XXII, 103). This form is not to be corrected to hirima (as Pischel, § 98, has done). It seems to owe its origin to forms like harīyate = lajjate (Majjh.-Nik. I, p. 120; Itivutt. 49; Therīg. 140; Jāt. IV, 171; Angutt.-Nik. III, 16).

2) Veṃdhiya = veḍhiya. See § 74. Possibly veṇṭala (occuring in Erz. 7, l. 22) is to be explained the same way, i. e. vṛitta + la > veṭṭala > veṇṭala (round-ish).

expanding its hood like a banner, uttering a hissing sound [1]).

254. Seeing the snake coming toward them, Mayaṇamanjarī clung to the neck of the prince, her body trembling with violent fear.

1) One is strongly tempted to read phaṇamaṇi, and this is represented in my translation. Still phaṇimaṇi, "its snake's jewels" is not senseless, only a little awkward and pleonastic. [C really reads phaṇamaṇi]. The notion that snakes carry jewels in their hoods is very common in India (cp. the Western idea of the snake's crown). Rāmāyaṇa XIII, 12 (maṇibhiḥ phaṇasthaiḥ; Çiçupālavadha phaṇamaṇiḥ); Rāvaṇavaha V, 39; VI, 72; VII, 69; IX, 45, 89; Uttarajjh. p. 346; Prabandhacintāmaṇi, p. 169. According to Gauḍavaha 348, 349 the brilliant feathers of the peacock are the transformed lustre of the jewels of the many snakes devoured by this bird. Where such a jewel lies there rises the cloud and begins to thunder, and then floors of lapis lazuli (vaidūrya, vālavāyaja) emit brilliant rays. Çiçupālavadha XIII, 58 and Mallinātha's scholion. It is also well-known that snakes are supposed to guard buried treasures. Samayamātrikā I, 27; Jātaka n°. 73; Crooke, Popular Rel. and Folklore etc. pp. 270, 271; Benfey, Pantschatantra I, p. 359; Winternitz, Sarpabali pp. 27, 37 sqq.; Hāla 577 and note; Gauḍavaha 198; Knowles, Folk-Tales of Kashmir p. 273 note. But that proves insufficient to prevent such treasures from shifting places and disappearing (a wide-spread Folklore notion). Cp. Khuddaka-Pāṭha VIII, 4. Therefore people in Old India chained them to the spot, as we gather from Gauḍavaha 499. Naturally the Nāgas, or Serpent Genii, are sometimes supposed to have a hand in the disappearance of buried treasures. Khuddaka-Pātha VIII, 4.

The compound dhamaṇīdhayamukkapukkāra I take as a dvandva. Dhaya = dhvaja. Dhaya cannot represent dvaya. So the first part may mean: "having inflated vessels (the hood) for a banner;" or, if we take dhamaṇī in the sense of "neck", "having a neck banner". We naturally suppose the hissing of the snake to issue from the mouth. Cp. Pariçishṭaparvan II, 206:

> Utphaṇāh phaṇinas te tu
> taṃ dashṭuṃ dushṭacetasaḥ
> phūtkārapavanam āsyair
> amucan dhamaṇīnibhaih.

But the compound may after all be understood differently and may be translated: "emitting a hissing sound from the banner-like inflated vessels" (or, "from the banner of its neck"). For we also read that the snake's hissing comes from its hood. Nāgānanda V, 17; Gauḍavaha 637. Dhvaja means a "distinctive mark". So still another rendering would be possible: "having hisses emitted from the bellow-like characteristic" (the hood).

255. "Do not fear", he said; down from the chariot stepped the valiant warrior, and when the snake came rushing on he suddenly paralyzed its movements.

256. Thereupon having paralyzed the snake's mouth and sported with it he left it. Mounting his peerless chariot he drove the horses swiftly on[1]).

257. After traversing somehow or other with great difficulty this tangled wood which was like a hell, he arrived at Sankhapura, gladdening the multitudes of the people in the city.

258. A delight to the hearts, and eyes of the people and giving gifts, he entered king Sundara's city, which was full of the splendor of apparel beautifully made.

259. When he had arrived in his own home he was then embraced by his mother and father with intense love and in great joy, and respectfully greeted by the people.

260. Thereupon at the end of the meal he was questioned about his adventures in foreign lands, and he told everything up to his arrival in his own house[2]).

261. While thus they experienced the greatest delight on account of their happy union and enjoyed the pleasures of royalty the time went by pleasantly.

1) Saṃjoiya cannot be = saṃyojita (Jacobi) in our passage. We would expect saṃcoiya. Saṃjoiya = samcoiya would perhaps not be impossible. There would be parallels. But I think, the root is jū, "to impel, drive on". Jū, juváti, and from this a-stem juv would be inferred. That would lead to jovai. Cp. ru, ruvai, rovai (§ 473); dhāv, dhuvai, dhovai; svap, suvai, sovai (§ 482, 497); and Pāli āyuvati (Jāt. VI, 27, stanza 1175) from yu, yauti (also in Skt.); luvati (Theragathā 762) from lū. From the present we get jovita > joiya. In all probability we have the same root in stanza 202. It would be better to translate there: "and when he drove the horses in the chariot on."

2) Lit., "till [he had] arrived in his own house".

262. Now one day in the spring, which imparts rapture to the hearts of people in love, the king went out into the park, accompanied by a numerous train of citizens.

263. Now thereupon that prince too, escorted by his friends[1]) and joined with his beloved, arrived there, the perfection of his beauty being gazed upon by the women of the city.

264. Together with Mayaṇamanjarī the glad-hearted prince amused himself with much laughter, mirth, lute-playing[2]), excellent dances, songs, and poetic compositions.

265. In the afternoon all the people, having made merry, quickly went to the peerless city; the king too came home, accompanied by his whole retinue.

266. But just when the prince, who had dismissed all his attendants, reached his peerless chariot, Mayaṇamanjarī was bitten by a ferocious snake.

267. Uttering cries of wail and woe and moaning likewise: "Bitten! bitten!" trembling in all her limbs, she dropped into the prince's lap.

268. Thereupon the prince said to her: "Do not, do not be afraid, lady with eyes like the petals of the blue water lily; in the mere twinkling of an eye I will render the poison of the poisonous snake powerless.

269. And while he was yet speaking thus that sweetheart of his became unconscious in a moment, her limbs being tormented with the terrible poison.

1) Suhi is not = sukhin (Jacobi), but = suhṛid. Jacobi has to change the same word in stanza 287 to sahi. But the reading of the MSS. is correct in both passages. The same suhi is found in Uttarajjh. XX, 9 and elsewhere in Devendra's ṭīkā.

2) Lit., "pastime with the vīṇā".

270. Knowing that she had been left by life, the prince lost his senses and wailed in pitiful tones, uttering cries of "Woe is me! woe is me!"

271. Collecting himself somehow or other with the utmost difficulty, the prince then built a pyre and put his wife on it.

272. Just as the prince after lighting the fire was casting himself into it, suddenly there arrived a pair of Vidyādharas from the sky.

273-274*a*. And as soon as they had come, one of the fairies addressed tender words to the prince: "Noble man, why do you cast yourself into the fire without a reason? In a mere moment I will make your wife's body scathless".

274*b*-275. Speaking thus he sprinkled [1]) her with charmed water. As if she had awoke at the end of a sleep the gazelle-eyed woman came to herself again. "What place is this"? she asked and rose immediately.

276. Having lifted up the prince's mistress and talked with him the pair of fairies flew up to their path [2]) in the heaven.

277. And accompanied by his beloved, the prince in that very instant went to an adjacent temple in the night that was filled with extremely dense darkness [3]).

278. At this time the prince said to his beloved in kind words: "Do you stay here for one moment while I fetch fire".

1) Lit., "struck, hit".
2) Or, "on their path".
3) Lit., "with the obscurity (gloom) of darkness". Andha is used as a neuter noun.

279. Having spoken thus he went and returned again, bringing fire with him. Then he saw in the temple the brightness of a light, which was a surprise to his mind.

280. When he had arrived, he with a heart full of suspicion said to her thus: "Noble lady, I have seen the brightness of a light in the temple".

281. And she answered: "My beloved, the brightness of the burning fire in your hands entered here; that you saw.

282-283. At this point, just as the prince after handing over his sword to his wife, blew into the fire with his two knees placed on the ground and his face bent down, the sword without the scabbard all of a sudden dropped out of her hand on the stone slabs of the temple with a very heavy stroke [1]).

284-285. Thereupon when he, who was of an artless character, asked his beloved all in a flurry: "Why did the sword fall to the ground divested of the sheath?" — then she said to him: "An exceedingly great bewilderment of the mind arose in me. Therefore, not being mistress of myself, I dropped the sword just now".

286. Thereupon having made the fire flame up, they passed the night [2]) in the temple and in the morning they went to their own house with hearts full of felicity.

287. And he told the whole story of the night to his relatives, friends, and household in the company of his mistress and with a heart that fluttered with impetuous joy.

288. And while these two thus clung to the pleasures

1) Nihāta = nighāta.

2) Lit., "the night having passed". The nom. absol. is interesting. Cp. St. 206.

their hearts desired and enjoyed the delights of the senses, the time passed pleasantly.

289. Now one day the good man, the prince, the royal scion, rode a steed of inverse training on the riding ground.

290. By that bad charger, who quickly carried him away before the very eyes of the people, he was taken thereupon into a most impervious wildwood, the abode of ascetics.

291. Rambling about the prince thereupon came to a temple of the Jina and he saw a perambulating monk, who was surrounded by a company of many saints.

And what kind of a man was he?

292-294. Like the moon among the planets and the stars, like the jewel Kaustubha among precious stones, like the wish-yielding tree among trees, like the Thousand-Eyed among the gods, like the moon in lovely gentleness, like the earth in patience, in brilliance like the sun, in beauteous form like the god of love; possessed of pure fourfold knowledge — named Sāhasagai —; by the power of his wisdom seeing all the affairs going on in the world; causing spiritual awakening in pious people by his preaching of the stainless law.

295. The prince went immediately and made a low obeisance to the lotus of his feet, and having thus received his blessing he sat down at his side.

296. Getting an opportunity then, the modest prince said: "My teacher, tell me. Full of curiosity, I would like to inquire about something.

297. "Master, who are these five noble men, radiant in bloom of youth, grace, and beauty, who entered the

path of indifference to the world and desire to take the vows?"[1]).

Thereupon the sage said:

298. "There is here in the midst of this country an inaccessible village, Camarī by name. A powerful Bhilla, Dharaṇidhara by name, ruled it.

299. "Now once upon a time, on a certain day, a son of a chief of men[2]) arrived in this Bhilla's territory, surrounded with horses, elephants, chariots, warriors, and heroes.

300. "Thereupon this commander of a host on the instant killed and destroyed his army and then commenced an equal fight with him[3]).

301. "They fought for a long time; and when neither of them could be vanquished the prince put in front his own wife, who made love [to the Bhilla].

302. "Thereupon while he, carried away by the god of love, cast his eyes on her, the prince found a weak point and hit him in a mortal spot.

303. "Having killed the lord of the Bhillas, the prince

1) Or perhaps, "Who are these five noble men? Radiant in the bloom of youth ... they desire ... Paḍihattha = pūrṇa; = uddhumāya (uddhmāta), apphunna (overwhelmed, flooded; from *āsphurṇa), ahiremaiya (flooded, lit. flood-covered, from *abhiremacita?) Paīyalacchī 81; = nirbhara ZDMG. 33, p. 46, st. 21 perhaps is = *pratibhāsta. Paḍihatthei (Rāvaṇavaha XII, 66)-may simply be = pratihastāyati, "to give a substitute, an equivalent, to equivalentise (sit venia verbo!), to requite".

2) Read with the MSS. naravarakumāra.

3) For sarisa = sadṛiça see § 245. Regarding sarisa in the sense "together with" (Jacobi) I have to confess my ignorance. In our passage the usual meaning fits quite well. Do we have to read -parisеṇa (from Parishad) in Erz. 72, l. 6? The mistake would be easy in the Devanāgarī writing. — Chalium in the next stanza probably is to be translated: "be outwitted, be undone". Bhiḍiya from bhid? Cp. raufen.

went home, accompanied by his beloved. But these five brothers of that Bhilla came speedily.

304. "Seeing their eldest brother deprived of life by a wound from an arrow, they set out on the track of the chariot, their lips quivering and shivering with anger.

305. "When they had gone to Sankhapura they saw the prince hemmed about with princes; and the five stayed there looking for an opening to kill him.

306. "Now one day they saw the prince, who had dismissed all his attendants, alone in the park with his own wife.

307. "Just as these men who were in an impassioned state of mind [1]), deemed this an opportunity for slaying him [2]), his wife all of a sudden was bitten by a vicious snake.

308. "When he, seeing her deprived of life, was casting himself into the fire a pair of Vidyādharas arrived; by them she was made hale and whole again.

309. "Quitting that park they went to a temple in the neighborhood. Thereupon the prince left that fawn-eyed woman [3]) and went after fire.

310. "Thus the five men, who had found a deceitful way [of killing him] and were therefore steeped in great joy, stood there concealed, their minds bent on compassing his death.

311. "And the youngest among them suddenly let his light, which he had hid for a long time, flash

1) This is better, I think, than Jacobi's "of a sorrow ful state of mind". Both kiliṭṭha and saṃkiliṭṭha are not uncommon in the sense of "tainted, sinful, impassioned". Cp. Pāli.

2) Or perhaps rather, "considered this means of killing him", reflected how they should utilize this opportunity.

3) Mayacchī = mṛigākshi.

out [1]) of the covered box in the middle of the temple.

312. "By the gleam of the light the young woman then saw their youngest brother, and she looked on him with soft eyes, that were full of extreme love.

313. "Then she said to him: "Slender youth, be my husband. If you think otherwise, then I shall destroy even my life" [2]).

314. "He, on the other hand, said to her: "Sweet innocent, I long for you; but if your husband knows of it, there is no life at all for me".

315. "Charming friend, I shall kill my lover before your eyes". Having spoken thus she instantly extinguished his light" [3]).

316. "At this point the prince suddenly arrived, bringing fire. And when he had arrived he said: "I saw a brightness here".

317. "Thereupon she said this: "The brightness of the burning fire that you hold in your hands gleamed into the temple, my dear, and was seen by you".

318. "While the prince after handing her his sword made the fire blaze up she drew the sword [4]) and dealt a blow at his neck.

319. "But this [younger brother], being of a com-

1) Lit., "made his light manifest (visible)".

2) Lit, "if you contemplate another thing". Or, "if you think of another woman" (Ballini). Less probable, "if you think of that other one (my husband), then I shall destroy even his life".

3) This seems to be the meaning of jhampio here. Cp. § 326. Uttarajjh. p. 189 also tells us: Āgacchantaṃ kumāraṃ dṛishṭvā tayā tatrastho dīpo vidhyāpitaḥ (vidhyāpayati, frequently used in Jaina Skt., is a wrong translation of Prākrit vijjhāvei [usually vijjhavai], Skt. vikshāpayati, Pāli vijjhāpeti [for instance, in Vinaya Vol. I, p. 31]). Cp. § 326.

4) Separate kaḍḍiya (gerund) from karavālaṃ and read muncai (C muccai).

passionate heart pushed the sword aside, and made it drop down. He told his brother the very strange doings of the woman.

320. "Seeing this[1]) most fearful regardless behaviour of hers they attained to the passionless state of mind and came to my side".

321. Having heard the story of his own life, the prince was agitated in mind and he meditated: "Ah, see the fearful doings of women!

"So this is true:

322. "The intelligent may know the sands of the Ganges, the waters in the sea, and the size of the Himavat —; woman's heart they may not know.

"And also:

323. "They weep and make you weep[2]), they tell lies and make you believe them[3]), and deceitfully they eat poison; they die, but they do not conceive a true affection[4]).

1) More literally, "Finding out this". Tayaṃ = ta + ka. I think we have this tayaṃ also in Kālācārya-Kathānakam stanza 12: tayaṃ paḍivajjia, "receiving this".

2) The present ruvai from ru (§ 473) forms a causative ruvāvayanti > ruvāayanti > rūvāyanti. But perhaps ruvāyai is on a par with viṃhāyai = vismāyayati. ZDMG. 34, p. 277, l. 25. The latter, though, admits of a double explanation too (Skt. vismāpayati furnishing the second).

3) § 487.

4) Khādanti > khāanti > khānti > khanti. Stanzas of similar import might be quoted by the dozen from Hindu literature. I cite only one, from the Tamil Garland of Wisdom.

> Trust you may the fatal poison,
> Trust the floods and raging storm,
> Trust you may the maddened elephant,
> Deem the tiger void of harm,
> Trust the Messengers of Yama,
> Robbers, hunters, murderers trust,
> But you trust the long-robed women,
> Helpless roam the streets you must.

See the charming and instructive little book Thillai Govindan: A Posthumous Autobiography. Edited by "Pamba". Madras 1903, p. 27.

324. "Woman indeed, as soon as she has fallen in love is all sugar like a piece of sugar cane; the very same woman surpasses the bitter nimba, as soon as her love is gone.

325. "In a moment women fall in love, but in a moment their love grows cold. Delighting in various loves and unstable in their affections, they are like the color of turmeric[1]).

326. "Cruel in their hearts and charming in body, speech, and glance, girls resemble a knife inlaid with gold[2]).

"So alas for my baseness that for her sake I stained my family and embraced dishonor. But indeed:

327. "So long shines renunciation of the world, intelligence[3]), noble extraction, and modesty only so long[4]); so long the sensitive[5]) dread of doing wrong, and fear of one's superiors only so long; so long control over one's senses, and the splendor of fame only so long, as man is not in the power of woman[6]), who bewilders the mind.

"Therefore out on the saṃsāra! There is nothing here that makes us happy. And it has been said:

328. "Say, how could there be happiness in the saṃ-

1) Which lasts but a very short time.

2) Skt. vicchurita has grown on Prākrit soil. The genuinely Sanskrit form would be vikshurita (from kshur, to cut), "carved", and hence "raised in some places and in others not", variegated, inlaid, covered with". The meaning "smeared", which is usually given, is all wrong.

3) According to Jacobi, "wealth".

4) Tāvahiṃ and jāvahiṃ in sense = tāva and jāva. These words are Apabhraṃça locatives sg. from the stems tāva and jāva (Skt. tāvat and yāvat) and correspond to Skt. tāvati and yāvati (used in Skt. in the same way). The aṇusvāra is not to be cancelled.

5) Taṇiya I take to be = tanīyas (the comparative of tanu). It is a counterpart to baliya = balīyas. Perhaps we rather should translate: "even the smallest dread of doing wrong".

6) If ramaṇihi be correct it may be the equivalent to ramaṇihe, the gen. sg. Probably, though, the anusvāra or the anunāsika (which so

sāra where greatness is seen one moment and vanishes in the next, where various joys and sorrows revolve [1]) in a moment, where union and separation last but a moment?"

Meditating in such and similar wise he was shaken to the foundation [2]), and falling at the feet of the holy man he said: "Blessed one, this is the story of *my* life. I am the slayer of their brother. And I shrink back from living in the saṃsāra. Therefore do me a kindness by conferring the vows on me". He was consecrated by the holy man. He became eager in the observance of çramaṇaship [3]), which is hard to follow [4]).

often are missing in the MSS.) should be added. Ramanihĩ would be loc. sg.: "so lange als er nicht beim Weibe in Knechtschaft steht". Here too we expect the genitive plur. But whether *ramaṇīshām (= ramaṇīnām) > ramaṇīsim > ramaṇihiṃ is permissible I do not undertake to decide. Cp. my note on Stanza 142 of Agaḍadatta.

1) Or, "change".

2) It will have been noticed that I try to reproduce the etymological and common meaning of saṃvega. It is a technical term with the Jainas, and the commentators render it by mokshābhilāsha. In many passages this is virtually correct. In others such a decided meaning cannot be intended. The word *itself* nowhere has that signification. It simply denotes the state of one who is stirred up in a religious way to the very depths of his soul. The "longing for final emancipation", of course, is a natural result and accompaniment of such a state. Tawney's "spirit of religious fervor" (Prabandhacintāmaṇi p. 83) is a happy rendering. Cp. Jacobi's Tattvārthādhigama under saṃvega.

3) Çramaṇa (one who exerts himself) is a Jaina monk or ascetic, now commonly called Yati.

4) In conclusion I call attention to the fact that our tale seems to have some connection with the Serpent Genii of India. Pits, subterranean dwellings, and treasures in the earth play an important part, and some of the names are suggestive of the same mythological or folkloristic ideas. The hero's name, Agaḍadatta, "Gift of the Well" immediately reminds even the Non-Sanskritist of Basnak Dau and Tulisā; and the name of Bhuyaṃgama, the sham ascetic and robber, who is killed by our Serpent Prince, means "the Snake". So our poem can claim kinship with tales and motifs that reach back for thousands of years. Apulejus' story of Cupid and Psyche is a link of that chain.

APPENDIX.

Geheimrat Jacobi kindly loaned me a MS. of Devendra's Ṭīkā, which had been sent to him from Ahmedabad by Vakil Keshavlal Premchand. My book was in the press already before I could use this MS. It is an oblong paper MS. of 396 leaves plus two lines on an additional leaf (397), evidently a copy from a most excellent original, but made in a very slovenly and unintelligent way.

I have compared Jacobi's text with this MS. and jotted down all the variants. In the following I give those which for one reason or the other seemed to me the most important. Since the MS. drops syllables, words, and longer or shorter passages very frequently through mere carelessness, I have, as a rule, not attached any importance to omissions. -essāmi for common -issāmi, -ettā for -ittā and similar phenomena may be expected to be very numerous, not to mention at all the well-known u for o and i for e. Of common occurrence is also o for u of Jacobi's text as a result of final a + initial u before geminated consonant. Such and similar things are rarely noticed in the following list. Ca (ya), tao etc. added or missing were passed by also; even one synonym for the other, in a number of cases, did not seem to require registration. As a matter of course, the host of lapsus calami are ignored likewise.

Since Fick's Eine jinistische Bearbeitung der Sagarasage and Jacobi's Die Jaina Legende vom Untergang Dvāravatī's (ZDMG. Vol. 42) are also taken from Devendra's Ṭīkā and are likely to be read by beginners in Prakrit I give the most significant variants to these, too. Fick has made rather many blunders in his little book; only a few I could rectify in connection with my little list of variants.

A number of passages I now view in a different way, a few of them on account of light afforded by the Ahmedabad MS. Whenever it was feasible I introduced slight changes or additions in the proof sheets, designating the Ahmedabad MS. by the letter C. Others follow in this Appendix.

At the end I give the text of three rather interesting stories found in the Ṭīkā and not edited as yet. For the Jaina King Çibi cp. Lanman's Sanskrit Reader pp. 335-36; for Citta and Sambhūta Leumann, WZKM. VI, 12 ff. The Faithless Wife etc. is the well-known tale Çukasaptati

XXXIII, for which compare my Daçakumāracaritam p. 103 and v. d. Hagen Gesammtabenteuer III pp. XXXV ff.; 163 ff.; LXXXIII ff.; 357 ff. These three little things cost me a great deal of time and trouble; and I fear the result is still not very satisfactory. Perhaps somebody who has access to other MSS. of the Ṭīkā will somewhere let us have the benefit. Only some of the blunders of the MS. appear in the foot notes.

Finally I have to thank Geheimrat Jacobi also for his very great kindness in reading over the MS. of my book. He jotted down on the margin some valuable remarks, part of which I have indicated in the notes while reading the proofs; others are mentioned in the following.

CORRECTIONS AND ADDITIONS.

P. 5, note 2. The form datta *is* found.

P. 7, notes 1 and 2. I now take vayaṇam in bhanjeūṇa v. = vadana (not vacana) and translate, "While they looked on, hearing, on account of their exquisite taste, only the howling of jackals and making wry faces, the singing (of the actors) proceeded (lit., issued forth)". Cp. note 2 on p. 69. Jacobi suggests kolhuyāṇaṃ va aṇṇakolhuyarasiaṃ souṃ, and C certainly favors this view, for it reads aisarao kolhuyāṇaṃ va anna-kolhugarasiaṃ souṃ "on account of the excessive noise (svara) like jackals hearing the barking of other jackals". But although this thrust at such "shows" is in the monkish spirit of the tale, our author seems to be too much in sympathy with these Caṇḍāla boys for comparing them to jackals. — Regarding vācaṃ bhindati cp. Finnish ei halaistua sanaa, "not a single (lit., cloven) word".

P. 10, note 1. Jininda must *always* be translated "the princely Jinas" and accordingly Jinavara "the excellent Jinas" (not "the best of Jinas").

P. 10 l. 1. In deference to Jacobi I have changed my rendering "conform to the good Law" and adopted his "Law of monks". Still I think that I was right and that sādhudhamma is here exactly = saddhamma Erz. 29, 30 (and suddhadhamma, which occurs so often). The "Law of monks" does not fit well into the context.

P. 13, note 2. C seems to favor Leumann's emendation. It reads jaha vaṇadavo vaṇaṃ davavassa jalio. Cp. also taḍataḍassa bandhaṇaṃ chettūṇa (German, "ritsch-ratsch"). C. fol. 36 *b*.

P. 23, l. 9. We have to follow MS. A, which is supported by C. Both read ālankiyaṃ. Transl., "his breast, which was adorned with a sirivaccha, was covered", etc. This sirivaccha on his body is the prophetic sign of his great destiny, and Varadhaṇu hides it in order that B. may appear like an ordinary mortal and thus avoid danger. Cp. ZDMG. 42 p. 500, l. 14.

P. 24, ll. 15-17. Better transl., "And forthwith V. was seen (by B.) being beaten by.... Yama (and thus) having come to a place far off". Cp. Erz. 10, 23; 61, 8; 77, 27; 40, 26; ZDMG. 42, p. 499, 24; 507, 32; C fol. 261 *a* jo ca tumhaṃ majjhe nayare bhamanto dīsihii.

P. 26, note 2. In Divyāvadāna ed. Cowell Neil p. 41 we find kuṭhāraṃ vahati; 254 āpaṇaṃ vāhayati (die Axt führen, einen Laden führen).

P 30, l. 18. Jāva frequently corresponds to German "indessen", i. e., 1) da, 2) dennoch. This "however" we have here and in Erz. 60, 33; ZDMG. 42, 501, l. 30; 502 l. 2 and elsewhere. Yāvad is used the same way in the Divyāvadāna.

P. 35, note 1. On cock-fights see F. v. Hellwald, Ethnograph. Rösselsprünge (Leipzig 1891) p. 118 ff.

P. 54, l. 7. Samāicchiūṇa I derive from the equivalent to Skt. sam + ā + ṛicchati. Interesting is the differentiation from acchai.

P. 61, note 3. In C fol. 110*b* sq. a goatherd is perforating the leaves of a fig tree in a similar way. A rājaputta who has been wronged by his brother sees him, makes him put out both eyes of the king, his brother, while he passes on the street. The rājaputta becomes king and gives a village to the goatherd, who plants sugar cane and gourds there and, eating the gourds with molasses, sings,

Aḍḍhamaḍḍhaṃ[1]) pi sikkhejja; sikkhiyaṃ na niratthayaṃ.
Aḍḍhamaḍḍhappasāeṇa khajjae gulatumbayaṃ.

Concerning the hells and narakabhūmi see Jacobi's edition of the Tattvārthādigama ZDMG. 60, pp. 309 ff. I regret that I could not utilize this most valuable work in the preparation of my book. Jacobi's edition came out two years later; and I can use it only now while I read the last proofs here in Chicago. Jaina terms should be looked up there by the student.

P. 77, note 2. Also v. d. Hagen, Gesammtabenteuer II, 631 ff.

P. 84, note 2. Tahāviha means "of such a nature (as to ....), apt (able) to bring about a certain thing", hence, it seems, "competent, worthy". Tahārūva is used the same way in the Ṭīkā. Cp. Erz. 1, 21; tahāvihaṃ kimpi kāūṇa (e. g. aṇuṭṭhāṇa) one was reborn as a god (this a number of times in the Ṭīkā); Sagarasage 11, 5 (wrongly transl. by Fick).

P. 102, note 1. Upayoga commonly means "mental sight". Pariçishṭap. V, 4; IX, 82 et al. loc. Cp. Jacobi's Tattvārthādighama II, 8 ("geistige Funktion, Vorstellen").

P. 106, l. 5. I derive addāva from *adrāpa (ādarpaṇa, darpaṇa). With darp: drap cp. darç: draç. The same way dāvei (dāvai) = *drāpayati. See § 554.

P. 107, note 2. In C folio 167*a* the 18 dosa are given as: Annāṇa, koha, maya, māṇa, loha, māyā, raī, araī, niddā, soya, aliyavayaṇa, aliyacāriyā, macchara, bhaya, pāṇivaha, pema, kīḍāpasanga, hāsa.

P. 110, l. 17. Read uruddho, i. e. oruddho (= avaruddha, checked etc.) Erz. 32, 24.

P. 114, l. 1. Interesting is anavarāgra Divyāvad. p. 197, which evidently answers to aṇavayagga. From anamatagga > anamadagga > aṇavaḍagga > aṇavaragga?

1) For ḍḍh one could also read ṭṭ since the two are not distinguished by the MS. Cp. end of Jātaka Nos. 107, 108, 373.

P. 114, last line 115. Better transl., "There his sister's son, King Kesi, the (whilom) Prince Kesi, who had been installed in kingship by him alone (by this very U.), was addressed by", etc. Cancel period in Jacobi's text.

P. 115, note 2. Add, So probably better "Let pautta... be given to him in the house of a herdswoman".

P 115, ll. 16-17. Better cancel the sentence, "Again.... ate". C omits puṇo vi bhunjanto devayāe nivārio (Erz. 34, 2). The sentence is evidently a thoughtless repetition, and it is clear that U. did eat and that he died of the poison.

P. 116, l. 6. Cp. the foregoing story with Divyāvadāna 544 ff. (N°. XXXVII). A picture of Buddha is sent to king Rudrāyaṇa of Rauruka by Bimbisāra. Rudrāyaṇa is converted. One day he plays the vīṇā, while his queen Candraprabhā dances. He notices signs that she is going to die in seven days. The vīṇā drops from his hand. "Have I danced poorly?" He tells her. She wants to become a nun. "If you instruct me (upadarçayitavyam) [1]) after having been reborn among the gods". She agrees, joins the sisterhood, becomes a goddess, appears to Rudrāyaṇa. He installs his son Çikhaṇḍin in royal power, wanders forth a monk, is killed later on during his return to his former realm by men in the employ of his son, who is persuaded by two bad ministers of state that R. wants back his realm. R. enters Nirvāna; but the city of king Çikhaṇḍin is buried by a rain of dust on account of an affront offered to the great monk Kātyāyaṇa. Two good men are spared, who build two new cities called after their names. The tutelary deity (devatā) of Rauruka follows Kātyāyana in his wanderings.

P. 116, last line. Transl. "expiated" instead of "repented". Bhandarkar, Report p. 98, note.

P. 123, note 4. C fol. 37 *a* has sāgāraṃ aṇasaṇaṃ, "qualified refusal of food (fasting)"? Or, "absolute"? Sāgāraṃ Erz. 43, 9 (transl. p. 154) may be taken as an adverb.

P. 124. The first stanza recurs in C fol. 37 *a* with the variant savvaṃ tiviheṇa instead of carime samayammi.

P. 128 note 2. C reads bhikkhaṃ laṭṭham *lashta = lashita, § 564), which tallies with my translation. Cp. C fol. 71 *a*, l. 4 nūṇaṃ ahaṃ annarāhiṃto laṭṭhayaro "surely I am more excellent than other kings".

P. 133, stanza. With ḍhikkiya cp. Skt. ṭhetkṛita.

P. 135, l. 2. Possibly better, "him who thus [becomes] a rough (ungainly, repulsive) goblin? Or, "a spectre, thus dwindling away (kshara)? Sosijjai could be taken as a passive in the sense of a future active (§ 550), "es wird ihn durch Alter und Krankheit vertrocknen". But I do not know if the impersonal expression can be used in Prākrit after this German and Russian fashion. Probably taṃ is no masc. acc. sg., but an adverbial neutre (German "da"), followed by nominatives sg. Transl. "Then (there) the resplendent man.... is soon dried up by old age and

1) Appear to me?

disease, thus (becoming, being) a repulsive goblin", etc., as just indicated. The metrically better jeṇ' of C also points in that direction. See Variants. Read ppamattau in Jacobs text? [1]).

P. 140, ll. 10-11 ("festival of her birth-day"). Vaddhāvaṇaya means any festival; so better, "had a festival celebrated", and accordingly on p. 159, second last line, "a festival was celebrated".

P. 150, l. 8. "With a confident heart". This is wrong. Transl., "abandoning all fear of another world, stabbed him whose heart was full of confidence".

P. 152, stanza. Better, "from intercourse with another man's wife and from greed for earthly possessions (i. e. para going with a dvandva dhaṇamehuṇa)? Pariggaha (parigraha) has this meaning often.

P. 157, last l. Transl., "In Jambudvīpa (instead of "India"), and see Jacobi's Tattvārthādhigama III, 7 ff.; IV, 14.

P. 164, note 1. Cp. the Buddhistic list of eight nurses recurring so frequently in the Divyāvadāna: 2 anka-, or, amçadhātrī, 2 krīḍanaka-(krīḍāpanaka) dhātrī, 2 maladhātrī, 2 kshīradhātrī. See esp. p. 475, where these terms are explained.

P. 166, l. 19. Better, "together with another nun". Although companies of Jains nuns are seen, they "habitually wander in couples". See J. C. Oman, The Mystics, Ascetics, and Saints of India (London 1903), p. 150. In Chapter VIII of this useful book we find a good account of Jaina monks and nuns of our days. — With the end of our tale (the many bracelets and the one bracelet) cp. p. 159 of that work.

P. 167, l. 10. C also has the bracketed words. Transl. "king C. did her reverence. The best seat was given to her. The king sat down on the ground (floor). The ladies of the harem heard of it. They too fell at the feet of the reverend lady, their eyes streaming" etc.

P. 194. The two Skt. stanzas are found in Amatagati's Subhāshitasaṃdoha (XXIV, 9 and 20). ZDMG. 61, pp. 300, 303. In the last pāda of the second stanza Amitagati offers tām bhajanti katham āpaṇayoshām — a horrible corruption, indeed. I cannot here discuss this interesting fact. In reading Amitagati's collection one is reminded continually of other Jaina stanzas. For instance Subhāsh. II, 29 is as close a Skt. equivalent of Erz. 3, last stanza (mūsuvavasu karai), as the different metre allows.

P. 202, note 1. Gaṇḍikā "piece" (of sandal wood) occurs at Divyāvadāna 31, 27, and gaṇḍa "piece" repeatedly in the same work.

P. 211, note 3. Read with the MSS. patta (not pattā). Pattapavarā would mean "accomplished" (lit., having attained the best, of excellent attainments). A and C read pattavarā "having obtained a bridegroom" (or same as pattapavarā).

1) Query, Read, jaṇa khaṇabhangurau jara | rogehi [thus C] sosijjai | rakkhaṃ taha (taṃ) kharauṃ (or, kharau with C, adjective), "old age by means of diseases will dry him up"? For the nom. jara see § 100.

P. 212, note 2. In Divyāvad. p. 579 the people in search of a king see that the boy Çyāma, who sleeps outside of the karvaṭaka, under a tree, is destined to be king, because the shade of *his* tree does not shift.

P. 216, note 4. Collaga is also the first of the ten "examples" (diṭṭhanta) which are used to show how difficult it is to attain for a second time existence as man. So we read C folio 165*b*: Kicchena māṇusattāisamaggī pāvijjai; akayadhammāṇaṃ sā nipphalā sampajjai; collagāidiṭṭhantehiṃ puṇo dullahā vaṇṇijjai, jao ahammeṇa jīvo kujonīsu bhamejjai. The ten are enumerated and explained in connection with Uttarajjh. III, 1 (Calcutta ed. p. 127 ff.). Collagaṃ is given there as paripāṭībhojana. The Universal Monarch Bambhadatta of our first story says to a Brahman: Maggasu jahecchiyaṃ. The Brahman goes back to his village in order to ask his wife what he should ask. She says, Kiṃ bahuṇā pariggaheṇa! Collagakaraṃ savva-Bharahe maggāhi! The Brahman returns to the king and maggio collagakaro jahā: "deva, paḍhamaṃ tumha ghare bhunjissaṃ, tao tuha causaṭṭhīe bhāriyāsahassāṇaṃ, battīsāe mahārāyasahassāṇaṃ, puṇo sāmantamantimahantagapurohiyārakkhagāṇaṃ, tao ettha nayare seṭṭhisatthavāhamāhaṇabaṇiyakoḍumbiya-m-āiṇa evaṃ savvanayaragāmāgarāīsu jāva savva-Bharahe. Tammi niṭṭhie puṇo vi tumha gehetti". The import is, he will never come back to B.'s palace. Folio 60*b*. Cp. Uttarajjh. 127 ff.

P. 218, note 2. Or, "make out the half of the duty", i. e. the half that he has to pay as tax? By the commentary to Jātaka N°. 528, stanza 177 the sixth, the tenth part., etc., are mentioned as toll, duty and the like. So "fix half of the duty" seems to be the best rendering.

P. 223, l. 13. Lit., "Let one employ some means". But the reading of C "Let your majesty (devo) employ" etc., is better.

P. 229 ll. 17—1. Even deva are addressed by Sakka with devānuppiya. C. fol. 304*a*.

Agaladatta. Stanza 75, note. With Eino Leino cp. Kalevala XXV, 144 ff. *Stanza 181.* C reads sāvayasayasaṃkale" "full of hundreds of wild beasts", which seems preferable. *St. 197.* Perhaps "however" would be better for jāva. *St. 204.* Divyāvadāna 333 gives four classes of poisonous nāga: drishṭivisha, çvāsavisha, sparçavisha, daṃshṭrāvisha. According to Amitagati (Subhāsh. XVII, 14) the snake of the deadly look is very black. *St. 253.* The correct translation would seems to be, "red-eyed, like a bellows emitting a hissing sound". C reads dhamaṇīvapamukkaphukkāraṃ, which might be = dhamaṇiṃ va pamukka-. Possibly-vaya- is intended (cp. A; p and y are confounded frequently), i. e. ≐ vrata "emitted in the manner of a bellows". Or = pada, place, region, etc.? *St. 260.* With jā patto cp. ZDMG. 42 p. 505, 2, 20; Divyāvad. 179 yāvat triptaḥ paribhuṅkshva. *St. 294.* Bhaviya means "convertible" (originally, I think, = bhavika, fit, proper, capable of being awakened; still bhavya is conceivable too). Dhammujjuyamaī[1]) C fol. 260*b* is a good equivalent.

1) = dharmodyatamati. Ujjuya (ujjhuya) and samujjuya from udyata occur also elsewhere in the Ṭīkā.

Cp. the Buddhistic vaineya, veneyya. *St. 309.* With the gen. jalaṇassa "for fire" cp. Divyāvad. 179 pushpānam enaṃ preshayāmi "I'll send him for flowers"; also bhikshūṇam (pushpāni) cāraya "pass them around to the brethren", 180. *St. 318.* Read muncai (C muccai).

VARIANT READINGS OF C.

1, 1 Sāgee (for Some); 4 bhikkhaṭṭhī; 6 dugunchaṃ; 10 rattiṃ pasuttā; 15 rāyahaṃsīe; add. jovvaṇaṃ pattā after-bhāvā; 20 add nayarīe after V.; **2**, 7 nayarīe paveso; 8 bhūmigaṃ; 10 avaguṇḍiya; 15 kumāratti (read thus); 16 vimaṇadummaṇā; 17 jovvaṇasohaggalāvaṇṇakalā-; 27 bhaṇiyā; 32 jogotti. **3**, 4 niccāḍāvio (*niçcāṭayati, cp. uccāṭayati); 9 add jaṃ (MS. jem) after khameha; 10 paḍisaṃhara tavaha teyam, i. e., paḍisaṃharaha tavateyaṃ (better than Jacobi's text); 14 avaiddhe; 18 tavaṃ, 22 tahā before stanza; uvavāsa; 24 duddharu; 36 suviiya; 37 phaṃseṇa. **4**, 1 paribhavaṇa; 2 ahiyam ummāhayaṃ; 5 maṇūsā; 10 navegā; 18 paraṃ pupphaṃ (but varaṃ fol. 242*b*, where this stanza and the preceding one are quoted in the story of Bharata); 31 havai; 24 ālae; 32 ibbhasuo. **5**, 1 ahivo; Kareṇadatto; 3—4 saṃvaccharaṃ; 21 maṇasā asahamāṇo; 23 om. bhaṇai; 24 suṇiya; 30 āli. **6**, 4 kaīvena; 9 parivuḍā (f. parigayā); 12 vahūsahiyassa; Varadhaṇusahāyassa; visajjiāsesa-; 25—26 gaṇḍayaṃ (f. muṇḍayaṃ); 26 pahirāvio kasāyavatthe; 28 vesa (f. vattha); 35 paṭṭocchāiya. **7**, 7 pūradesaṃ; 18 sarayāsamayaṃmi; 24 dacchattaṇao; 25 kīlāhiṃ; instead of lines 27—33 we have: Io tao paribhamanto pecchai girinaivaṃsakuḍangī (= iṃ). Ditthaṃ olambiyaṃ khaggaṃ. Taṃ gahiya chinnā vaṃsayālī. Vaṃsantarālaṭṭhiyaṃ ca nivaḍiyaṃ ruṇḍam ekkaṃ (MS. nivaṭṭhiyaṃ ruṃtuṃḍaṃ ikkaṃ) daraphurantahoṭṭhauḍamanoharāyāraṃ etc. **8**, 2 sattamabhūmigāe; 12 ruyasu; 20 tuhe (f. tuha); 21 tubhantiyam itaṃ nivārehī; sāhissai ya sā etc. **9**, 7 mahāsarovara; 31 niggoha; 36 desaṃ (f. paesaṃ). **10**, 6 add gahio bef. gao; 10 om. na (which seems better); 23 suṭṭhulaṇhāo; 24 jai na hu; tā (f. to); 27 anguṇisaṃmara; 28 sūīo taḍio (Jacobi's text, I think should be read "kaḍḍiūṇālakkhaṃ piva sūīo bheḍio", taking away the needles, he freed etc.; bheḍiya may be Skt. bhedita "separated"); 32 add. te after pīe; 33 om. tan. Then, nehanijantiyāṇa tesiṃ tattheva ṭhiyāṇaṃ (not sure of reading; MS. seems to read ḍiyāṇaṃ) annayaradine; 36 samappiyaṃ. **11**, 20 divasāṇi; 33-34 tīe vi soum iṇam evaṃ? (MS. soussa iṇamamevaṃ). **12**, 1 tumh' eso kahio leha-; 4 rayaṇavaī three times; 6 aṇṇesamāṇase (f. aṇṇesamāṇassa se?); 10 paccaīya (the usual form in the MS.); 11 vaīyara (usual form of MS.); 13, 21 eyaṃ (f. evaṃ). **13**, 6 pahipaharanteṇa (paḍi-? pahe? doubling by mistake?); 17 na najjaṇohā bhāya (= bhāi)-Varadhaṇuṇi kiṃ mao etc.; 26 -ābhimuhaṃ, vitiṇṇo āvāso; 29 mitto patto: 32 pahāra. **14**, 2 ya after tattha (I would prefer to take tattha with the following sentence. This reading favors my alteration); 3 nimmaviyaṃ; 11 Sivamandiraṃ; 12 Jalasiṃho; 21 khaṇabhanguraṃ (MS. khaṇaṃ); 28 teṇa bhaṇiyaṃ. **15**, 2 add. dhammadesaṇāe after -vayaṇehiṃ; 10 muṇiya;

15 indayāla. **16**,9 ahivaiṇā; 11 diṇā; 16 purisāgārehiṃ; payaṭṭe; 21 ullasio; 27 tacchattanao (i. e. daccha-); 31 sarisaṃ (reading of MSS. should not be changed). **17**,1 atthi kiṃci vatta(vvaṃ) mae saha tee (i. e. tae); 4 hatthisaṃgamāo; 5 hatthi[ṃ]khambham uccariyāe; 9 ukiriya (i. e. ukk-); 11 ṭṭhiyaṃ; 14 lajjāe (better!); 15 saddhi (= saddhiṃ, Skt. sārdham); 16 avassā; 18, 26 vatto; Kareṇutto (i. e. Kareṇudatto); 31 appaṇā; 36 uṭṭhio. **18**,1 saṃdhukkhiyāṇalo; 7 mahīcakka-; 12 daṃsaissāmi; 13—14 kusumeddhaṃ, 36 vaçagataparishaj-; 38 mocitaḥ kadarthakebhyaḥ. **19**,12 vishayādās; 28 -māhātmyād annamātradānenāpy; 32 -prasare; 34 add. pariṇate cānne bef. pratyūshasi; anyonyanijam. **20**,4 tato jñātavṛittāntotpannakopena saputra-; 7 svasukham; 9—10 svasukhākurvan (MS. svakhā-); 15 bhariyā, tāṇa putto coddasa-; 30 taruṇīyajaṇamajjhaṭṭhiyaṃ. **21**,5 ṇayavaḍaṇuṭṭhio (i. e. calaṇaya-?); 6 avagūḍho; 9 bhīsaṇe raṇṇe; 19 ṇuvanno (= aṇuvanno?); 20 atthi (f. tattha); 36 maṇorahotti (I will fullfill; yours is the wish, you only have to wish?). **22**,2 oḍa; 6 rajjuvva; 9 uddhaṃ; 13 sikkaro; 30 pavatto; 31 indayāla. **23**,9 vatto. **24**,22 kālaṃ nei (Uttarajjh. p. 527, l. ult. kālaṃ nayati); 27 diṭṭho tammi diṇe (f. ṭhio tiṇṇi diṇe); 29 mulamulanta; 35 -āhiṃ cittatavo-. **25**,2 jhāṇeṇa; 15 ceiyāṇaṃ pūyaṃ; 23 tao muṇiṇā. 26 marisejjaha (mṛish). **26**,3 vijjāharajjhanda; 21 tubbhe (so often for tumhe); 27 gāmei (also elsewhere for gamei); 33 'dayāto (atīta); 36 tti bhaṇie Indeṇa bhaṇiyaṃ. **27**,5 teṇa bhaṇanti; 8 paḍicchaha; 29 Rāhāyariya; 32 bhamiyā; 34 cṃakūraṃchiliyātakkeṇa (read ambiliya? b and ch are as similar as b and v); 36 bhattaachando. **28**,1—2 sattaladdhīo; 17 Vīībbhae (Vīibbhaya or Vīibhaya throughout); 18 Uddāyaṇo (so nearly throughout); 21 Mahāseṇa; 22 tiṇṇiseyaccatta (i. e. chatta); 30 vatthāvāo; 31 Vijjamāla. **29**,12 pavisihitti (read thus); 22 cittam (citra, for vittaṃ); 23 sappahāse ya; 29 suddhammā (sudhamma? suddhadhamma? saddhamma?). **30**,4 saṃdesaha; 12 cheṭṭūna; chubhai; 19 parusaṃ (so throughout); 24 siddhi; but we have to read siṭṭhi also in line 21, so transl. there, — "the creator of the whole world"; 28 saṃjutto. **31**,1 apuṇubbhava (read thus); 6 duṭṭhu (cp. suṭṭhu); 9 dīsinti; 18 allīṇo; 23 pariggahāvarao; 33 kaṇaga; 27 erisī; **32**,2 abhibhūo ya (f. abhiruio); 8 navaraṃ acchai tti; 24 okkhanda (= avaskanda, which seems better). 27 pajjosamaṇā-; 28 saṃjāyāṇi (which is probably correct, "I worked under a delusion: I did not know" etc.); pajjosavaṇaṃ; 29 ranno. **33**,14 abhiogaṃ; 15 add. ahaṃ after naṃ; 16 samucchie (i. e. saṃmucchie); 36 parihario. **34**,7 pāḍiyaṃ. So avahīrau aṇavarāhitti; 9 paṃsūo (*nom. pl.*) acchanti; 13 māṇaseṇa (which seems better); 26 kilāhaṃ. **35**,2 om. hatthī; 4 pekkhai; 5 jāhitti; 29 paṭṭhiyā (better, f. paviṭṭhā); 31 amho. **36**,1 gacchejjasu; 2 sāhuṇīyamūlaṃ; pavattaṇī; 6 kkaraṇo; 13 nāe maiharīe; 17 karemitti; 19 dikkarūvāṇi (Skt. dikka, young elephant; so "youngster"); 24 vaṃsakuḍange; 33 tahiṃ jaṃ savvasampayā; 34 pullaḍā ya daddā. **37**,2 paḍicchiyavvao; 6 om. vaḍḍhio, add. bhaṇai ya "eeṇa mama kajjaṃti": 15 aṃsaṃ vilaggo; 18 tu (f. ca); 22 genha (better!);

23—25 leham dei "dehi mama egaṃ gāmaṃ, aham ..... vā taṃ demi", so ruṭṭho; 27 osārettā; 37 jayā ca (read thus). **38**, 2 visaho; 3 vasahaṃ; paṭṭuehiṃ; 9 paḍḍuyaparighaṭṭaṇaṃ; 15 pāuvalaggaṃ; 17 vintarā; 27 tahā jeṇ' ummatta (jeṇa — taṃ "wie — so"? Or, "where — there"?); 28 aireṇa vi jaṇa khaṇabhanguraū; 30 kharaū; 36 samekkhaṃ. **39**, 2 vaṃsobbhāvo; 10 vikarīo (Skt. vikara earth-pit); 17 sumiṇaya; 27 dehā Nalagirihatthī Aggisīrū; 32 pāikka (f. payāi); 35 add. kameṇa after tao. **40**, 8 navara; 13 om. dhario; 19 sukavvabandhā; 19—20 daṃsenti ditth. ind. indayālino; dijjaṃti tambolo (read tambolā?); 22 muyangāṇi; 24 om. aṇammi diṇe (which seems better); 30 ca samekkha. **41**, 7 jogaṃ; 19 pavirāvajjasu (= pavīra + āvajjasu? probably blunder); 25 sampatto; 36 nivannā. **42**, 1 loettha (f. ma ettha); 7 dharaṇivaṭṭe; 8 akajjaṃ kayaṃti. **43**, 1 thovavelāe; suhajjhāṇovagao; 3 avassa; 8 vaṇapālehiṃ; 10—11 ghuruharanti (f. -huranti?); phekkāranti (Skt. phetkāra the howling of the jackal); bhasuyāo (f. sivā, Skt. *bhashuka, cp. bhashaka barker). **44**, 1 mayaṇavattho; 3 vavatthie; add mayā bef. keṇai; 4 Naṇdīsaravaradīvaṃ; 9 solasasudahimuhesu (om. selesu); 19 pauttī (this ī for im in acc. very frequent); 22 caurāsīi; 29 titthe bahuvolīṇe suguru in text; 34 Mihilāe (so also further on); 36 pacchau (or, patthau) piyā putto bhavissaitti. **45**, 14 moḍadhārī; 20 luppanti; 26 ṇisuṇesu; 37 mīliyāhiṃ (om. vi). **46**, 3—5 piyaṃ suhaṃ (both times); 23 saṃciṭṭhai; 24 rāiṇā (as emendated by Jac.); 29 uvabhunjamāno (better!). **47**, 8 Namibhaṇiyaṃ; 15 soūṇa (f. nāūṇa). **48**, 6 jjhaṇajjhaṇaraveṇa āūrijjai; 9 khalahalanti; 13 muccāmi (as in Jacobi's text); 15 Seyaṇagarāyatthaṃ (or, cchaṃ) attāṇam; nanditūraghoseṇa; 17 kahaṃ (f. kahiṃ). Kahaṃ should probably be retained. "How (is that)? Have I etc."). **49**, 5 tassa ya veī- (ceī?) hare pūiūṇa; 21 disāe; 35 nerikkhejjā (i. e. nir-, nirīksh). **50**, 1 Kaṇayamanjarī; 5 ḍiṇṇo; 16 suṇesu; 21 om. eyaṃ; 24 Caubhujo; 29 sampai. **51**, 10 gayam (Skt. gada sickness, disease? Blunder f. gavvam?); 12 uvasantamāṇo; 19 uvarayagaha(r. geha?) -vāraṃ; 20 attavaggeṇa, om. vā. **52**, 13 sasaṇehaṃ; 17 add. daṃsiyāiṃ after nivaḍiyāiṃ; 20 karemitti; veraggam uvāgao pavajjam abbhuvagao; 22 om. eyaṃ; 31—32 mayā cintiyante (i. e. cīntayanteṇa?) "esā piuṇā saha mā gamissaitti"; 33 mayaṃgaṃ (i. e. mayagaṃ). **54**, 4 kahaṃ; 7 suhaṃ suheṇa; 9 aiukkaṇṭhayāe (on account of excessive yearning); 13 suranganāsahio; 15 uciya (i. e. -ṃ?) samullāveūṇa; om. taṃ; 18 aṇumantasu (anumantrayati); 26 pancamapancamadiṇassa (better!); 36 rajjaṃ pālantassa. **55**, 1 manjarīe puputtaspapphaphalayāiyaṃ (i. e. pattapupphaphalayāiyaṃ, "leaves, flowers, fruits twigs, etc. in clusters [bunches]". Read phavāla, pavāla f. phala?); 18 jayā (f. jaha). **56**, 7 add. aīva, om. rūva; 15 mahāsatta; 17 veāsaṃjogo, 24—25 vimhiyacittamaṇāe; 26 lāvaṇṇarūvadhārī; 28 viyaddha; 36 sagabbhā. **57**, 2 bālo; 11 karayalapphāso; 14 uttima; 26 jāṇei; 28 desaesu. **58**, 1 jalaṇihisaṃghaḍieṇa; 2 vujjhanti; 12—13 ko tuha mayankaseva habhiṇa (hasiṇa?) paḍibaṇdhaṃ? Tumha sayala etc.; 15 haru; 18 mosaṇu; 19 veu (veda, f. devu); 20 kajjaakajju; 21 taṇusaṃtāvaṇe kugaipahe (with tahiṃ jūi); 22 tahiṃ piya; 32 aloṇiyaṃ koi caṭṭei silaṃ; 27 piyasāmī. **59**, 10 anaṃmi diṇe; 13 guṇḍiyāo; 19 eso va; 20 aliyaṃ; 24 nibheṇa; 30 pottiyaṃ; 33 viṇāsae; tūliganḍuyaṃ; 35 khalī. **60**,7 lacchī (? The MS. never distinguishes between tth and cch); 14 Binnāyapuḍa, 16 om. metta; labbhai; tā; 18 kedūraṃ. **61**,5 hiṇḍiuyam (i. e. hiṇḍiuṃ ya); 24 avarovvi. **62**,5 paho; 7 mahantaṃ; 15 uvajjhāveṇa; 30 bhaṇiehiṃ; 33 ṇuvanno. **63**, 3 pāragao; 7 add. saha bef. saṃvayahāro; 29 abhiruiyaṃ; 32 rajjaṃ pi tassa savv'-eyaṃ; 33 tā (f. tāhe); 34—35 aṇunnāyūṇa, pujjantu (*pūryantu) maṇorahā ee amhaṃ; 35 vibhaveṇaṃ (better!). **64**, 4 bhāreūṇa (but 6 bhareūṇa); 8 seṭṭhī; 9 uvarigo; 11 phopphala; 20 thagamalinta; jāṇesu; 31 evaṃ soūṇa; 36 devīe kao pāṇo (probably original reading, devīe kao pāṇapasāo); 38 parihāvio. **65**, 9 nirao (f. pasatto); 10 gaḍotti; jāṇudese; 11 litte (but probably litto is intended since ya follows paṭṭo); 12 uvajīvai; caṁkhamanto ya; dhārieṇa (prob. f. dhārieṇa); kilaṃmanto; 13 caṃkamai; rattiṃ khattiṃ; 14 nikkhivai; 16 āṇei; 17 puvvannatthā; 18 kūve; tattheva vivajjai; 19 vaccai nagaraṃ; 19 taṃ before geṇhium; 20 bahū; om. ya; 22 tīrai; 23 add. devo after kareu; 24 ṭhavei; sakkai; 25 niggao; 26 so ya (instead of Mūladevo); 26 nivanno acchai; bhaṇai; 27 acchai; bhaṇṇai; 28 maṇussaṃ; 29 subahuṃ; 30 paṭṭhiyā ya nayarabāhiriyaṃ. **66**,1 ei; 2 pāhuṇagassa; tāhe (f. tāe); kūvaṃtarasaṃniviṭṭhe; tīe; 4 aīva; 6 nassaha; 7 bolo; om. y'; kaṭṭhiūṇa; 8 rāyamagge ai —; 11 karei; 14 subahuṃ (also in 17); 15 bhagiṇī; 15—16 se bhogasaṃpayā dattā; 16 vi gaesu; 17 diṇṇaṃ; saṃpūio; 18 aīva sakkāraṃ; 19 pauṃjai; davāviyaṃ; 19 bhagiṇī se pucchai, tāe bhaṇṇai; puvvaviiya-; 21 om. davvaṃ; dāvāveūṇa. **68**, 29 tīe kulapabhūo. **69**,6 bhaṇiuṃ (as in Jacobi's text); 10 pavaḍḍhiya; 11 bandhāiṃ; 15 purīya; 34 evaṃ kila so. **70**, 9 annadiyahaṃmi: 10 hu (f. u); uṭṭhio (f. vaḍḍhio); 31 ya (f. u); 34 hohī; 36 angā. **71**, 4 kāmassa; 14 pavasissaṃ (but *85*,₃ also pavisio, where pavasio = pauṭṭha would likewise seem more natural); 39 pitthiṭhīe. **72**, 7 suravataṃ; 38 nei (f. no); 39 bahuniuṇo. **73**, *12* roravaissa va mandiraṃ; 32 ne. **74**, *1* taha (f. aha); cayau; 3 maraṭṭhi; 19 etthantaraṃmi bhanio kumāro teṇaṃ; 26 savvaṃ (f. kajjaṃ); 31 turiyagayaṃ; piṭṭhiṃ; 38 joe vi bhittisaṃdhi (read, saṃdhiṃ examines, etc.? But probably blunder); 38 niggamaṇagūḍhaṃ. **75**, 5 imaṃ duṭṭhaṃ. **76**, 6 dummiyā; 16 gheppahiṃ: vijjā; 17 lajjai; 18 jovvaṇiṇa; 19 duggijjhau; mahilahaṃ; 27—28 pabhāsaí pāvaka me bhāuyaṃ vahanto; 32 chaṭṭhiṃ; chaṭṭhīe; 37 naravarassa (should not be changed. Vara "the most excellent, the prince" is used for-pai (-vai) *very* often). **77**, 4 turayāṇaṃ; 17 niyajīyaṃ ("since" [or, while] my life is departing, therefore [or, during that time] etc.); 36 karahāruhā. **78**, 9 Mayaṇamanjarī; 20 samaggaṃ; 27 chaladappieṇa; 28 ya ghaṇabaddhaṃ. **79**, 1 sakkejjā; 7 diṭṭhī; 17 ne (f. no); 25 tumha; 35 bhaṇiyaṃ. **80**, 2 tisūlavakkeṇa (cakkeṇa?) ya saṇāho (MS. has -kkoṇa, but o for e is frequent in MS. Metathesis?); 4 tiyassī; 10 davvanivaho; 11 naravaisuyassa; 16 payaṭṭho; 18 pāhuṇṇaṃ; 28 neya (i. e. ne [no], ya ?). **81**, 30 palovei. **82**, 7 sadaṁ; 8 samuhaṃ; 10 veṃṭiya; 17 vaya (i. e. pada "place" MS. vapa); 17 phukkāraṃ; 22 kuṇiyaṃ (i. e. kuṇiya, hardly kuṇium); 25 nivahe. **83**, 19 sajjasarīraṃ; 23 -iṇiṃ (i. e. paṇaiṇim); 26 add.

aha after pacāsanne; 38 vaṭṭe. 94,1 om. tā (read ya?); 7 suhi; 12 turayaṃ; 22 Sāhasanaī; 26 viṇayajutteṇaṃ; 27 suha guru (or, suhaguru); 32 so (f. taṃ); 34 naravai; 35, 39 tā (f. to). 95,7 jovintā; 15 tatto; 29 vaṇhī; 34 muccai pahāraṃ (correct to muncai pahāraṃ and read thus); 37 taṃ yam (taṃ ya? tayaṃ?). 96,1 santanto (saṃtānta "distressed", but most probably blunder); 7 ruyāvanti; 17 citti (but C fol. 133*b*, where this stanza occurs again, vitti; there maṇa f. maṇu in l. 20; cp. Amitagati's Subhāsh. XXV, 2); 19 hi (f. i.); 20 ramaṇihiṃ maṇumohaṇihiṃ; 38—29 parivālaṇojjuo.

UNTERGANG DVĀRAVATĪS.

495,20 vuggaheūṇa. *496*,33 gahiyā; 37 parisakkantehiṃ. *497*,11 ato mahāsattā; 31 puvvajamma; 33 bāhasamupphulla; *498*,32 maṇahāu (read, pāvaenam aṇāhā (o)ḍajjhae; *499*,7 Baravaiṃ (f. puravariṃ); 13 sīso haṃ samāṇo nimmamo haṃ, to savva-; 17 Paṇhava; 22—23 parighāviyā (read -dhāviyā?); 34 bhayapuṇṇa. *500*,3 paribhava; 14 jāo atacchaloya-(atathya); 19 kuttiyāvaṇaṃ (for pūiya-, which clearly means "Kuchenbäcker", from pūpa; he gets bhakkha there (cp. Uvāsagadasāo I, 34; and bhakshyakāra is Kuchenbäcker); 22 Baladevākārī; 23 C also viyaṇṇo (possibly the two similar akshara ṇṇ and gg are confounded. Read viyaggo = vyagra heedless, reckless? Or = vikarṇa deaf, inattentive, regardless?); 27 kuddhasaṇṇā; 34 aṃsuppappuya (açruprapluta); 38 savvabhāgayāṇaṃ. *501*,32 aṃsusamupphala. *502*,4 kumārasamūhā; 14 turiyaturiyaṃ; 29 sajjhāyajhānarayāṇaṃ. *503*,2 pakkhalijjanto ("being staggered", which is the meaning also of pakkhulijjanto, I think. Cp. p. 504, l. 34); 16 mahāraha (f. mahārāya); 31 dāṇavu; mukku (for cukka; 32 mukku (f. sukka); *505*,8 karemi; 9 pulinaṃmi jjhāmemo; 28—29 pabhāyāe rayaṇīe tehiṃ etc.; 28 sāmiṃ; 37 mahākaṭṭhaṃ. *506*,1 tiṇṇi tiṇṇi (both times); 2 satta satta; 11 -katthahāraehim (but 13 kaṭṭhā-); 16 kiccaṃ (krityā magic); 21 mahākarālamuhā bībhaccha-; dāruṇa; 30 ṭhiyam uvaviṭṭhaṃ va (scil. paḍivannā). Pāsa-. *507*,16 samupphulla; 20 mandabhāgī.

SAGARASAGE.

1, l. ult. Jaṇhukumāro. *2*,2 paribbhavāsi (i. e. -vāmi. This form occurs frequently and is not incorrect. Cp. § 251); 7 kaṇagamayacau-; *3*,8 bhīyā (f. mīya, which = mīta hurt, harmed?); 20 nāsāe or nasoe (no sāhae perfectly in order. Transl. "erreicht seinen Zweck nicht" [sādhayati]). *4*,3 pauttovahī (he sees the snakes flee and learns the cause (the state of affairs) by means of ohi. Cp., by the way, ZDMG. 42, p. 503, l. 35—36 ohiṇāṇeṇa Balaṃ pecchiuṇa); 7 tavvahaṇatthaṃ (f. tattha haṇaṇattham); 3 bhaṇiaṃ pautto. *5*,3 niyapurisamāsannaṃ; Sāmantāmaccehiṃ ya etc. 5 ekkapaese; om. amha (which is superfluous); 12 saṃbharai; 14 aṇāhamaṃḍayaṃ (but read, aṇāhaṃ maḍayam, "an abandoned corpse");

6,5 ghare ghare; 6 vijjovaditthabhūīpala(ṃ)bho. 7,1 paharagaṃmī (cf. ZDMG. 42 p. 504, l. 37); 9 also C vihalaṃghalo. Read-aṃgalo "überwältigte Glieder habend"? Or, vihalaṃdhaloyano = vihvalāndhalocana?); 14 deha me tumhe virahaduhaṭṭassa daṃsaṇaṃ. *8*,2 appaṇo (i. e. appaṇā). *9*,8 om. ārāhio (Fick wrong. Bhagīrahī fasts for 3½ days and thus causes the king of the Snakes to yield to his desire — a case of prāya). 13 tatthā (which should be retained. There is no "Ungenauigkeit" in the text. Transl. "Dort wurde die Gangā, viele Tausende von Flüssen mit sich führend, ins Meer hinabgelassen"). *10*,10 kammam aṇeṇa. (after which put period. In Fick's text stop after mahantaṃ. Kappamaṇa "von tüchiger (frommer) Gesinnung", or, "auf guten Wandel bedacht"; cp. kappa in Kalpasūtra ed. Jacobi). *11*,1 also C māivāhattāe (a small "Lebewesen" is meant also by kodaviya. Cp. Uttarajjh. XXXVI, 129); 4 paribhaviūṇa; 12 saṃvegam uvagao gao bhayavantam vandiūṇa sabhavaṇaṃ.

CITTA AND SAMBHŪYA.

Je te do vi govadārayā Citta-Sambhūyapuvvabhavamittā sāhuaṇukampāe laddhasamattā kālaṃ[1]) kāūṇa devaloge uvavannā te tao cuyā Khiipaiṭṭhie nayare ibbhakule do vi bhāyaro jāyā. Tattha tesiṃ anne vi cattāri ibbhadāragā vayaṃsayā jāyā tattha vi bhoge bhunjiūṇa tahārūvāṇaṃ therāṇaṃ antie dhammaṃ soūṇa savve vi pavvaiyā. Sucirakālaṃ saṃjamam aṇupāleūṇa bhattapacchakkhāṇaṃ kāūṇa Sohamme kappe Paummagumme vimāṇe chāvi jaṇā caupaliovamaṭhiīyā devā uvavannā. Tattha je te govavajjā devā[2]) te caiūṇa Kurujaṇavae Usuyārapure ego Usuyāro nāma rāyā jāo, bīo tass' eva mahādevī Kamalāvaī nāma saṃvuttā, taio tassa ceva rāiṇo Bhigū nāma purohio saṃvutto, cauttho tassa ceva purohiyassa bhāriyā saṃvuttā Vāsitthī gotteṇa Jasā nāma. So ya[3]) Bhigū purohio gāḍhaṃ tappae avaccaṇimittaṃ uvāyaṇae[4]) devayāṇi pucchai nemittie. Te ya do vi puvvabhavagovā devabhave vaṭṭamāṇā jāṇiuṃ jahā: "amhe eyassa Bhigussa purohiyassa puttā bhavissāmo" tao samaṇarūvaṃ kāūṇaṃ uvāgayā Bhigusamīvaṃ. Bhiguṇā sabhārieṇa vandiyā. Suhāsaṇatthā ya dhammaṃ kahanti. Tehiṃ dohiṃ vi sāvayavayāṇi (çrāvakavratāni) gahiyāṇi. Purohieṇa bhaṇṇai: "bhayavaṃ, amha avaccaṃ hojja na vatti". Sāhūhiṃ bhaṇṇai: "bhavissanti duve dāragā, te ya ḍaharagā ceva pavajjaissanti; tesiṃ tubbhehiṃ vāghāo na kāyavvo pavvayantāṇaṃ. Te subahuṃ jaṇaṃ sambohissanti". Bhaṇiūṇa paḍigayā devā. Nāicireṇa ya caiūṇa tassa purohiyassa bhāriyāe Vāsiṭṭhīe duve vi udare paccāyāyā. Tao so purohio sabhārio nagarāo

1) Missing in MS. — With "Citta and Sambhūta" cp. also Jāt. N°. 509.

2) MS. kūetigovaccādevā. Read je te govajīvavajjā in accordance with Uttarajjh. 420 l. 8 tatra ye te gopajīvavarjā devāç catvāra?

3) MS. vasitthāgotteṇajasāya.

4) Denom. fr. uvāyaṇa, Skt. upāyana. MS. uvāiṇae.

niggantum paccantagāme [1]) ṭhio. Tattheva sā māhiṇī pasūyā, dārayā jāyā. Tao "mā pavaissantitti" kāum māyāvittehim vuggāhiyā jahā "ee pavvaiyagā ḍekkarūvāṇi (children, cp. Skt. dikka) ghettum mārenti, pacchā tesim mamsam [2]) khāyanti; tam mā tubbe kei eesim alliissaha" (ā + li). Annayā te tammi gāme ramantā bāhim niggayā. Io ya addhāṇapadivannayā sāhū āgacchanti. Tao te dārayā sahū daṭṭhūṇa bhayabhīyā palāyantā egammi vaḍapāyave ārūḍhā. Sāhuṇo vandium gayā ammapiusamīvam [3]). Māyāvitteṇa pavvaiyā. Devīe rāyā sambohio, tāṇi (these people) pavvaiyāṇi; evam tāṇi chāvi kevalaṇāṇam pāviūṇa nevvāṇam uvagayāṇi.

A JAINA KING ÇIBI.

Annayā ya posahasālāe ṭhio [4]) Vajjāuho devindeṇa pasamsio jahā: "dhammāo na sakkai devehim cāleum Vajjāuhakumārotti". Tao ego devo tam asaddahanto āgao, āgantūṇa ya viurūvio [5]) parevao, so ya bhayasambhanto Vajjāuham allīṇo māṇusabhāsāe "saraṇāgaotti" bhaṇamāṇo Vajjāuheṇa diṇṇe saraṇe tayā sannitthio. Tayanantaram ca samāgao lāvago, teṇa vi bhaṇiyam jahā: "mahasatta, esa mae chuhākilanteṇa pāvio, tā tam muñca eyam; annahā natthi mama jīviyamti". Tao tam āyaṇṇiūṇa Vajjāuheṇa bhaṇiyam: "Na juttam saraṇāgayasamappaṇam. Tujjha vi na juttam eyam, jao

Hantūṇa parasappāṇe appāṇam jo karei sappāṇam
appāṇam divasāṇam kae sa nāsei appāṇam.
Jahā jīviyam tuha piyam niyayam taha hoi savvajīvāṇam;
piyajīviyāṇam jīvāṇam rakkha jīvam sajīvam ca.
Khaṇamittam tuha titti, imassa puṇa cayai jīviyam jīvo;
tamhā u na juttam iṇam cadupphadantam vivāeum [6]).
Iya evam aṇusiṭṭho raṇṇā mahurakkharehim so sauṇo
padibhaṇai: "Bhukkhio ham, na maham dhammo maṇe ṭṭhāi".

1) MS. pamvvamtagā.

2) MS. samam.

3) Something is missing. Cp. Uttarajjh. p. 420: Tau dārakau ekasmin vatapādape ārūḍhau, sādhavas tu tasyaiva vaṭapadapasyādhaḥ pūrvam gṛihītaçanādibhojanam kartum pravṛittāh. Vaṭārūdhau tau kumārau svabhāvikam annapānam paçyataḥ etc. They begin to reflect, remember former existence, become pratibuddha. Sadhūn vanditvā gatau etc.

4) MS. posahalae (i. e. posahālae?) thio. Cp. Uttarajjh. p. 537 f. and for the whole story Benfey, Pantschatantra I pp. 388 ff.

5) So MS. Probably viuvvio is intended.

6) He who gives (preserves) life to his own self by killing other living beings ruins his own self for the sake of a few days. As thy own life is dear to thee so it is to all living beings; do thou preserve (spare) the life of life-loving living beings and thy own life (i. e. in having regard for the life of others you secure your own welfare). For thee it is only the satisfaction of a moment; but the soul of this

Tao punar avi bhaṇiyaṃ rāiṇā: "Bho [1]) mahāsatta, jai bhukkhio tumaṃ tā annaṃ demi tuha maṃsaṃ". Paḍibhaṇai sauṇo: "Niyavāvāiyamaṃsadullalio haṃ, na roei majjha [2]) paravāvāiyamaṃsaṃti". Rāiṇā bhaṇiyaṃ: "Jettiyamettaṃ pāro tulei tettiyamittaṃ demi niyadehāo [3]) kattiūṇa maṃsaṃ; tumaṃ khāhi". Tao lāvao paḍivannaṃ rāiṇo vayaṇam [4]). Āṇio nārāo [5]), pakkhitto ekkaṃmi pāsaṃmi pārāvao, bīyapāse

Ukkattiūṇa dehaṃ. rāyā jaha jaha parikkhivai maṃsaṃ,
taha taha ya hoi sauṇo garuyaro devamāyāe.
Daṭṭhūṇa tayaṃ rāyā hāhāravamuhalapariyaṇasamakkhaṃ [6])
āruhai sayaṃ ciya varatulāe niyajīyanikkhankho [7]).
Iyatuliyadevamāyaṃ daṭṭhūṇa vimhio devo [8])
daṃsei niyaṃ rūvaṃ maṇikuṇḍalabhūsiyasarīraṃ.

Aṇusāsiūṇa niyabhāvaṃ harisāūriyahiyao vimhiamāṇaso [9]) gao sadhāmaṃ [10]).

THE FAITHLESS WIFE AND THE TWO DEITIES ENAMORED OF CLEANLINESS.

Atthi Varāḍavisae Sadhannauranāmā saṃniveso. Tatth'ego mayaharaputto. Tassa bhajjā dussīlā paiṃmi parokkhe ḍiṇḍiyasasarakkheṇa [11]) samaṃ coriyaramiyaṃ karei. Annayā tattha naḍapekkhaṇaṃ jāyaṃ.

one (whom you kill) loses life. Therefore it is not right to kill the one who trembles with fear. The MS. has many mistakes in these and in the following stanzas (e. g. param appāṇe; vivasāṇam kae na; titi; vivāeu). The word cada (cadu?) clearly means "fear" or something similar. Ca dupph. (i. e. dush — "badly") seems out of the question. Read vahu (vadha, killing)? With upphaḍai "to start, palpitate" (emporfahren) cp. upphiḍai p. 104, note 2. The sense is not quite natural if we retain jīvo. I propose to read jīva and vayai (vrajati, although cayai, tyajati as an intransitive would do, too; cp. Erz. 74, 1 vayau. where C reads cayau) — "but, o soul (living being), this one's life departs".

1) MS. so.

2) MS. roe vajjha.

3) MS. dehatu.

4) So accord. to the MS. Probably tuṭṭho (Uttarajjh. tatas tushto lāvakaḥ) has dropped out. Else we would have to read lāvaeṇa. The MS. reads lāvau.

5) Scales. Skt. nārāca?

6) MS. guhala.

7) Or, nikkhankhī. The MS. has nikkhankhā.

8) Something seems to have dropped out in this line. Read -māyo eyaṃ (or, tayaṃ) daṭṭhūṇa?

9) Or, -maṇo so (MS. maraṇaso).

10) MS. sahasādhaṃ.

11) For sasarakkha Uttarajjh. (p. 549) here has nagarārakaha, and later on talārakaha. Sasarakkha = svasvaraksha, "protector of one's own self", i. e., = ātmaraksha, "body-guard"? Transl., "body-guards" on p. 104 (l. 3).

Tammi ya paṇaccio ego taruṇanaṭṭo itthirūveṇa. Tīe nicchaiyaṃ "puriso esotti"; jāo nadeṇa rāo [1]). Pacchannaṃ ca bhaṇio naṭṭapeḍayamayaharo: "jai imiṇā veseṇa mae samam kīlai imo, tao aham aṭṭhasayaṃ demi". Paḍivannaṃ ca teṇa. Bhaṇiyā ya esā: "Gaccha tumaṃ sampayaṃ puvvaṃ [2]) ceva". Na gao esa, pucchiyaṃ gharaṃ; sāhiyaṃ. Imīe sūraddhā [3]) naṭṭanimittaṃ khīrī. Āgao niyamayaharapesio naṭṭo, kayaṃ calaṇasoyaṃ, uvaviṭṭho bhunjium [4]), bhariyaṃ khīrīe bhāyaṇam, dinnaṃ gulahiyaṃ. Jāva na bhunjai tāvāgao sasarakkho. Tīe bhaṇio ya naṭṭo; "Uṭṭhehi, tiloyarae [5]) pavisa jāv' eyaṃ paṭṭhavemi" [6]). Paviṭṭho naḍo. Āgao sasarakkho. Jāvā na ceva bhunjai tāv' āgao se paī. Tīe bhaṇiyaṃ: "Lahuṃ uṭṭhehi, pavisa ettha tilovarae, na gantavvaṃ dūraṃ, sappo ciṭṭhaitti". Paviṭṭho sasarakkho, āgao se paī. Bhaṇiyaṃ ca ṇeṇa: "Kim eyaṃ?" Tīe bhaṇiyaṃ: "bhukkiatti jemeni". Iyareṇa bhaṇiyaṃ: "Ciṭṭha tāva tumaṃ, ahaṃ jememi". Iyarīe bhaṇiyaṃ: "Ajj' aṭṭhamī, kaham aṇhāo jemesi?" Teṇa bhaṇiyaṃ: "Tumaṃ ṇhāyatti". Iyarīe bhaṇiyam: "Mā evaṃ karehi, na esa dhammo. Sayaṇeṇaṃ [nivesau tuha ghare eyam Umā-Mahesaraṃ]" [7]). Balā ya bhutto eso. Io ya bhukkhiotti bhakkhaṇanimittaṃ phuṃsiyāmatilā [8]) naṭṭena. "Sappotti" palāṇo sasarakkho, avaro "avasarotti" piṭṭhao naṭṭho vi. Diṭṭhā [9]) niggacchamāṇā mayaharaputteṇa. "Kim eyaṃti" pucchiyā ghariṇī sā. Nivveyaṃ jaṃpiyam imīe: "bhaṇio mae tumaṃ: "Mā evaṃ karehi, na esa dhammo, sayaṇeṇaṃ nivesau [10]) tuha ghare eyaṃ Umā-Mahesaraṃ". Ajja aṇhāyabhoyaṇadhammabhangeṇaṃ niggayaṃ" [11]). "Hā duṭṭhakkayaṃ" visanno mayaharao [12]). Bhaṇiyam ca ṇeṇa: "Ko itth' uvāyo?" Tīe bhaṇiyaṃ: "Nāeṇa davvam ajjiṇiya savviḍḍhīe pūyaṃ karehi, tao pavisai eyaṃti" [13]). Gao mayaharautto Dasaṇṇavissae. Laggo vādakamme; nipphattīe [14]) vi dattā dasagaddiyāṇagā [15]).

1) Read, naḍe 'ṇurāo?

2) MS. tumam sampayaṃ paṃ (= sampayaṃ sayaṃ [i. e. svayam] or simply, sampayaṃ?).

3) So MS. Read yāraddhā?

4) MS. bhujiuṃ.

5) I. e. tilovarae (Uttarajjh. 549 tilagrihodare).

6) Ex conj. MS. only -vemi. Uttarajjh. has nivartayāmi. But that would regularly give nivattemi, although nivattāvemi is possible, I think.

7) Bracketed words supplied by me from below.

8) Or probably better, phuṃsiyā āmatilā (MS. has phuṃsimāyatila).

9) MS. sasarakkho avasarotti piṭṭau naṭṭho viṃdhā. Read, sasarakkho, avasarotti piṭṭhao naṭṭo vi (scil. palāṇo)? The MS. has naṭṭho for naṭṭo once before.

10) MS. nivesatuṃ. Read, nivesai tumha ghare?

11) MS. niggaṃggaṃ.

12) Read mayahara(p)utto?

13) I. e. umā-Mahesaraṃ. Probably better everywhere saviḍḍhīe "with all splendor (abrundance)".

14) MS nippatie. Maybe the period ought to be put after mayaharautto.

15) Uttarajjh. 550, daçagadyāṇakasuvarṇaṃ.

"Appotti" na tuṭṭho. Vitteṇa [1] tahavi payaṭṭo niyadesaṃ. Aḍavīe pippalamūle vīsamai. Etthantare avahario āseṇa samāgao taṃ uddesaṃ [2] Dasaṇṇabhaddo rāyā. Diṭṭho mayaharao. Teṇa daṃsiyaṃ udakam, uppallāṇio [3] āso, vissāmio rāyā. Thevavelāe samāgao pariyaṇo. Tao uvagāritti pucchio mayaharaputto raṇṇā: "Ko tumaṃ, kim vā te kīrau?" Jahaṭṭhiyam eva sāhiyaṃ. Mayaharautteṇa bhaṇio rāyā: "Tā savviḍḍhī[4]pūyāsaṃpāyaṇatthaṃ kareu kiṃci devotti". Rāiṇā cintiyaṃ: "Ujjugo [5] varāgo ghattio [6] mahilayāe. Tā imaṃ ettha pattayāle [7] nemi paṭṭaṇam, tao jahājuttaṃ aṇucitthissāmotti". Nīo saṇayaram, sampāḍiyaṃ [8] bhoyaṇāiṃ, cintiyaṃ ca rāiṇā: "Aho se vavasāo, asantagaṃ pi viḍhaviya savviḍḍhīe pūyaṃ sampādei. Dhammapuriso khu eso. Tā kiṃ imassa kīrau?" Etthantare niveiyaṃ rāiṇo pauttikabagehiṃ jahā: "Deva, bhagavaṃ Mahāvīro samāgao". Parituṭṭho rāyā; vandiuṃ tattheva bhāveṇa dinnam pāusiyaṃ. Cintiyam ca ṇeṇa: "Jai nāma [9] esa mayaharaputto visiṭṭhaviveyarahio vi niyadevayāṇaṃ savviḍḍhipūyāsaṃpāyaṇatthaṃ [10] evaṃ parikilissai, tā amhārisehiṃ sārāsāravibhāgaviyāṇaehiṃ samaggasāmaggiehim tihuyaṇa-cintāmaṇissa bhagavao Mahāvīrassa viseseṇa saviḍḍhipūyā kāuṃ jujjaitti". Tā kallaṃ savviḍḍhīe tahā vandissaṃ bhayavaṃ jahā keṇai na vandiyavvotti" [11]. Bīyadivase pahāyasamae ya kayagosakicco ṇhāyavilittālaṃkiyadeho udārarūvo jovvaṇalāvaṇṇanevaccheṇa, pancasaikeṇa varoheṇa saddhiṃ maṇḍiyālaṃkiyāe cāuraṅgiṇīe [12] senāe parigao pavarajāṇārūḍhehiṃ bahūhiṃ sāmantamantiseṭṭhisatthavāhapaurajaṇasahassehiṃ aṇṇijjamāṇo bhambhābheri-m-āiyāujjaravabaṃhiriyadigantaro, paḍhantehiṃ māgahehiṃ, gāyantehiṃ gandhavvehiṃ, naccantīhiṃ vilāsiṇīhiṃ gao bhayavaṃvandaṇatthaṃ. Visujjhamāṇabhāveṇa vandio bhayavaṃ. "Kayatto mhi" [13] harisio rāyā mayaha-

1) Possibly, na tuṭṭho vi teṇa? (Or, of course, tuṭṭho vitteṇa. Tahavi).

2) MS. tammudesaṃ. Read, mayaharautto. Tena etc in following? (MS. mayaranauṭṭeṇa).

3) Unsaddled.

4) The MS. wavers between savaḍḍhī and savviḍḍhī throughout (and it would be just as possible to read -ṭṭī).

5) Ṛijuka; cp. Jacobi's edition of Kalpasutra sub ujjuya.

6) Uttarajjh. vipratāritaḥ.

7) Prāptakāla. Read pattayālaṃ? MS. pattayāla.

8) MS. sampadiyaṃ.

9) Hardly, Pāusiyajuvaivayaṇeṇa jai nāma (i. e. *prādushitayuvativacanena). MS. reads, pāusiyacitiyavaṇena. It also has baṃdiu (hardly for bandiṇo). The sense seems to be, "In his mind he gave on the spot "someting for the rainy season"" (to Mahāvīra and his monks? Probably garments for that season are meant. Or, shelter?) Hardly connected with Pāli dussaṃ.

10) MS. saṃpāyatthaṃ.

11) Probably we have to read, vandiyapuvvo.

12) Correct to cāuraṅgiṇīe and the preceeding varoheṇa to avaroheṇa?

13) MS. kayattho mhe.

rautto ya. Etthantareṇa Sakkeṇa cintiyaṃ: "Mahāpuriso Dasannabhaddo paḍibujjhissai imiṇā vaiyareṇa. Ao mahāvibhūīe vandāmi bhayavantaṃ". Viuvvyiyā Erāvaṇamuhae [1]) aṭṭha dantā, dante dante aṭṭha pokkharaṇīo [2]), pokkharaṇīe pokkharaṇīe aṭṭha paumā, paume paume aṭṭha pattā, patte patte battīsa baddhā rāsapekkhaṇā. Evaṃ vibhūīe Erāvaṇaṃ payāhineūṇaṃ vandio bhayavaṃ devindeṇaṃ. Taṃ daṭṭhūṇaṃ cintiyaṃ Dasannabhaddeṇaṃ: "Aho khalu tuccho haṃ jeṇ' imīe vi tucchāe sirīe gavvo [3]) kao. Ahavā

> Adiṭṭhabhaddhā theveṇa vi honti uttuṇā [4]) nīyā.
> Naccai uttālakaro hu mūsago vīhim āsajja.

Kao ya ṇeṇa suddhadhammo; ten' erisī [5]) riddhı. Tā ahaṃ pi taṃ ceva karemi. Kim ettha visāeṇa! Uktaṃ ca

> Samasaṃkhyāvayavaḥ san purushaḥ purusham anyaṃ kim atyeti? [6])
> Puṇyair [7]) adhikataraç cen, nanu so'pi karotu tāny eva!

Iccāisaṃvegabhāvaṇāe paḍibuddhe khauvasamaṃ [8]) uvāgayaṃ [9]) cārittamohaṇīyaṃ; bhaṇiyaṃ ca teṇa: "Bhayavaṃ nivvinno haṃ bhavacāragāo. Tā kareha me vayappayāṇeṇāṇuggahaṃ ti. Dikkhio mayaharaputteṇa samaṃ bhagavayā, vandio ya Sakkeṇa pasaṃsio ya. "Dhanno kayattho tumaṃ jen' erisī [10]) riddhī [11]) sahasacciya paricattā saccaviyā ya painnā tume, jao davvavandaṇāe [12]) bhāvavandanā pahānatti" pasaṃsiūṇa gao suraloyaṃ Sakko.

1) MS. only Eravae.
2) MS. om. But further on, apparently by careless repetion, aṭṭhabaṭṭīsa.
3) MS. mavvo.
4) Puffed up, proud. See Gauḍavaha sub voce. Nīyā = nīcāḥ.
5) MS. erisā.
6) MS. and Uttarajjh. 551 abhyeti.
7) MS. Puṇyor, Uttarajjh. puṇyair.
8) Acc. of direction. Cp. Amitagati's Subhāshitasaṃdoha VII, 26; IX, 2, where I read tannāçikarmaprakṛitau, naçin "destructive" (ed. Schmidt & Hertel, ZDMG. 59, pp. 315, 331). See in Tattvārthādigama ed. Jacobi ZDMG. 60 the passages given in the index under kshayopaçama, cāritramohanīya etc.
9) MS. seems to read uvegayaṃ.
10) MS. erisā (which possibly should not be tampered with).
11) MS. rivvī.
12) MS. add. ya.